Rousseau, Nietzsche, and the Image of the Human

Rousseau, Nietzsche, and the Image of the Human

PAUL FRANCO

The University of Chicago Press
Chicago and London

The University of Chicago Press, Chicago 60637
The University of Chicago Press, Ltd., London
© 2021 by The University of Chicago
Published 2021
Printed in the United States of America

30 29 28 27 26 25 24 23 22 21 1   2 3 4 5

ISBN-13: 978-0-226-80030-1 (cloth)
ISBN-13: 978-0-226-80044-8 (e-book)
DOI: https://doi.org/10.7208/chicago/9780226800448.001.0001

Library of Congress Cataloging-in-Publication Data

Names: Franco, Paul, 1956– author.
Title: Rousseau, Nietzsche, and the image of the human / Paul Franco.
Description: Chicago ; London : The University of Chicago Press, 2021. |
    Includes bibliographical references and index.
Identifiers: LCCN 2021000640 | ISBN 9780226800301 (cloth) |
    ISBN 9780226800448 (ebook)
Subjects: LCSH: Rousseau, Jean-Jacques, 1712–1778. | Nietzsche, Friedrich Wilhelm,
    1844–1900. | Philosophical anthropology. | Self. | Woman (Philosophy) |
    Political science—Philosophy. | Philosophy, Modern.
Classification: LCC B2137 .F73 2021 | DDC 128–dc23
LC record available at https://lccn.loc.gov/2021000640

♾ This paper meets the requirements of ANSI/NISO Z39.48-1992 (Permanence of Paper).

Who, then, amidst these dangers of our age, will dedicate himself, as sentinel and champion of humanity, to the inviolable sacred treasure gradually accumulated by the most various generations? Who will erect the *image of the human*, when all feel in themselves the worm of selfishness and dog-like fear, and have fallen from that image into bestiality or even into rigid automatism?

NIETZSCHE, "Schopenhauer as Educator"

Contents

Abbreviations

References to Rousseau's and Nietzsche's works appear parenthetically in the text with the following abbreviations. I have generally relied on widely available English translations, though in a few instances I have modified the words slightly. For Nietzsche's untranslated notebooks and correspondence, I have used my own translations of the German text in the *Kritische Studienausgabe*. For Rousseau, references are to page number unless otherwise noted. For Nietzsche, references are to aphorism or section number unless otherwise noted.

Rousseau

C   *The Confessions*. In *The "Confessions" and Correspondence*, edited by Christopher Kelly, Roger D. Masters, and Peter G. Stillman, translated by Kelly. Hanover, NH: University of New England Press, 1995.

E   *Emile, or On Education*. Translated by Allan Bloom. New York: Basic Books, 1979.

EOL   *Essay on the Origin of Languages*. In *The "Discourses" and Other Early Political Writings*, edited and translated by Victor Gourevitch. Cambridge: Cambridge University Press, 1997.

FD   *First Discourse*. In *The "Discourses" and Other Early Political Writings*, edited and translated by Victor Gourevitch. Cambridge: Cambridge University Press, 1997.

GenMS   "Geneva Manuscript." In *"The Social Contract" and Other Later Political Writings*, edited and translated by Victor Gourevitch. Cambridge: Cambridge University Press, 1997.

GP   *Considerations on the Government of Poland*. In *"The Social Contract" and
         Other Later Political Writings*, edited and translated by Victor Gourevitch.
         Cambridge: Cambridge University Press, 1997.

J   *Julie, or The New Heloise*. Translated by Philip Stewart and Jean Vaché.
         Hanover, NH: University of New England Press, 1997.

LB   *Letter to Beaumont*. In *"Letter to Beaumont", "Letters Written from the
         Mountain", and Related Writings*, edited by Christopher Kelly and Eve
         Grace, translated by Kelly and Judith R. Bush. Hanover, NH: University of
         New England Press, 2001.

LD   *The Letter to D'Alembert on the Theatre*. Translated by Allan Bloom. In *Poli-
         tics and the Arts: Letter to M. D'Alembert on the Theatre*. Ithaca, NY: Cornell
         University Press, 1960.

LF   "Letter to Franquières." In *"The Social Contract" and Other Later Political
         Writings*, edited and translated by Victor Gourevitch. Cambridge: Cam-
         bridge University Press, 1997.

LMal   "Letters to Malesherbes." In *The "Confessions" and Correspondence*, edited
         by Christopher Kelly, Roger D. Masters, and Peter G. Stillman, translated by
         Kelly. Hanover, NH: University of New England Press, 1995.

LO   "Letter to D'Offreville." In *"The Social Contract" and Other Later Political
         Writings*, edited and translated by Victor Gourevitch. Cambridge: Cam-
         bridge University Press, 1997.

LR   "Last Reply." In *The "Discourses" and Other Early Political Writings*, edited
         and translated by Victor Gourevitch. Cambridge: Cambridge University
         Press, 1997.

LV   "Letter to Voltaire." In *The "Discourses" and Other Early Political Writings*,
         edited and translated by Victor Gourevitch. Cambridge: Cambridge Univer-
         sity Press, 1997.

LWM   *Letters Written from the Mountain*. In *"Letter to Beaumont", "Letters Written
         from the Mountain", and Related Writings*, edited by Christopher Kelly and
         Eve Grace, translated by Kelly and Judith R. Bush. Hanover, NH: University
         of New England Press, 2001.

LU   "Letter to Usteri." In *"The Social Contract" and Other Later Political Writ-
         ings*, edited and translated by Victor Gourevitch. Cambridge: Cambridge
         University Press, 1997.

ML   "Moral Letters." In *Autobiographical, Scientific, Religious, Moral, and Liter-
         ary Writings*, edited and translated by Christopher Kelly. Hanover, NH:
         University of New England Press, 2007.

OW   "On Women." In *Autobiographical, Scientific, Religious, Moral, and Literary
         Writings*, edited and translated by Christopher Kelly. Hanover, NH: Univer-
         sity of New England Press, 2007.

PE   *Discourse on Political Economy*. In *"The Social Contract" and Other Later Political Writings*, edited and translated by Victor Gourevitch. Cambridge: Cambridge University Press, 1997.

PN   "Preface to Narcissus." In *The "Discourses" and Other Early Political Writings*, edited and translated by Victor Gourevitch. Cambridge: Cambridge University Press, 1997.

R   *The Reveries of the Solitary Walker*. Translated by Charles E. Butterworth. Indianapolis: Hackett, 1992.

RJ   *Rousseau, Judge of Jean-Jacques: Dialogues*. Translated by Judith R. Bush, Christopher Kelly, and Roger D. Masters. Hanover, NH: University of New England Press, 1990.

SC   *On the Social Contract*. In *"The Social Contract" and Other Later Political Writings*, edited and translated by Victor Gourevitch. Cambridge: Cambridge University Press, 1997. Cited by book and chapter number.

SD   *Second Discourse*. In *The "Discourses" and Other Early Political Writings*, edited and translated by Victor Gourevitch. Cambridge: Cambridge University Press, 1997.

Nietzsche

A   *The Antichrist* (with *Twilight of the Idols*). Translated by R. J. Hollingdale. Harmondsworth: Penguin, 1968.

AOM   *Assorted Opinions and Maxims*. In *Human, All Too Human*, translated by R. J. Hollingdale. Cambridge: Cambridge University Press, 1986.

BGE   *Beyond Good and Evil*. Translated by Walter Kaufmann. New York: Vintage, 1966.

BT   *The Birth of Tragedy*. Translated by Walter Kaufmann. New York: Vintage, 1967.

D   *Daybreak: Thoughts on the Prejudices of Morality*. Translated by R. J. Hollingdale. Cambridge: Cambridge University Press, 1997.

EH   *Ecce Homo* (with *On the Genealogy of Morals*). Translated by Walter Kaufmann. New York: Vintage, 1967.

GM   *On the Genealogy of Morality*. Translated by Maudemarie Clark and Alan J. Swenson. Indianapolis: Hackett, 1998.

GS   *The Gay Science*. Translated by Walter Kaufmann. New York: Vintage, 1974.

GSt   "The Greek State." In *On the Genealogy of Morality*, edited by Keith Ansell-Pearson, translated by Carol Diethe. Cambridge: Cambridge University Press, 1994. Cited by page number.

HC   "Homer on Competition." In *On the Genealogy of Morality*, edited by Keith

Ansell-Pearson, translated by Carol Dieth. Cambridge: Cambridge University Press, 1994. Cited by page number.

HH   *Human, All Too Human.* Translated R. J. Hollingdale. Cambridge: Cambridge University Press, 1986.

KSA   *Sämtliche Werke: Kritische Studienausgabe in 15 Bänden.* Edited by Giogio Colli and Mazzino Montinari. Berlin: Walter de Gruyter, 1980. *Nachlass* cited by volume, notebook, and, in brackets, note number. Where available, I have drawn on the English translations of the unpublished fragments in *The Complete Works of Friedrich Nietzsche* (Stanford: Stanford University Press, 1995–).

RWB   "Richard Wagner in Bayreuth." In *Untimely Meditations,* translated by R. J. Hollingdale. Cambridge: Cambridge University Press, 1983. Cited by section and page number.

SB   *Sämtliche Briefe: Kritische Studienausgabe.* Edited by Giorgio Colli and Mazzino Montinari. Berlin: Walter de Gruyter, 1986. Cited by volume and page number.

SE   "Schopenhauer as Educator." In *Untimely Meditations,* translated by R. J. Hollingdale. Cambridge: Cambridge University Press, 1983. Cited by section and page number.

TI   *Twilight of the Idols.* Translated by R. J. Hollingdale. Harmondsworth: Penguin, 1968.

UDH   "On the Uses and Disadvantages of History for Life." In *Untimely Meditations,* translated by R. J. Hollingdale. Cambridge: Cambridge University Press, 1983. Cited by section and page number.

WP   *The Will to Power.* Translated by Walter Kaufmann. New York: Vintage, 1968.

WS   *The Wanderer and His Shadow.* In *Human, All Too Human,* translated by R. J. Hollingdale. Cambridge: Cambridge University Press, 1986.

Z   *Thus Spoke Zarathustra.* Translated by Walter Kaufmann. Harmondsworth: Penguin, 1966.

1

Introduction

Among philosophers, Jean-Jacques Rousseau and Friedrich Nietzsche are perhaps the two most influential shapers and explorers of the moral and cultural imagination of late modernity. This statement is not very controversial with respect to Rousseau, about whom Henry Maine famously observed, "We have never seen in our own generation—indeed the world has not seen more than once or twice in all of history—a literature which has exercised such prodigious influence over the minds of men, over every cast and shade of intellect, as that which emanated from Rousseau between 1749 and 1762."[1] Maine wrote this in 1861, eleven years before Nietzsche made his philosophical debut with *The Birth of Tragedy*; but I do not think it is any more controversial to say that Nietzsche exercised a similarly powerful influence over the minds of twentieth century thinkers and writers with the works he produced between 1872 and 1888, and this influence shows no sign of abating. Leo Strauss sums up the revolutionary impact these two thinkers had on their respective intellectual milieus in this way: "Nietzsche changed the intellectual climate of Germany and perhaps the whole of continental Europe in a way similar to that in which Rousseau had changed that climate about 120 years before. And I do not think that a comparable change of the intellectual climate had occurred in the time between Nietzsche and Rousseau."[2]

What, in the first instance, made Rousseau and Nietzsche such influential figures was that they both offered penetrating critiques of modern liberal, Enlightenment civilization—*our* civilization. Rousseau, of course, led the way in this regard. In his 1750 *Discourse on the Sciences and Arts* and his 1754 *Discourse on the Origin and Foundations of Inequality among Men*, he leveled a devastating critique of the inequality, immorality, and inauthenticity of modern, "enlightened" society. Above all, he criticized what he was the first to pejoratively refer to as the "bourgeois," the man who is "always in contradiction with himself, always floating between his inclinations and his duties," and thereby incapable of being "either man or citizen" (*E* 40). In his classic work *From Hegel to Nietzsche: The Revolution in Nineteenth-Century Thought*, Karl Löwith credits Rousseau with offering the "first and clearest statement of the human problem of bourgeois society," which "consists in the fact that man, in bourgeois society, is not a unified whole."[3]

One hundred twenty years later, beginning with *The Birth of Tragedy* (1872), Nietzsche extended Rousseau's critique of the Enlightenment and of the artificiality of modern society. Like Rousseau, Nietzsche lamented the loss of unity in modern life, but his critique focused more on the fragmentation of modern culture that had resulted from the growth of the sciences, especially history, and the decline of religion as a unifying cultural practice. Like Rousseau, Nietzsche, too, heaped scorn on the bourgeois, but the burden of his critique fell less on the selfishness and duplicity of this modern character and more on his pettiness, his craving for security and comfort, his aversion to risk and danger, his singularly unheroic disposition. This aspect of Nietzsche's critique of modern society received its most memorable expression in Zarathustra's portrait of the bourgeois "last man," who has his "little pleasure for the day and his little pleasure for the night" and imagines that he has "invented happiness" (*Z* 1, prologue, 5)

In their critiques of modern bourgeois society, Rousseau and Nietzsche ruthlessly fulfilled what the latter called the "inescapable task" of all "extraordinary furtherers of man whom one calls philosophers"—namely, serving as the "bad conscience of their time" (*BGE* 212). But what made them both more than mere critics was that their critiques were in the service of constructive projects aimed at delivering modern human beings from corruption and showing them a new path to fulfillment. In this regard, Rousseau spoke of "changing the objects of [men's] esteem and thus perhaps slowing down their decadence" (*RJ* 213); while Nietzsche, more ambitiously, urged philosophers to find "a *new* greatness of man, a new untrodden way to his enhancement" (*BGE* 212). In short, Rousseau and Nietzsche both put forward powerful alternative visions of how we ought to live and constructed imaginative ideals to counter what they perceived as the selfishness, weakness, and aimlessness of their respective ages.

Nietzsche himself recognized this crucial constructive aspect of Rousseau's philosophy in his early essay "Schopenhauer as Educator." There he mentioned Rousseau—along with Goethe and Arthur Schopenhauer—as having provided one of the three great images of the human being to counter the atomistic and self-seeking tendencies of the age and to "inspire mortals to a transfiguration of their own lives." He added that, of these three images, Rousseau's "possesses the greatest fire and is sure to produce the greatest popular effect." With its condemnation of the corruption of modern society and its appeal to "holy nature," Rousseau's image of the human "has promoted violent revolutions and continues to do so" in the form of socialist agitation (SE 4:150–51). More recently, Pierre Manent has also called attention to the constructive dimension of Rousseau's philosophy, calling him the "last great reformer of the West (Friedrich Nietzsche is in this respect only a distant second). As a philosopher, Rousseau above all wants to understand, but as a reformer, as someone who wants to change men's objects of esteem, he formulates a philanthropic project."[4]

Manent is right to characterize Nietzsche as a reformer in the mold of Rousseau, but his claim that he is "only a distant second" to Rousseau in this regard seems to seriously underestimate the German thinker's philanthropic project. One would be hard pressed to find another late-modern philosopher who is more concerned to change the objects of men's esteem than Nietzsche (see *KSA* 9:11 [76]). This, in the end, is what the project of the revaluation of all values is all about. Indeed, I would argue that the change Nietzsche seeks to effect in the objects of men's esteem is more radical than anything found in Rousseau. Be that as it may, Nietzsche, like Rousseau, often appeals to antiquity to suggest an alternative scheme of values to the one modern human beings currently operate under. And his imagination is just as fertile as Rousseau's in inventing ideals to counter the idols that modern human beings worship. We may therefore slightly alter Manent's formula to come up with the guiding premise of this book: Rousseau *and* Nietzsche are the last *two* great reformers of the West, and as such, an examination of their critiques of modern society and their philanthropic projects to reform it is of the utmost importance.

There are many parallels in Rousseau's and Nietzsche's reformist projects. Perhaps the most salient is that both thinkers appeal to nature, albeit in complex ways, to ground their visions of the good or meaningful life. In the case of Rousseau, the natural human being—whether in the state of nature or in society—is characterized by independence, self-sufficiency, and freedom from the inflamed *amour propre* or vanity that makes the life of civilized man so frenetic and inauthentic. In the case of Nietzsche, nature takes on a more terrifying, less sentimental aspect, and the natural human being is characterized by sublimated cruelty, will to power, and freedom from the conventional morality that makes the life of civilized man so bland and mediocre. In the final year of his sane life, Nietzsche summed up his fundamental difference with Rousseau in this way: "I too speak of a 'return to nature,' although it is not really a going-back but a *going-up*—up into a high, free, even frightful nature and naturalness" (*TI*, "Expeditions," 48).

I examine Rousseau's and Nietzsche's respective conceptions of human nature in chapter 2 in connection with their critical genealogies of modern civilization. Besides leveling devastating critiques at modern, enlightened bourgeois society, Rousseau and Nietzsche both embed those critiques in a historical account of how human beings came to be in the degraded condition in which they find themselves. For Rousseau, the progressive corruption of humanity results from the growth of inequality and the activation of an unhealthy form of *amour propre* that leads human beings to constantly compare themselves with one another and compete for advantage. He thus provides a "genealogy of vice" (*LB* 28). Nietzsche, on the other hand, sees the leveling, weakening, and diminishing of modern humanity as the result of the progressive moralization and taming of human beings. He therefore provides a "genealogy of morality." Nietzsche sums up the difference between his and Rousseau's genealogies in this way: "If it is true that our civilization has something pitiable about it, you have the choice of concluding with Rousseau that 'this pitiable civilization is to blame for our *bad* morality,' or against Rousseau that 'our *good* morality is to blame for this pitiableness of our civilization'" (*D* 163). He, of course, ultimately opts for the latter explanation.

In chapters 3 through 5, I take up specific aspects of Nietzsche's and Rousseau's constructive or reformist projects. In chapter 3, I consider their respective understandings and ethics of the individual self. A common way of characterizing the monumental shift in the moral life of modern Europe that was initiated by Rousseau and radicalized by Nietzsche is in terms of the ideal of authenticity. Charles Taylor highlights the crucial role Rousseau played in this shift, arguing that the latter's emphasis on the inner voice of conscience and sentiment of one's own existence introduced a "massive subjective turn" in modern culture, a "transformation towards a deeper inwardness and a radical autonomy. The strands all lead from him."[5] Taylor sees Nietzsche as ushering in a new understanding of authenticity that severs it from morality and identifies it instead with artistic self-creation.[6] In chapter 3, I fill out, refine, and complicate this picture of the relationship between Rousseau's and Nietzsche's respective conceptions of the authentic self. With respect to Rousseau, I argue that his conception of authenticity is not as subjectivist as Taylor suggests. Sincerity or authenticity does not mean conformity to some inner self but being free of the dependence on others that leads to the dissimulation and hypocrisy Rousseau deplores. Such independence requires that our desires and the power to satisfy them are in equilibrium, and this ultimately requires the sort of self-mastery Rousseau identifies with moral virtue. It is

precisely this identification of authenticity with morality that Nietzsche rejects, emphasizing instead the uniqueness and elusiveness of the self and re-
conceiving authenticity in terms of a rich doctrine of self-creation.

A key element of Rousseau's reformist project involves the relationship
between men and women and their respective roles in the family. Rousseau
takes up this theme in books 4 and 5 of *Emile*, where he argues that women
should receive a different education from men that trains them to rule in-
visibly from within the family while ceding authority to men in the public
spheres of the economy, politics, and science. Rousseau's differential treatment of men and women has, of course, been much criticized for being sexist,
but when viewed against Nietzsche's notorious remarks on women, it looks
positively progressive. This, no doubt, is a rather crude statement of Rousseau's and Nietzsche's complicated and challenging views on the contentious
subject of the relation between the sexes. In chapter 4, I offer a more nuanced
discussion of their views and the fundamental differences between them.
Rousseau and Nietzsche both agree about the importance of sexual difference and its role in establishing a complementary relationship between men
and women. Where they differ is in how they conceive of this complementarity: whereas for Rousseau it gives rise to a harmonious interdependence that
supports morality, for Nietzsche it provides the basis for a creative antagonism that promotes the enhancement of the species. Though neither of their
views on women has many defenders in our postfeminist world, both raise
thought-provoking questions about the standard liberal-egalitarian understanding of the relation between the sexes.

Perhaps the most striking difference between Rousseau and Nietzsche relates to their visions of politics, which I take up in chapter 5. Rousseau attacks
the liberal political tradition he found articulated in Locke and Montesquieu
from the left, advocating a more egalitarian and republican type of politics
based on what he calls the "general will." Nietzsche attacks the democratic tradition of politics spawned by Rousseau and reflected in the French Revolution
from the right, advocating an aristocratic politics based on the will to power.
The one thing that unites Rousseau and Nietzsche is their common hostility
to the bourgeois liberal tradition and the extremity (and, for many, the un-
savoriness) of their political prescriptions. In chapter 5, I argue that the most
serious charges that have been leveled against their political philosophies—
that they are somehow authoritarian, tyrannical, or totalitarian—are largely
misguided. This is especially true in the case of Rousseau, who, despite his
criticism of the classical liberal tradition, ends up defending a version of liberal democracy that has individual liberty as its goal, political and economic
equality as its condition, and impersonal law as its guarantee. The case of

Nietzsche is more difficult, partly because his aristocratic political vision is so ambiguous and elusive. Nevertheless, I show that this vision has more to do with a set of values rather than an actual arrangement of political institutions, and that it is ultimately compatible with democratic political institutions that serve the needs of the mediocre many. I also argue that Nietzsche succeeds in identifying a real problem in Rousseau's highly individualistic and juridical vision of politics, and that his own perfectionist and aristocratic vision, while no doubt flawed, offers a more promising starting point for reflection on the politics of culture today.

It is clear from what has been said so far that, in their critiques of modern society and their visions of a new ideal for humanity, Rousseau and Nietzsche are united by deep similarities and divided by fundamental differences. Not surprisingly, Nietzsche emphasized the differences and identified Rousseau as a key philosophical antagonist. Here at the outset, I would like to lay out in some detail Nietzsche's critical engagement with Rousseau because it raises important questions about the relationship between the two thinkers— questions that will serve to frame the analysis that follows.

From quite early on in his career, Nietzsche identified Rousseau as the source of the revolutionary spirit of the age, both democratic and social- ist. This is evident in the passage from "Schopenhauer as Educator" on the Rousseauian image of the human, and it receives expression in a slightly later aphorism from *Human, All Too Human* on the delusion involved in revo- lutionary ideology. There Nietzsche writes that, in the "political and social fantasists who with fiery eloquence invite a revolutionary overturning of all social orders," one hears the "echo of Rousseau's superstition, which believes in a miraculous primeval but as it were *buried* goodness in human nature and ascribes all for the blame for this burying to the institutions of culture in the form of society, state and education" (*HH* 463). Above all, Nietzsche identifies Rousseau with the French Revolution and its vengeful doctrine of equality (*HH* 463; *D*, preface, 3; *TI*, "Expeditions," 48; *WP* 94). In an aphorism from the second volume of *Human, All Too Human*, he writes that the fanati- cism of the French Revolution "had, before the Revolution, become flesh and spirit in Rousseau," who thereby diverted the Enlightenment from its moder- ate course as represented by Voltaire, to whom Nietzsche originally dedicated *Human, All Too Human* (*WS* 221; see also *WP* 99, 100).[7]

Nietzsche sees the French Revolution as itself an expression of the moral fanaticism and romanticism of the eighteenth century in general, which again he traces back to Rousseau. In the second volume of *Human, All Too Human*, he speaks of the "stream of moral awakening" that flowed through Europe in the eighteenth century: "If we seek the sources of this stream we find first of all Rousseau, but the mythical Rousseau constructed out of the impression produced by his writings." Out of this mythical Rousseau came the moralism of Kant, Schiller, and Beethoven (WS 216). In his later writings, Nietzsche ceases to make the subtle distinction between the real and the mythical Rousseau. He refers to Kant simply as a "moral fanatic à la Rousseau" (WP 101) and claims that Kant's moral "enthusiasm" was the result of his having "been bitten by the moral tarantula Rousseau" (D, preface, 3). Rousseau himself, he says, was preoccupied with the "moral reprehensibility of man," and with such moralism he sought to "stir up the instincts of the oppressed" (WP 99). Romanticism, too, Nietzsche sees as the echo of the "eighteenth century of Rousseau," which elevated feeling, sentiment, idealism, enthusiasm, and women. Nietzsche contrasts the idealism and sentimentalism of Rousseau's eighteenth century with the realism, "animalism," and fatalism of the nineteenth. He concedes that there is a certain gloominess to the nineteenth-century image of the human, but he ultimately sides with it against the eighteenth century because it is "truer" and "more honest" (WP 62, 94, 95, 100, 1017, 1021).

One of Nietzsche's most intriguing references to Rousseau appears in the aphorism "Descent into Hades" (Hadesfahrt), from the second volume of Human, All Too Human. Part of the interest of this aphorism lies in the appreciation of Rousseau it exhibits and in its acknowledgement of Nietzsche's debt to him. There are four pairs of thinkers, Nietzsche writes, with whom he has long conversed and whose judgment he has constantly consulted: Epicurus and Montaigne, Goethe and Spinoza, Plato and Rousseau, and Pascal and Schopenhauer; "whatever I say, resolve, cogitate for myself and others: upon these eight I fix my eyes and see theirs fixed on me" (HH, 463). Obviously, the thinkers in each of these pairs are linked in Nietzsche's mind in an important way. Epicurus and Montaigne advocate a life of moderation and simple pleasure; Goethe and Spinoza embody the life of disinterested contemplation; and Pascal and Schopenhauer epitomize the religious response to the misery of existence. But what is the link between Plato and Rousseau? A clue comes in one of Nietzsche's later notes, where he lumps Plato and Rousseau together as moral fanatics who resisted the moral liberality of their respective ages: Plato condemned the moral corruption of Periclean Athens in the same way Rousseau condemned the moral corruption of Voltaire's Paris (WP 747). In the end, therefore, the Hadesfahrt aphorism reflects the same judgment about Rousseau's moralism that Nietzsche expresses more explicitly elsewhere. Nevertheless, it also indicates Nietzsche's high regard for Rousseau, which sometimes gets lost in his more polemical comments on the Swiss thinker.

I stated earlier that what links Rousseau and Nietzsche first and foremost in our minds is that they offer two of the most powerful critiques of modern society. But as Nietzsche makes clear in the aphorism "Contra Rousseau," from which I have already quoted, they have very different ideas on what exactly has gone wrong: whereas Rousseau blames our pitiable civilization for "our *bad* morality," Nietzsche blames "our *good* morality" for the "pitiableness of our civilization." For Rousseau, the inequality and competitiveness of modern society has made us into moral hypocrites who ultimately seek to profit at our neighbors' expense. For Nietzsche, on the other hand, it is morality itself that has transformed us into weak, comfort-seeking herd animals devoid of any genuine individuality: "Our weak, unmanly social concepts of good and evil and their tremendous ascendency over body and soul have finally weakened all bodies and souls and snapped the self-reliant, independent, unprejudiced men, the pillars of a *strong* civilization: where one still encounters *bad morality*, one beholds the last ruins of these pillars" (*D* 163).

Like Rousseau, Nietzsche measures the corruption of modern humanity against the standard of nature; but once again he emphasizes the differences in their respective conceptions of that standard. Though he, too, speaks of a "return to nature," it is to be understood not so much as a "going-back" as a "*going-up*" (*TI*, "Expeditions," 48). Nature for Nietzsche is not where we start but where we end; it is an achievement. As he puts it in a late note: "*Not* 'return to nature'—for there has never yet been a natural humanity. . . . Man reaches nature only after a long struggle—he never 'returns'—nature: i.e., daring to be immoral like nature" (*WP* 120). It is the uncovering of nature in this immoral sense that Nietzsche sees as the distinctive achievement of nineteenth-century reflection on human nature, over and against the sentimental image of the human that belongs to Rousseau's eighteenth century. Again, a late note captures Nietzsche's point: "In place of the 'natural man' of Rousseau, the nineteenth century has discovered a *truer image of* 'man,'" one that is more terrible and animalistic. Nor is the natural man in this truer, more terrible sense to be found in the past; rather, it is a cultural achievement to be progressively realized in the future: "Increase in the terribleness of man is an accompaniment of every increase in culture" (*WP* 1017; see also 95, 382).

As many scholars have noted, Nietzsche's interpretation of Rousseau is something of a caricature and exaggerates the differences between the two thinkers.[8] His attribution to Rousseau of a desire to "return to nature" is a good example of such caricature. As any attentive reader of Rousseau knows, he does not advocate a simple return to nature. Likewise, Nietzsche's emphasis on his differences with Rousseau obscures the profound similarities in their philosophical positions. As W. D. Williams puts it in his early study of the Nietzsche–Rousseau relationship, though Nietzsche continually attacks Rousseau, "the violent scorn and hatred masks a real affinity."[9] He goes on to elaborate on this affinity: "Nietzsche's mind is from the start fundamentally like Rousseau's, and he stands in direct line of descent from him. . . . In its deepest implications his attack on Rousseau is an attack on his own alter-ego, and his own attitude is fundamentally akin to the Frenchman's throughout."[10] Leo Strauss makes a similar point in a seminar he taught on Rousseau in 1962: "Perhaps the greatest historical injustice which Nietzsche committed was never to make clear how much he owes to Rousseau. . . . He detested so much Rousseau and what he stood for that he neglected to emphasize that his position is unintelligible except as a reply to Rousseau above all."[11]

Though scholars are right to point to the distortions and simplifications contained in Nietzsche's interpretation of Rousseau and his relationship to Nietzsche's own thought, there nevertheless remain important differences between the two thinkers, and these differences in many ways reflect an important shift in the moral and cultural life of Europe from the late eighteenth to the late nineteenth century.[12] Specifying these differences in a more nuanced and historically just manner than Nietzsche does will be a crucial part of the chapters that follow. And once we have gained a more precise understanding of the differences that divide Rousseau and Nietzsche, we cannot avoid the fundamental question of the relative merits of their positions and whether the movement from the one to the other—the trajectory of nineteenth-century moral, cultural, and political thought—ultimately constitutes an advance or decline. Taylor, for example, seems to point to the latter,[13] as does Keith Ansell-Pearson (at least with respect to politics) in his pioneering study of Nietzsche's relationship to Rousseau.[14] My own position inclines in the other direction. Without taking anything away from Rousseau's pathbreaking achievement, I argue that Nietzsche's critique of modernity speaks more directly to our current nihilistic predicament and that his solutions therefore provide more useful guidance in trying to escape from it.

Perhaps an even more fundamental question than that of the relative merits of Rousseau and Nietzsche goes not to their differences but to what they have in common, asking whether their whole critique of the Enlightenment and of the bourgeois liberalism that belongs to it has been misguided. There are two responses to make to those critics who attack Rousseau and Nietzsche in the name of Enlightenment liberalism. First, though this liberalism has certainly given modern human beings many good things, enumerated most recently and dogmatically by Steven Pinker,[15] its weak spot has always been the sort of human being it promoted: one who is preoccupied with comfortable self-preservation and driven by the calculation of self-interest rather than imagination and lofty goals. Rousseau and Nietzsche both speak to this moral and cultural deficit in modern Enlightenment liberalism. The second point to make, though, is that Rousseau and Nietzsche are not to be understood as simply antimodern or anti-Enlightenment thinkers. Both embody important aspects of the Enlightenment—its commitment to intellectual probity and valuing of individual personality, for example—and question modernity from within the modern horizon itself. For this reason, Arthur Melzer refers to Rousseau as the "first *defector*" from the Enlightenment, its "first 'dialectical' opponent."[16] I would argue that Nietzsche is another such "defector" or "dialectical opponent."[17]

There is another set of critics who also find the shift in the moral and cultural life of Europe inaugurated by Rousseau and radicalized by Nietzsche to be problematic, but they do so not because they see these two thinkers as traitors to the Enlightenment or modernity but because they see them as dialectical outgrowths of it. This is in many ways the position taken by Melzer, who argues that Rousseau's extreme individualism "is only an extension and radicalization of the bourgeois individualism of Hobbes and Locke," leading to "an intense and redoubled longing for individuality" and "an obsession with sincerity."[18] Allan Bloom and Daniel Bell make the point even more polemically, arguing that the ideal of sincerity or authenticity that Rousseau and Nietzsche articulate has led to a shallow culture of narcissism and solipsism and to a kind of cult of nonconformity and creativity.[19]

It is no doubt true that the ideal of sincerity or authenticity has been debased, trivialized, and commercialized in our time; but that is no reason to abandon it altogether. In this regard, despite my disagreement with his specific conclusions, I follow the approach of Charles Taylor, who maintains that while the modern ideal of authenticity "has degraded," it is nevertheless "very worthwhile in itself, and indeed . . . unrepudiable by moderns. So what we need is neither root-and-branch condemnation nor uncritical praise. . . . What we need is a work of retrieval, through which this ideal can help us restore our practice."[20] It is in just such a work of retrieval that I engage in this book, not only with respect to the ideal of authenticity, but with respect to the whole movement of moral, cultural, and political reflection that runs from Rousseau to Nietzsche. My central claim is that in order to understand ourselves as modern human beings, we must engage with Rousseau's and Nietzsche's profound analyses of the discontents of modernity and their attempts to create a new, psychologically richer, and more spiritually nourishing image of the human.[21] We may not fully accept their specific diagnoses of our cultural malaise or their specific prescriptions to cure it, but we must come to grips with them if we are to confront the challenges of modernity intelligently.

Genealogies of Modernity

Any comparison of Rousseau and Nietzsche must begin with their radical critiques of modern society. This is the similarity that stands out most immediately when viewing the two thinkers side by side. Both lament the degraded condition into which modern, "enlightened" humanity finds itself, albeit for different reasons. In the case of Rousseau, it is the inequality of modern society and the hypocrisy, self-division, and loss of civic virtue it has spawned that inspires his impassioned critique. Nietzsche takes almost the opposite position on what ails modern humanity. It is precisely democratic equality that poses the greatest danger to modern man, reducing him to a perfect herd animal, "the dwarf animal of equal rights and claims" (*BGE* 203), a mediocre, blinking being who craves nothing more than peace, security, and bourgeois comfort.

Besides leveling devastating critiques of modern, enlightened bourgeois society, Rousseau and Nietzsche both embed those critiques in a historical account of how human beings came to be in the degraded condition in which they find themselves. Here, too, the similarities give way to important differences, corresponding to their different interpretations of the fundamental problems of modern society. Thus Rousseau traces the progressive corruption of humanity that results from the growth of inequality and the activation of an unhealthy form of *amour propre* that leads human beings to constantly compare themselves with one another and compete for advantage. Nietzsche, on the other hand, sees the leveling, weakening, and diminishing of modern humanity as the result of the progressive moralization and taming of human beings; it is our good morality that accounts for the pitiableness of our civilization, not the pitiableness of our civilization for our bad morality (*D* 163).

Though Rousseau and Nietzsche place the blame for our degraded condition on different factors in their genealogies, they both identify an initial condition prior to that degradation that serves to denaturalize it. The degraded condition in which modern humanity finds itself is not the product of human nature as such, but of historical circumstances and decisions that were not inevitable and therefore are not irremediable. This denaturalizing function of Rousseau's and Nietzsche's genealogies of modernity is what ultimately gives them not only their critical but also their constructive power. Again, though, their conceptions of the initial situation and of human nature more generally differ fundamentally. Rousseau's genealogy of vice rests on his conception of the natural goodness of man. Nietzsche dismisses this conception as a piece of unhistorical "superstition" or "fantasy" (*HH* 463), reflective of the mendacious sentimentalism and moralism of the eighteenth century (*WP* 95–96). In its place, he offers a more terrifying, less sentimental image of *homo natura*.

Whether Nietzsche's conception of human nature is more accurate than Rousseau's and, more generally, whether his genealogy of modernity's discontents is more profound are questions the ensuing analysis will try to answer. In many ways, how one answers these questions depends on where one comes down on Rousseau's and Nietzsche's respective diagnoses of the fundamental problem of modernity. If one sees inequality and the inflamed *amour propre* that grows out of it as the fundamental problem, then Rousseau's analysis will be more compelling.[1] If mediocrity, spiritual flattening, and the loss of human greatness seem to be our greatest danger, then Nietzsche's analysis will come out on top. On the specific question of human nature, a more definitive answer can be ventured. While I show that Rousseau's conception of the natural goodness of man is not as naïve or sentimental as Nietzsche supposes, I also argue that Nietzsche goes considerably further than Rousseau in uncovering the nonmoral and animalistic bases of human nature. In this regard, he is right to see himself as sharing in the greater realism, historical sense, and intellectual honesty of the nineteenth century, which has discovered a "*truer image* of 'man'" than the natural man of Rousseau (*WP* 1017; see also 95).

Rousseau on Natural Goodness

In his prizewinning *Discourse on the Sciences and Arts* of 1750, Rousseau launches his famous critique of the insincerity of modern European morality, a morality that possesses "the appearances of all the virtues without having a single one." What is most problematic about this morality, from his point of view, is that it hypocritically conceals motives that are the exact opposite of the ones it pretends to act on. Beneath the "deceitful veil" and "vaunted urbanity which we owe to the enlightenment of our century," there lies nothing but suspicion, hatred, and betrayal (*FD* 7–8). Rousseau ultimately traces this hypocrisy back to the bourgeois social system that puts "men in a position where they can only live together by obstructing, supplanting, deceiving, betraying, destroying one another," a system in which "everyone pretends to be working for the profit or reputation of the rest, while only seeking to raise his own above theirs and at their expense" (PN 100). He elaborates on this fatal contradiction at the heart of the bourgeois social system in the *Second Discourse*, where he urges readers to "look through [their] frivolous displays of beneficence to what goes on in the recesses of men's hearts." There it will be found that despite the pretense of concern for the welfare of others, each man harbors the secret desire to cut "every throat until he is sole master of the universe" (*SD* 197–99; see also 170–71).

Rousseau's critique of the insincerity of bourgeois morality points toward another key aspect of his critique of modern society—namely, the self-interestedness of liberal politics that comes at the expense of the public good. In contrast to the civic spiritedness that animated ancient Sparta and Rome, politics in the emergent liberalism of Rousseau's day has ceased to be the focal point of the citizen's activity and instead merely provides peace and security so that individuals can pursue their own private interest, often at one another's expense. In this liberal system of politics, commerce and luxury replace civic participation and virtue as the principal objects of individual endeavor. As Rousseau succinctly puts it in the *First Discourse*, "Ancient politicians forever spoke of morals and virtue; ours speak only of commerce and money" (*FD* 18). This is the basis of his famous diatribe against representatives in the *Social Contract*. The whole purpose of having representatives, he argues there, is to relieve people of the duty to participate in the public's business so that they can focus on their own private business. This is exactly the reverse of what happens in a well-constituted state, where public business takes precedence over the private and "citizens do everything with their own hands and nothing with money" (*SC* 3:15).

As momentous as Rousseau's critique of modern, liberal bourgeois society is, it is his genealogical account of the ills he diagnoses that constitutes his most original contribution to late-modern moral and political thought. His key insight is that these ills are not inherent in human nature but have been brought about by human beings themselves through the social institutions they have created. This is what I have referred to as the denaturalizing function of Rousseau's genealogical project. In the "Preface to Narcissus," he draws attention to this denaturalizing function when he states that his originality does not consist in exposing the various self-contradictions of the social system; these have been pointed out by hundreds of sermonizers. His distinctive contribution consists, rather, in laying bare the causes of the evils perceived: "Above all I point out something highly consoling and useful by showing that all these vices belong not so much to man, as to man badly governed" (PN 101; see also *SD* 197; LV 233–34).

The fundamental premise on which Rousseau bases his argument that man's miseries are of his own making is that "man is naturally good" (LR 70; *SD* 197; LMal 575), that "there is no original perversity in the human heart" (*E* 92; *LB* 28). In his *Dialogues*, Rousseau claims that the idea that "nature made man happy and good, but that society depraves him and makes him miserable" is the great principle that runs through all his writings (*RJ* 213). In particular, he cites the *First* and *Second Discourses* and *Emile* as the three writings in which this principle is most fully developed (LMal 575). In this section, my focus will be on Rousseau's account of man's natural goodness in the *Second Discourse*. This account forms the crucial backdrop for Rousseau's genealogy of vice that I take up in the next section. It is also the account that bears most directly on Nietzsche's own genealogical investigations.

The magnificent opening paragraph of the *Second Discourse* discloses the key presupposition of Rousseau's genealogical enterprise in that work— namely, that human nature cannot simply be equated with the condition of human beings as they have come to be today. It is precisely because human beings have changed dramatically over the course of time that knowledge of human nature is extremely difficult to acquire. Comparing human nature to the mythological statue of Glaucus, "which time, sea, and storms had so disfigured that it less resembled a God than a ferocious beast," Rousseau maintains that the human soul has been radically altered over the course of time by the acquisition of knowledge, errors, and alien passions to the point that it is now "almost unrecognizable" (*SD* 124). Knowledge of human nature therefore requires an act of radical historical excavation in which all the accidental accretions of time are wiped away so that the original thing itself can be seen in all its pristine otherness. This is the task of the first part of the *Second Discourse*, which is devoted to describing what human beings were like in what Rousseau calls the "pure state of nature" (*SD* 132, 146, 214, 215).

In inquiring into the condition of human beings in the state of nature, Rousseau of course follows in the footsteps of his great predecessors Hobbes and Locke. But he makes clear that he intends to go further than they did in uncovering original human nature: "The philosophers who have examined the foundations of society have all felt the necessity of going back as far as the state of nature, but none of them has reached it. . . . All of them, continually speaking of need, greed oppression, desires, and pride transferred to the state of nature ideas they had taken from society. They spoke of savage man and depicted civil man" (*SD* 132). Rousseau does not mention Hobbes or Locke by name in this passage; but in a slightly later writing, he explicitly refers to Hobbes—"one of the finest geniuses that ever lived"—as the author of the error that confuses natural man with the men one sees around one. He adds: "A superficial philosopher observes souls kneaded and risen a thousand times over in the leaven of society and believes he has observed man." Philosophers in general "only know what they see, and they have never seen nature. They know well enough what a Londoner or a Parisian is; but they will never know what a man is" (*SW* 164–65; see also *LP* 227).

Rousseau points to the lack of historical sense on the part of philosophers in several places (see, e.g., PN 101n; *SD* 209–11); and his profound awareness of the historicity of human beings, his recognition that "the mankind of one age is not the mankind of another age" (*SD* 186), is one of the things that most closely links him with Nietzsche.[2] Rousseau does not, however, offer a strictly empirical account of human beings in the state of nature but, rather, one that is hypothetical or conjectural, "better suited to elucidate the nature of things than to show their genuine origin" (*SD* 125; see also 132).[3] The primitive human being that lies at the end of this regressive analysis is as close to being an animal as a human being can possibly be. He is limited to "purely animal functions," and the "only goods he knows in the universe are food, a female, and rest." Because he has only physical needs that are easy to satisfy, he has no occasion to reason or to acquire knowledge, and this ensures that his desires never exceed his physical needs or his capacity to satisfy them. Above all, the primitive human being has no imagination, the faculty most responsible for creating an excess of desires over the capacity to fulfill them and thereby for bringing about human unhappiness. Without imagination, foresight, or curiosity, the primitive human being lives completely in the present, yielding to "the sole sentiment of [his] present existence, with no idea of the future, however near it may be" (*SD* 142–43; *E* 80–83).

Though the primitive or natural human being resembles an animal in almost every way, Rousseau nevertheless indicates that he differs from an animal in two important respects. First, he possesses free agency. Whereas an animal is "nothing but an ingenious machine" in which natural instinct does all the work, man has the ability to act independently of and even against natural instinct (*SD* 134–35, 140–41). Rousseau admits, however, that there are potential difficulties with this metaphysical idea of free agency[4] and therefore turns to another specific property that can less controversially account for the peculiar open-endedness and plasticity that differentiates human beings from animals: namely, perfectibility. This is the faculty that, "with the aid of circumstances, develops all the others." Whereas "an animal is at the end of several months what it will be for the rest of its life," human beings have an almost unlimited capacity to develop their faculties in a multitude of ways. Unlike animals, human beings are given almost nothing; they have to learn everything. That is why they are capable of becoming imbeciles, of losing through old age what they have acquired over a lifetime. While this "distinctive and almost unlimited faculty" of self-perfection allows human beings to go beyond their given, natural endowment and achieve enlightenment and progress, Rousseau dwells less on the progressive implications of perfectibility and instead emphasizes how it draws man "out of that original condition in which he would spend tranquil and innocent days" and leads to all his miseries (SD 141; see also E 61–62).

In the pure state of nature, however, man's perfectibility remains *in potentia*; several conditions prevent it from becoming activated. The first and most important of these conditions—also the least plausible, from a purely historical point of view—is that the primitive human being is an absolutely solitary creature, having no more need for another human being than a monkey or wolf has for its own kind (SD 149). Most radically, Rousseau denies that human beings in the pure state of nature are even united in families. In this primitive state, where there were no "houses or huts or property of any kind, everyone bedded down at random and often for one night only; males and females united fortuitously, according to chance encounters" (SD 145). In arguing for the solitariness of human beings in the state of nature, Rousseau radicalizes the individualism of Hobbes's state of nature. But unlike Hobbes, Rousseau does not see this individualism as leading to a state of enmity or war; indeed, just the opposite. Precisely because human beings are solitary and self-sufficient, they have no need of others, and they certainly have no need to compete with or dominate others. Because "the state of nature is the state in which the care for our own self-preservation is least prejudicial to the self-preservation of others, it follows that this state was the most conducive to peace and the best suited to mankind" (SD 151).

Where Rousseau departs most radically from Hobbes, of course, is in denying that pride or *amour propre* has any place in the pure state of nature. Because the primitive human being sees himself as the only spectator in his universe, he does not make comparisons between himself and others; nor is he subject to feeling undervalued or disrespected, the true source of the desire for vengeance. Even if he does happen to come into conflict with another human being—over a piece of food, for example—the matter is quickly settled "without the slightest stirring of arrogance or resentment": "Since pride has no share in the fight, it ends with a few fisticuffs; the victor eats, the vanquished goes off to seek his fortune, and everything is once again at peace" (*SD* 199, 218; see also 154).

In a way, the absence of *amour propre* in the primitive human being, the fact that he is driven exclusively by nonrelative, noncomparative *amour de soi*, makes up almost all of what Rousseau understands by the natural goodness of man. Natural goodness in this sense has nothing to do with moral goodness or virtue; it consists merely in the absence of the wickedness or perversity that derives from *amour propre* (*SD* 150–52). Rousseau provides an important gloss on this negative definition of natural goodness in the *Letter to Beaumont*, where he says that "the only passion born with man, namely *amour de soi*, is a passion in itself indifferent to good and evil." Insofar as he is indifferent to good and evil, the natural human being also lacks conscience, which develops only with our understanding and our ability to make comparisons. Such a human being "knows only himself. . . . He neither hates nor loves anything. Restricted to physical instinct alone, he is null, he is stupid. This is what I have shown in my *Discourse on Inequality*" (*LB* 28).

There is one sentiment that belongs to the primitive human being, however, that gives his natural goodness a more positive dimension. This is the sentiment of pity, or the "innate repugnance" to see one's fellow human beings suffer. Rousseau is careful not to overidealize this natural sentiment, which is "prior to all reflection" and can even be found in animals. The "maxim of natural goodness" that flows from natural pity—"*Do your good with the least possible harm to others*"—falls far short of "that sublime maxim of reasoned justice *Do unto others as you would have them do unto you*" (*SD* 152, 54). In order for pity to develop beyond this limited natural sentiment, it needs to be stimulated by reflection, comparison, and especially imagination (*EOL* 267–78). Rousseau brings this out in his discussion of fully developed pity in *Emile*, which in hardheaded fashion also emphasizes the role of selfishness and *amour propre* (*E* 221–31).[5]

Rousseau's discussion of natural pity in the *Second Discourse* is perfectly in keeping with the unsentimental and realistic character of his entire account of man's natural goodness in that work. It is important to underline this realistic, even "scientific" character of Rousseau's account because Rousseau is so often accused of being naïve, tender-minded, and idealistic for attributing natural goodness to human beings. Nietzsche himself falls prey to this stereotypical mistake when he criticizes Rousseau's concept of natural goodness as an "insipid and cowardly" attempt to read Christian morality into nature (*WP* 340). He often contrasts Rousseau's idealism and sentimentalism in this regard with the greater realism, animalism, and intellectual honesty of the nineteenth century (*WP* 95, 102, 117, 120, 1017). As we have seen, though, Rousseau's naturally good human being is nothing if not animalistic; and his concept of natural goodness, far from being idealistic or moralistic, consists essentially in the primitive human being's not being subject to *amour propre* and not gratuitously harming his fellow human beings.

Precisely because man in the state of nature is not much more than a "stupid, limited animal" (*SC* 1:8; see also *LB* 28), he does not represent Rousseau's ideal. Against the common primitivist misunderstanding of his intention, Rousseau in no way advocates a return to the state of nature. He explicitly rejects the notion that societies should be destroyed, mine and thine annihilated, and "men return to live in the forests with bears." Because the original simplicity of most human beings has been irrevocably destroyed, they "can no longer live on grass and acorns, nor do without laws and chiefs" (*SD* 203; see also *LP* 227; *RJ* 213). And even if it were possible to return to the pure state of nature, Rousseau is quite clear it would not be desirable to do so. Had we remained in it, we would never have developed our highest faculties or "tasted the most delicious sentiment of the soul, which is the love of virtue" (GenMS 154–55).

This is not to say that Rousseau's account of man's goodness in the state of nature does not have important normative implications. In the first place, as we have seen, it serves to denaturalize the current degraded condition of human beings, showing that this condition is not the result of human nature per se but, rather, has been brought about by human beings through the social institutions they have created (PN 101; *SD* 197; LV 233–34). What previous thinkers had attributed to the evil inherent in human nature, Rousseau attributes to social and historical circumstances. And the optimistic implication that can be drawn from this tracing of our ills back to social and historical circumstances is that what human beings have done to themselves can be undone or redone by human beings as well. While it is an exaggeration to say that Rousseau considered human beings to be "infinitely malleable"[6]—we will see that his solutions to the problems of modern society generally involve the manipulation of fixed features of human nature (for example, *amour de soi*, pity, and even *amour propre*)—it is nevertheless true that he holds out the hope that human beings can be reshaped and transformed in fundamental ways.

But does Rousseau's account of man's natural goodness in the pure state of nature offer any more determinate guidance for the reshaping of human beings and human society? The answer is yes, and in two different ways. In the first place, the naturally good human being serves as a formal model of the kind of wholeness, independence, and freedom that we no longer enjoy. Though we cannot return to the simple wholeness, independence, and freedom of primitive human life, Rousseau nevertheless hopes to reestablish these qualities for modern human beings on completely different grounds— rational and social—from those found in the state of nature. The pure state of nature also provides normative guidance by identifying the principles of self-preservation and pity from which "all the rules of natural right" flow. Again, Rousseau points out that because we no longer live in the state nature, reason must subsequently reestablish these rules of natural right "on other foundations, when by its successive developments it has succeeded in stifling nature" (*SD* 127).[7] But this is the task of the *Social Contract*. In the *Second Discourse*, Rousseau is more concerned to use the model of the state of nature as a benchmark from which to trace the genealogy of modern humanity's vices. It is to that genealogy that we now turn.

Rousseau's Genealogy of Vice

In his *Letter to Beaumont*, Rousseau provides a retrospect of his writings, repeating that the "fundamental principle" running through all of them is the natural goodness of human beings. From this principle it follows that "all the vices imputed to the human heart are not natural to it; I have stated the manner in which they are born. I have followed their genealogy, so to speak, and I have shown how, through continuous deterioration of their original goodness, men finally become what they are." How did this deterioration take place? Rousseau describes it largely in terms of the fundamental contradiction of the social system that is such a prominent part of his critique of modern society. Once individuals begin to associate with one another and their particular interests come into conflict, *amour de soi* "changes into *amour propre*," men regard one another as "born enemies," and "none finds his own good except in someone else's ill." Of course, no one pursues his selfish interest overtly but, rather, hypocritically conceals it under the pretense of devotion to the public good (*LB* 28–29; see also PN 100; *SD* 197–99). Rousseau later goes on to claim that it is this contradiction of the social system that ultimately explains "all the vices of men and all the ills of society" (*LB* 52; see also LMal 575).[8]

The genealogy of vice that he lightly sketches in the *Letter to Beaumont* Rousseau develops at much greater length in the second part of the *Second Discourse*. There he makes clear that the degeneration he traces was not a necessary consequence of human nature but, rather, the product of a series of chance events. Human perfectibility and the faculties it spawned existed only in potentiality in the state of nature; in order to develop, "they needed the fortuitous concatenation of several foreign causes which might never have arisen and without which [man] would have remained in his primitive condition" (*SD* 159; see also 139). This, again, follows from the fundamental principle of the natural goodness of man. Wickedness or vice is in no way sown into human nature; it must come from elsewhere (*LB* 35). This is the lesson not only of the *Second Discourse* but also of *Emile*, a book Rousseau describes as a "treatise on the original goodness of man, destined to show how vice and error, foreign to his constitution, enter it from the outside and insensibly change him" (*RJ* 213).

Though contingent, the developments Rousseau describes in the *Second Discourse* are by no means arbitrary, and sometimes they seem almost inevitable. This is no more true than of the development of the first distinctively human faculties in response to the inevitable difficulties that supervened on the pure state of nature. Human beings had to figure out how to get food from inaccessible places, compete with other animals who wanted this food, avoid or combat ferocious beasts, deal with harsh climates and the variability of seasons, and so forth. These challenges and the need to respond to them gave rise to comparative ideas such as fast and slow, strong and weak, and bold and fearful, and eventually human beings became aware of their superiority to other animals. This "aroused the first movement of pride (*orgeuil*) in [man]"; and though at this point he considered himself only "in the first rank as a species," the ground was being prepared for the emergence of that *amour propre* by which he would later "claim first rank as an individual." It was at this point, too, that human beings sometimes came together to accomplish a common project—for example, capturing a deer—thus giving rise to a rudimentary and purely ad hoc form of sociality (*SD* 161–63).

As important as these initial developments were, Rousseau's genealogy of vice takes on deeper significance when it turns to what he calls the "first revolution" in human history, that which "brought about the establishment and differentiation of families and introduced a sort of property." This revolution came about when human beings began to construct huts for themselves and live together as families, a development that "gave rise to the sweetest sentiments known to man, conjugal love and paternal love." More fateful developments of the human heart soon followed. As families came to live next to one another, young people of the opposite sex began to spend more time together. Comparing one another on the basis of merit and beauty, they began to experience "sentiments of preference." Rousseau describes the revolution of the human heart now taking place with exquisite ambiguity: "A tender and sweet sentiment steals into the soul, and at the least obstacle becomes an impetuous frenzy; jealously awakens with love; discord triumphs, and the gentlest of all passions receives sacrifices of human blood" (*SD* 164–65).

Rousseau here describes the momentous emergence of *amour propre*, a sentiment that "originates in comparisons" (*SD* 218) and leads every individual to seek to be first among his fellows. This, too, seems to be an almost inevitable development (see also *E*, 241–15, 235), and its fatefulness becomes increasingly evident as Rousseau proceeds. He relates how increased contact among young men and women led them to gather in front or their huts or around a tree (in the *Essay on the Origin of Languages*, they gather around wells [*EOL*, 277–78]). They began to amuse themselves by singing and dancing, and this led them to make ever more comparisons about who was the best singer or dancer, who was the handsomest or most eloquent. As a result, "everyone began to look at everyone else and to wish to be looked at himself, and public esteem acquired a price." Rousseau makes clear that this unleashing of *amour propre* constitutes a crucial transition in his genealogy of vice: it was "the first step at once toward inequality and vice: from these first preferences arose vanity and contempt on the one hand, shame and envy on the other" (*SD* 166).

Rousseau indicates that this is the stage of development reached by most of the "savage" peoples observed by his contemporaries, and he warns that it should not be confused with the pure state of nature described earlier in the *Second Discourse*. Whereas men in the pure state of nature were gentle and largely indifferent to their fellows, men at this later stage are particularly sensitive to the harms done to them by others, perceiving in them an intentional slight to their dignity and contempt for their person. As a result, "vengeances became terrible, and men bloodthirsty and cruel." And yet Rousseau famously does not condemn this stage of human development. Insofar as it occupied "a just mean between the indolence of the primitive state and the petulant activity of our *amour propre*," he says it "must have been the happiest and the most lasting epoch," the one that was "least subject to revolutions, the best for man" (*SD* 166–67). Among other things, this suggests that blame for our current degraded condition cannot be placed on *amour propre* alone.[9] Something else was needed to transform this relative sentiment awakened by love and the desire to be loved into the source of human misery.

That something else was the division of labor and economic interdependence introduced by the discovery of metallurgy and agriculture. With this second revolution in the state of nature we arrive at the decisive turning point of Rousseau's genealogy of vice. Prior to the advent of metallurgy and agriculture, human beings were economically self-sufficient, doing all the things necessary for survival by themselves. As long as human beings "applied themselves only to tasks a single individual could perform, and to arts that did not require the collaboration of several hands," Rousseau claims, "they lived free, healthy, good, and happy." The discovery of metallurgy and agriculture destroyed this primitive independence, leading men to specialize in one or the other of these arts and to exchange the surplus of what they produced for what they otherwise lacked. Rousseau leaves us in no doubt about the disastrousness of this development: "As soon as one man needed the help of another, as soon as it was found to be useful for one to have provisions for two, equality disappeared, property appeared, work became necessary, and the vast forests changed into smiling fields . . . where slavery and misery were soon seen to sprout and grow together with the harvests" (SD 167–69).

This passage, along with so many others in Rousseau's writings, makes clear that he sees mutual dependence of the sort found in an economy based on the division of labor, self-interest, and exchange to be the true source of human misery and vice. We will see more fully why this is so in a moment, but for now it is worth underlining that if there is a villain in Rousseau's genealogy of vice, this is it. As he puts it earlier in the Discourse: "Everyone must see that since ties of servitude are formed solely by men's mutual dependence and reciprocal needs that unite them, it is impossible to subjugate a man without first having placed him in a position of being unable to do without another" (SD 159). He makes a similar point in Emile, arguing that the genuinely free and happy individual is one who "has no need to put another's arms at the end of his own" and that "dependence on men . . . engenders all the vices" (E 84, 85).

Rousseau highlights two fundamental consequences of the new situation in which "one man needed the help of another": property and inequality. With respect to the first, he argues that once land began to be cultivated as a result of the discovery of agriculture, it was necessary that it be divided. There would be no motivation to cultivate the land unless one was assured of not being despoiled of the harvest. As the process of planting and harvesting was repeated from one year to the next, continuous possession of the land soon transformed itself into property (SD 144, 169). At the outset of his genealogy of vice in part 2 of the Discourse, Rousseau famously identifies property as the principal cause of the "crimes, wars, murders . . . miseries and horrors" that have afflicted humanity, and he calls the first man who enclosed a piece of ground "the true founder of civil society" (SD 161).

But property would not have had these pernicious effects if everyone had been equal in talents and had the same ability to appropriate equal amounts of property. However, this was not the case. In the pure state of nature, Rousseau argues, there was relatively little inequality of talents because everyone partook of the same simple manner of life; and what little inequality there was had almost no influence because of the lack of relations between people. This changed with the advent of the division of labor, mutual dependence, and property. Now being stronger, more skilled, or more ingenious allowed one to acquire more property; and having more property allowed one to enjoy a way of life and education that exacerbated the original inequality of talents. In this way, the differences between men that had little existence or effect in the pure state of nature became "more perceptible, more permanent in their effects, and [began] to exercise a corresponding influence on the fate of individuals" (SD 157–58, 169–70).

Of course, it is not the sheer fact of inequality that makes it so pernicious, according to Rousseau, but that it forces everyone to become consumed with the perpetual and restless desire to achieve comparative economic advantage over his fellows. Because everyone's rank and fate is determined not only by the amount of goods he has but by the qualities that enable him to acquire them—strength, beauty, eloquence, intelligence—men soon began to affect or simulate these qualities; "for one's own advantage, one had to seem other than one in fact was. To be and to appear became two entirely different things" (SD 170; see also 187). And because everything depends on one's relative position in such a system, there is no genuine common interest between people; everyone seeks to profit at everyone else's expense. This "instills in all men a black inclination to harm one another, a secret jealousy that is all the more dangerous as it often assumes the mask of benevolence in order to strike its blow in greater safety" (SD 170; see also 197–98). Rousseau never bought into the eighteenth-century orthodoxy that economic interdependence produces a common interest among men, obliging each "to contribute to everyone else's happiness in order to secure his own." Rather, he consistently argues that such interdependence puts "men in a position where they can only live together by obstructing, supplanting, deceiving, betraying, destroying one another," leading to a situation in which "everyone pretends to be working for the profit or reputation of the rest, while only seeking to raise his own above theirs and at their expense" (PN 100; see also LB 29).

It is not necessary to follow in detail the rest of Rousseau's genealogy of vice in the Second Discourse, since it mainly shows how the establishment of the right of property in civil society and the institution of government to protect it merely codified and deepened the peculiar evil that had already emerged with the rise of the division of labor, property, and inequality in the state of nature. In any event, the central thrust of Rousseau's genealogy has become abundantly clear: the source of human vice and misery is not to be sought in human nature but in the social institutions and practices that have corrupted it, above all in the system of mutual dependence and inequality based on property that has given *amour propre* its peculiarly destructive bent.

Nietzsche's genealogy will take a different tack, placing the blame for the degradation of modern humanity not on our bad social institutions but on our "good morality" (*D* 163). We must now consider it.

Nietzsche on *Homo Natura*

As with Rousseau's, Nietzsche's genealogical investigations grow out of a radical critique of modern humanity and civilization. But whereas Rousseau's critique focuses on the insincerity and hypocrisy of the modern bourgeois, Nietzsche's emphasizes the latter's loss of direction, purpose, and meaning and his consequent lack of passion, energy, and aspiration. In Nietzsche's early writings he blames science and the historical sense for this nihilistic situation, but in his mature writings he increasingly comes to see morality as the primary culprit—specifically, the morality of pity or altruism that derives from Christianity, what he sometimes calls "herd morality" or the "morality of timidity" (see *BGE* 197–201). Concerned above all with comfortable self-preservation, such a morality seeks to abolish suffering while striving after "the green-pasture happiness of the herd, with security, lack of danger, comfort, and an easier life for everyone" (*BGE* 44). Democracy is the ultimate political expression of this morality (*BGE* 202), and its ultimate product is the blinking "last man," without passion, longing, or love (*Z* 1, prologue, 15), "the dwarf animal of equal rights and claims" (*BGE* 203).

Like Rousseau, Nietzsche sees modern humanity's degraded condition as the product of a historical process; human nature cannot simply be equated with what human beings have come to be today. This is where almost all previous philosophers have gone wrong, in Nietzsche's view: they have taken human beings as they currently exist and assumed that they are "eternal facts" embodying a fixed and constant nature. "Lack of historical sense," he writes, "is the family failing of all philosophers" (*HH* 2). Rousseau, however, is no exception to this rule, according to Nietzsche. Despite titanic efforts to uncover original human nature in all its pristine otherness, Rousseau's conception of the natural goodness of man ends up being nothing more than an unhistorical "superstition" or "fantasy," embodying an "insipid and cowardly"—that is, Christian—conception of nature (*HH* 463; *WP* 100, 340). Nietzsche intends to approach his genealogical task in a more radical and historically rigorous manner. Writing in the wake of Darwin and the deepening historical sense of the nineteenth century, Nietzsche uncovers something far more terrifying and animal-like than Rousseau's gentle and compassionate beast.

Nietzsche's differences with Rousseau regarding human nature are evident even in his earliest writings. In *The Birth of Tragedy*, for example, he describes

the satyr chorus out of which Greek tragedy grew as a chorus of natural beings who live "behind all civilization" and provide the civilized human being
with the metaphysical comfort that "life is, at the bottom of things, despite all
changes of appearances, indestructibly powerful and pleasurable." Similar to
"the idyllic shepherd of more recent times," the satyr reflects "a longing for
the primitive and the natural." But Nietzsche makes clear that the satyr comes
much closer to the "real truth of nature"—the Dionysian ground of existence
consisting of the "'witches' brew' of sensuality and cruelty"—than the "sentimental, flute-playing, tender shepherd" does. Interestingly, he adds that the
satyr is "not a mere ape" but represents "the highest archetype of man, the
embodiment of his highest and most intense emotions" (BT 7–8). Already in
The Birth of Tragedy, it is clear that Nietzsche finds Rousseau's image of the
naturally good human being in the pure state of nature too sentimental and
insufficiently natural. We need to dig deeper to unearth the genuine *homo
natura.*

Nietzsche begins this more radical project of excavation in his middle
works, especially *Daybreak*. Instead of simply focusing on the Greeks, he extends his attention backward to primeval times, when the most fundamental
changes in human nature took place (see *HH* 2; *D* 18). Nietzsche's newfound
interest in primitive society and morality was no doubt influenced by post-
Darwinian theorists of evolutionary ethics such as his friend Paul Rée and
Herbert Spencer. But unlike these thinkers, Nietzsche is not interested in
merely providing a secular, utilitarian foundation for the prevailing morality
of altruism; rather, he uses his investigations of primitive society precisely
to undermine this morality. Like Rousseau, he seeks to denaturalize current
moral prejudices. This denaturalizing impulse is captured well in the first
aphorism of *Daybreak*: "All things that live long are gradually so saturated
with reason that their origin in unreason thereby becomes improbable. Does
not every precise history of an origination impress our feelings as paradoxical
and wantonly offensive? Does the good historian not, at bottom, constantly
contradict?" (*D* 1).

This aphorism also reveals an important difference in Nietzsche's genealogical approach at this stage of his career from that of Rousseau. Nietzsche
does not seek to uncover a pristine nature with which to contrast humanity's
current unnatural condition. No such pure or holy origin exists. Writing in
the wake of Darwin, Nietzsche states: "Formerly one sought the feeling of
the grandeur of man by pointing to his divine *origin*: this has now become
a forbidden way, for at its portal stands the ape, together with other gruesome beasts, grinning knowingly as if to say: no further in this direction!"
(*D* 49). In his genealogical investigations in *Daybreak*, Nietzsche seeks simply

to uncover the irrational origins of morality; his concern is solely to debunk. There is nothing in our human beginnings that can serve as a normative standard by which to judge our current degradation; nature has no normative status, even in the limited sense it had in Rousseau's genealogy. We will see that this outlook changes in Nietzsche's mature work. But in order to appreciate this change fully, we must first examine his initial attempt at a genealogy of morality.

Nietzsche refers to the primeval morality he investigates in *Daybreak* as the "morality of custom" (*Sittlichkeit der Sitte*). The name expresses the chief proposition of that morality—namely, that "morality is nothing other (therefore no *more!*) than obedience to customs, of whatever kind they may be; customs, however, are the *traditional* way of behaving and evaluating." For Nietzsche, unlike Rousseau, the primitive human being is not an asocial individual but a thoroughgoing creature of society and its customs. He comments that because we moderns are used to thinking of morality in terms of individual utility—in this respect, following in the footsteps of Socrates—we find it extraordinarily difficult to comprehend the thoroughly anti-individualistic morality of custom. The demands it imposed on individuals were made "*not* on account of the useful consequences [they] may have for the individual, but so that the hegemony of custom, tradition, shall be made evident in despite of private desires and advantages: the individual is to sacrifice himself" (*D* 9). Nietzsche devotes many aphorisms to showing just how arbitrary, fanciful, and unscientific these traditional customs were (see, e.g., *D* 10–13, 24, 33); nevertheless, he insists that they served the crucial purpose of reminding the individual of "the perpetual compulsion to practice customs." Without such compulsion, primitive society would have fallen apart. The "first proposition of civilization" is that "any custom is better than no custom" (*D* 16).

The purpose of Nietzsche's genealogy of morality in *Daybreak* is to show that though considerably weakened, the morality of custom still exerts an influence on current morality: "Under the dominion of the morality of custom, originality of every kind has acquired a bad conscience; the sky above the best men is for this very reason *to this very moment* gloomier than it need be" (*D* 9; italics added). At the same time, he acknowledges that modern human beings have also come to think differently about morality and individuality than our primitive forebears did. He makes this latter point even more emphatically in *The Gay Science*, stating that during the "longest and most remote periods of the human past," when herd morality reigned supreme, "nothing was more terrible than to feel that one stood by oneself"; individuality, freedom of thought, and egoism were considered painful, and the desire to live "according to one's own weight and measure" was considered "madness." But in the modern world, human beings have learned to think and feel differently about themselves, so much so that it is difficult for us to grasp the crudity of primitive morality. "Today," Nietzsche writes, "one feels responsible only for one's will and actions, and one finds pride in oneself. All our teachers of law start from this sense of self and pleasure in the individual, as if this had always been the fount of the law" (*GS* 117).

Apart from rigid obedience, Nietzsche highlights one other aspect of the primitive morality of custom in *Daybreak*, an aspect that sharply differentiates his conception of original human nature from Rousseau's: namely, cruelty. "Of all pleasures," he writes, the one that is "the greatest for men of that little imperiled community which is in a constant state of war" is "the pleasure of *cruelty*." In language that anticipates the later *Genealogy of Morality*, he states that "cruelty is one of the festive joys of mankind." Living in fear and feeling powerless in the face of enemies and the elements, primitive man enjoys "the highest gratification of the feeling of power" in the exercise of cruelty. And inferring from his own delight in cruelty that the gods too must enjoy the spectacle of suffering, primitive man engages in voluntary suffering and self-torture to provide such a spectacle. Indeed, anyone who sought to stir up "the inert but fertile mud of customs" needed to exhibit not only madness but also voluntary self-torture in order to inspire belief and counteract the bad conscience that always accompanied innovation. Again anticipating a point he makes repeatedly in his later writings, Nietzsche states that "every step in the field of free thought . . . has always had to be fought for with spiritual and bodily tortures. . . . Nothing has been bought more dearly than that little bit of human reason and feeling of freedom that now constitutes our pride" (*D* 18; see also *GM* 2.6; *BGE* 188).

But we must be careful about too closely assimilating Nietzsche's early genealogy in *Daybreak* to his later one in *The Genealogy of Morality*. As the examples above indicate, in *Daybreak* Nietzsche associates cruelty largely with voluntary suffering and self-torture and the feeling of power it produces with impotence. With respect to the latter, he claims that "because the feeling of impotence and fear was in a state of almost continuous stimulation so strongly and for so long, the *feeling of power* has evolved" to a high degree of subtlety; "the means discovered for creating this feeling almost constitute the history of culture" (*D* 23).[10] And at the end of this long ladder of culture "stands the *ascetic* or martyr," who derives the "liveliest feeling of power" from the sight of his own self-torment; never before has there been such a "voluptuousness of power" (*D* 113; see also *HH* 136–43). Again, Nietzsche's primary purpose here is to debunk, to expose the unsavory origins of our highest cultural practices—in particular, the intoxicating effects of Christianity à la

St. Paul and Pascal and of romantic art à la Wagner. The "feeling of power" is not yet the "will to power" with which Nietzsche identifies *homo natura*.

Nietzsche's definitive treatment of the genealogy of morality is, of course, found in the work of that name. As I have already suggested, the key difference from his earlier genealogy is that Nietzsche now contrasts the decadent morality of pity he wishes to criticize with a healthier, more natural morality that preceded it. As a result, this decadent morality is now characterized as "antinatural," which suggests that the opposite, natural system of valuation carries normative significance. In this way, the formal pattern of Nietzsche's genealogy comes to look more similar to Rousseau's. Nevertheless, despite this similarity in form and function, Nietzsche's *homo natura* looks very different from Rousseau's naturally good human being. This is what we now need to unpack.

Toward the beginning of *The Genealogy of Morality*, Nietzsche distinguishes his genealogical approach from that of "English psychologists" like his friend Rée (who was, of course, German) and Spencer. These post-Darwinian, utilitarian historians of morality, he claims, "lack the *historical spirit* itself. . . . They have been left in the lurch precisely by all the good spirits of history" (*GM* 1.2). Though Nietzsche's genealogical inquiries *are* driven by the historical spirit, they are not strictly based on historical fact. Despite his familiarity with the most advanced anthropological knowledge of his day, found in English writers like Walter Bagehot, John Lubbock, and Edward Tylor, his "hypotheses concerning [human] origins" are just as hypothetical as Rousseau's (*GM*, preface, 4). As he says about one of his conclusions in *Genealogy*, "This [is] stated as conjecture: for it is difficult to see to the bottom of such subterranean things" (*GM* 2.6). Because the exact sequence of Nietzsche's conjectural history is not always clear—differing in this regard from the more linear narrative of Rousseau's *Second Discourse*—I will sometimes draw on Nietzsche's other mature works as well as notes to reconstruct the steps leading from humanity's animal past to the establishment of primitive communities based on the morality of custom. In the next section, I will take up Nietzsche's account of the corruption of humanity through Jewish and Christian morality.

With respect to the animal human being prior to the establishment of fixed communities or "states," Nietzsche, unlike Rousseau, gives only the briefest of indications. Prior to finding themselves "enclosed once and for all within the sway of society and peace," he writes, human beings were "half animals who were happily adapted to wilderness, war, roaming about, adventures." Like Rousseau's "savages," these half animals possessed "an enormous quantity of freedom," but this freedom expressed itself not in the solitary enjoyment of the sweet sentiment of existence—again, Nietzsche rejects Rousseau's unhistorical claims about the asociality of primitive man—but in violence, cruelty, and aggression. The "instinct for freedom" found in the state of nature is, in other words, the "will to power" (*GM* 2.16–18). This understanding of *homo natura* in terms of the will to power constitutes the new element in Nietzsche's genealogy of morality in his mature writings (see *WP* 391). Nevertheless, his conception of human nature as violent, cruel, warlike, and victory-loving goes back to his earliest writings. This emphasis on the aggressive character of human personality is what distinguishes Nietzsche's view of human nature from Rousseau's from start to finish.

It is at this point in the story that Nietzsche introduces his notorious notion of the blond beast. How did the freely roaming animals mentioned above come to be enclosed within the confines of society? What was the origin of the oldest form of the state? Nietzsche does not resort to romantic or legal fictions to describe this "most fundamental of all changes" that human beings ever experienced. He declares that "some pack of blond beasts of prey, a race of conquerors and lords, which, organized in a warlike manner and with the power to organize, lays its paws on a population enormously superior in number perhaps, but still formless, still roaming." There is nothing here that resembles the ahistorical and rationalistic notion of the social contract: "Whoever can give orders, whoever is 'lord' by nature, whoever steps forward violently, in deed and gesture—what does he have to do with contracts!" And just as the oldest form of the state began in violence and compulsion, so it continued to exercise formative violence and compulsion long after its initial founding: "The oldest 'state' accordingly made its appearance as a terrible tyranny, as a crushing ruthless machinery, and continued to work until finally such a raw material of people and half animals was not only thoroughly kneaded and pliable but also *formed*" (*GM* 2.17; see also *BGE* 257).[11]

Nietzsche's account of the origin of the primitive state appears, of course, in the context of his larger hypothesis about the origin of the "bad conscience." I will take up this hypothesis in the next section; but first we must trace the more proximate consequences of the enclosure of the animal human being in the peace of the community. Given the forcible nature of the founding of the state, it is clear that its social structure initially had to consist of the powerful conquerors ruling over the weak, conquered population. Among the former, there develops the knightly-aristocratic morality described by Nietzsche in the first essay of *Genealogy*. This morality is characterized by a noble mode of valuation in which "good" refers to the qualities and actions of the powerful ruling group and "bad" refers to the qualities and actions of the powerless commoners; it has nothing to do with the morality of altruism or unegoistic action celebrated by "English" historians of morality (*GM* 1.2, 10). Rather, it is a morality of "self-glorification" in which "the noble human being honors himself as one who is powerful, also as one who has power over himself, who knows how to speak and be silent, who delights in being severe and hard with himself and respects all severity and hardness." It is not an individualistic morality; it is a morality that has "profound reverence for age and tradition," is intolerant, and discourages variation or deviation (*BGE* 260, 262). And though the members of the ruling caste are disdainful of the powerless commoners over whom they rule, they treat one another with "exquisite courtesy," exhibiting tremendous inventiveness in the various forms of "consideration, self-control, tact, loyalty, pride, and friendship" (*GS* 13; *GM* 1.11).

But this is only half the story. The violence and aggression that allow the powerful nobles to found the state do not simply die out once peaceful conditions have been established. The old animal instincts still lurk beneath the severity of morals and demand an outlet, which they find in the world outside the peaceful community. With respect to the outside world, the exquisitely mannered and severely restrained nobles "are not much better than uncaged beasts of prey." There, Nietzsche writes,

> they enjoy freedom from all social constraint; in the wilderness they recover the losses incurred through the tension that comes from a long enclosure and fencing-in within the peace of the community . . . At the base of all these noble races one cannot fail to recognize the beast of prey, the splendid *blond beast* who roams about lusting after booty and victory; from time to time this hidden base needs to discharge itself, the animal must get out, must go back into the wilderness. (*GM* 1.11)

It goes without saying that the return to the wilderness Nietzsche describes here has nothing in common with Rousseau's pastoral state of nature.

So much for the noble, powerful founders and rulers in the earliest communities. What about the formless roaming beasts they conquered and rule over? It is among these weaker animals who desire peace more than war that Nietzsche finds the origins of herd instinct and herd morality. Here it is important to bear in mind that we are dealing with the earliest form of the herd prior to being transformed and made sick by decadent religions. Nietzsche indicates that "there is nothing sick about the herd animal, it is even invaluable"; it has only "been made sick by the priest" (*WP* 282). Again in the next section, we will take up the process by which the herd animal becomes sick; here we are concerned with it only in its earliest, healthy form.

From what has been said so far about the origin of human communities, it is clear that the quality most prominently displayed by the weak herd animals who submitted to the powerful lords was obedience. Nietzsche writes: "At all times, as long as there have been human beings, there have also been herds of men (clans, communities, tribes, peoples, states, churches) and always a great many people who obeyed, compared with the small number of those commanding" (BGE 199). The "herd instinct of obedience" was crucial for the preservation of the earliest communities, and Nietzsche makes clear that preservation or survival was the preeminent concern of these early communities, which were surrounded by all sorts of dangers (BGE 201; GS 354; WP 260). Other qualities also contributed to the preservation of the community: "consideration, pity, fairness, mildness, reciprocity of assistance," what Nietzsche refers to as "little herd-animal virtues," the virtues of "little, good-natured sheep." But these qualities were always understood to be secondary to the warrior virtues that protected the community against external dangers—virtues that sprang from dangerous and aggressive drives like "an enterprising spirt, foolhardiness, vengefulness, craftiness, rapacity, and the lust to rule." In those early, endangered communities, fear of the external enemy always trumped love of neighbor (BGE 201; WP 203, 281).

The process of making the wayward herd animals in primitive communities more uniform, calculable, and communicable is ultimately the work of the morality of custom that Nietzsche has already described in *Human, All Too Human* and *Daybreak*. This morality receives its fullest and most graphic treatment in the second essay of *Genealogy*, where Nietzsche considers the painful process by which animal human beings became responsible beings and acquired the "right to make promises." The first step in this process involved creating a memory in human beings. Nietzsche points out that because forgetfulness is an essential part of living, necessary for the healthy "incorporation" of our experiences, extraordinary means were required to "burn" a memory into human beings: punishments, sacrifices, mutilations, and much blood and torture. In addition to memory, promising also presupposes that human beings are able to stick to what they have promised, to maintain their will over a long period of time in the midst of changing circumstances. "To be able to stand security for *his own future*," a human being "must first of all become *calculable, regular, necessary.*" This is the fundamental labor accomplished by the morality of custom. Though it involved the most gruesome "severity, tyranny, stupidity, and idiocy," it was only through the "morality of custom and social strait-jacket [that] man was actually *made* calculable" (GM 2.1–3; see also BGE 188).

As in the earlier *Daybreak*, cruelty plays a large role in Nietzsche's account of the morality of custom in *Genealogy*; virtually quoting from *Daybreak*, he says that it "constituted the great festival pleasure of more primitive men" (*GM* 2.6). Similarly, in *Beyond Good and Evil*, he claims that cruelty is a fundamental part of the "eternal basic text of *homo natura*." But in this latter aphorism, he also makes clear that cruelty encompasses more than the brutality of the blond beast, that it takes on more spiritual forms such as the intellectual conscience of the free-spirited seeker after knowledge (*BGE* 230; see also 229). Cruelty, aggression, love of victory, and the desire to overpower are all undeniable aspects of human nature, but they can be channeled in productive as well as destructive ways. This is an idea that Nietzsche articulated as far back as his early essay "Homer on Competition," wherein he claimed that the Dionysian Greek, who channeled his cruelty and "tiger-like pleasure in destruction" in civilized competition, was superior to the Dionysian barbarian (HC 187–89; *BT* 2).

All of this underlines that Nietzsche does not advocate a simple return to nature in its rawest or purest form any more than Rousseau does. Indeed, given his radically inhuman conception of nature as a witches' brew of cruelty and sensuality, he rejects this primitivist alternative even more emphatically than Rousseau does and paradoxically sees less of a tension between nature and history or nature and culture. For this reason, Nietzsche considers Rousseau's question whether man becomes morally better through civilization an amusing one, "since the reverse is obvious and is precisely that which speaks in favor of civilization" (*WP* 382). As we have seen, Nietzsche even appreciates the crucial role the harsh and capricious morality of custom played in subduing the wild and wayward animal in primitive humanity. In *Beyond Good and Evil*, he captures this paradoxical relationship between nature and culture, arguing that it is only by tyrannizing nature and submitting to seemingly capricious laws that poets, orators, and logicians have been able to achieve the beauty, rigor, and integrity of their creations: "The curious fact is that all there is or has been on earth of freedom, subtlety, boldness, dance, and masterly sureness . . . has developed only owing to the 'tyranny of such capricious laws.' Indeed, it is likely that such tyranny against 'nature' is precisely what is most 'natural'" (*BGE* 188).

Nietzsche conceives of the tyranny over "nature" by which human beings paradoxically become more "natural" as a crucial step in the progressive empowerment and liberation of humanity. In a late note, he speaks of the "evolution of man" as taking place in two stages. First, man had to gain power over nature and himself; and for this "morality was needed so that man might prevail in his struggle with nature and the 'wild animal.'" Second, once this power over nature has been achieved, it can be employed "in the further free development of oneself: will to power as self-elevation and strengthening" (*WP* 403; see also *WS* 44, 350). It is because Nietzsche sees nature and culture working together in this way that he can claim what Rousseau never could: "In my own way I attempt a justification of history" (*WP* 63). Of course, Nietzsche is not Hegel and sees much of history in terms of degeneration and decadence. It is to this aspect of his genealogy of morality that we now turn.

Nietzsche's Genealogy of Morality

In his genealogical investigations, Nietzsche goes much deeper into the past than Rousseau to unearth the roots of our current discontents. Whereas Rousseau traces our woes largely to the emergence of property and inequality that eventually gives rise to modern commercial and bourgeois society, Nietzsche goes back to the premodern foundations of European civilization in Jewish and especially Christian morality. The decisive event in his genealogy of decadent morality is the inversion of the noble values of antiquity by the Jews, who thus inaugurated the "slave rebellion in morals" (*BGE* 195; see also 260).

Interestingly, this slave rebellion did not begin with the slaves but with certain members of the ruling aristocracy: namely, the priests. Nietzsche complicates his story about the earliest societies by pointing out that alongside the warrior rulers—whose knightly-aristocratic values grew out of their "powerful physicality" and "overflowing health"—there emerged another caste of men who, lacking these attributes, developed an alternative set of values based on nonphysical qualities. Unable to compete in war, the hunt, or athletic contests, the priestly aristocrat made his claim to being the highest human type on the basis of "purity," esoteric knowledge, and a special relationship to the divinity. His abstention from action and brooding inwardness resulted in various physical illnesses; but more dangerous than these illnesses were the unscientific medicines the priest came up with to cure them. "With priests," Nietzsche concludes, "*everything* becomes more dangerous." But he adds that it was through priests that human beings also began to differentiate themselves from animals and acquire depth: "It was on the soil of this *essentially dangerous* form of human existence, the priestly form, that man first became *an interesting animal*, that only here did the human soul acquire *depth* in a higher sense and become *evil*—and these are, after all, the two basic forms of the previous superiority of man over other creatures" (*GM* 1.6; *WP* 139).

Nietzsche recognizes that there were several different kinds of priestly aristocracy in the ancient world, and not all of them were bad—for example, the Aryan priestly aristocracy governed by the law book of Manu; also the Mohammedan priestly aristocracy (*WP* 145; *TI*, "Improvers," 3; *A* 56–57). But in *Genealogy*, he focuses on the Jews because in them the impotence of the priest developed into the most terrible vengefulness—the Jews are the "priestly people of ressentiment par excellence"—and led to the most fateful act of spiritual revenge in human history: the radical revaluation of the noble values of the primitive knightly aristocracy. "It was the Jews," Nietzsche writes, "who in opposition to the aristocratic value equation (good = noble = powerful = beautiful = happy = beloved of God) dared its inversion," identifying the miserable, poor, powerless, sick, and suffering with goodness, and the noble, powerful, lustful, and cruel with evil (*GM* 1.7, 16). Nietzsche can hardly contain his astonishment at this brazen and mendacious reversal of values by which weakness was made to seem meritorious and sickness holy, and he gives brilliant satiric expression to it in *Genealogy* in the parables of the lambs and birds of prey and the workshop where ideals are fabricated (*GM* 1.13–14).

As historically significant as the Jews are for Nietzsche, he places the greatest blame for the corruption of humanity on Christianity, the "calamity of millennia" (*EH*, "Wise," 7), the "*one* great curse, the *one* great intrinsic depravity, the *one* great instinct for revenge . . . the *one* immortal blemish of mankind" (*A* 62). Though he devotes only a few sections of the first essay in *Genealogy* to Christianity, he makes the fundamental point there that runs through all his writings on the subject: namely, that Christianity, with its gospel of love, was not the opposite of Jewish hate or revenge but its most sublime and seductive expression (*GM* 1.8, 14–15). Primitive Christianity took the Jewish slave rebellion in morals to its logical conclusion, overthrowing the last vestige of ruling power in the form of the Jewish priest. The "political criminal" Jesus instigated a revolt against the Jewish church and the priests who presided over it. This was a revolt of the chandala, who rejected all forms of caste, privilege, and social hierarchy. Though the political instinct was already much diminished among Jews living under Roman rule, the early Christians destroyed what little was left of the "profoundest national instinct . . . the toughest national will to life which has ever existed on earth" (*A* 27; see also *WP* 182, 184).

How did the radical revaluation of values inaugurated by Judaism and brought to completion by Christianity succeed, especially among the noble and powerful? Nietzsche puts a great deal of emphasis on the seductiveness of Christianity, often comparing it to Circe. According to him, the New Testament is a masterpiece of seduction, appearing modestly to champion humility and compassion but in fact seeking arrogantly to impose its narrow herd ideal on everyone. As we saw in the previous section, Nietzsche does not simply dismiss the healthy herd animal and the conditions necessary for its preservation. What he objects to is the imposition of those conditions on the nonherd animal. With respect to Christianity, he objects to its arrogant and shameless appropriation of "the whole fascinating force of virtue." He considers Christianity's absolute identification of virtue with the petty qualities of "little, good-natured sheep" to be the "most fateful kind of megalomania that has ever existed on earth . . . as if only the 'Christian' were the meaning, the salt, the measure and the *ultimate tribunal* of all the rest" (*WP* 172, 199, 202–4, 210, 249; *A* 44).

Again, Nietzsche is primarily concerned with the effect this megalomania had on noble and powerful human beings. By bringing the "more valuable qualities of virtue and man into ill repute," he argues, Christianity "set the bad conscience of the noble soul against its self-sufficiency" and "led astray, to the point of self-destruction, the brave, magnanimous, daring, excessive inclinations of the strong soul" (*WP* 205). How did this happen? Again, Nietzsche draws attention to the seductive, Circe-like character of Christian morality. Building on his earlier insight that it was through the priest that human beings became interesting and acquired depth, he remarks that Christianity "*raised the temperature of the soul* among those cooler and nobler races that were then on top," showing them that "the most wretched life can become rich and inestimable through a rise in temperature" (*WP* 175). He even claims that the seductive power of Christianity may work most strongly on "such natures as love danger, adventure, and opposition—as love all that involves risking themselves while at the same time engendering a *non plus ultra* of the feeling of power" (*WP* 216; see also *BGE* 51). This is what he thinks happened to his beloved Pascal, and it is what he most opposes in Christianity: that it wants to break the strongest and noblest souls by converting "their proud assurance into unease and distress of conscience" and turning their will to power back upon themselves until they "perish of self-contempt and self-abuse" (*WP* 252; see also *A* 5; *BGE* 62).[12]

The reference to noble souls turning their will to power back upon themselves brings us to the second prong of Nietzsche's genealogy of decadent morality, which focuses on the element of self-cruelty in it. The first prong, treated in the first essay of *Genealogy*, is concerned with the revenge-driven revaluation of the values of the knightly aristocracy by the powerless commoners. Nietzsche portrays this revaluation largely as a power play on the part of the weak against the strong, an egregious example of the "politics of revenge." In a work subtitled "A Polemic," this is perhaps the most polemical aspect of Nietzsche's genealogy of morality. His tone is ironic, especially in the sections on the lambs and birds of prey and the workshop where ideals are fabricated, and he constantly emphasizes the mendacity of the slaves' revaluation. The analysis that belongs to the second prong, treated in the second and third essays of *Genealogy* and concerned with the "bad conscience" and its exploitation by the ascetic priest, is quite different. It is less political and more psychological, focusing on the inner turmoil of the sick and suffering rather than the outward expression of their ressentiment against the healthy and powerful. Above all, it is less polemical, showing the morality of decadence to be not merely a mendacious weapon of the weak but an ideal that filled a genuine psychic need.

In order to grasp Nietzsche's hypothesis about the origin of the bad conscience, we need to go back to the violent founding of the primitive state by the blond beasts. This event, Nietzsche claims, brought about the "most fundamental of changes [man] ever experienced." Having been used to roaming about freely in the wilderness, the animal man suddenly found himself "enclosed once and for all within the sway of society and peace." No longer able to rely on his instincts or discharge them outwardly, he felt the most profound misery and "leaden discomfort." But the old instincts did not simply disappear; they turned inward. And this, Nietzsche hypothesizes, is the origin of bad conscience: the internalization of the instinct for freedom or will to power. The aggression and cruelty he had previously discharged outwardly man now exercised on himself; "wedged into an oppressive narrowness and regularity of custom, [he] impatiently tore apart, persecuted, gnawed at, stirred up, maltreated himself." Nietzsche does not stint in evoking the gruesome psychic cruelty and sickness involved in the bad conscience. But as in his earlier treatment of the priest, he also recognizes the crucial role bad conscience played in deepening the human animal and creating the human soul: "With the appearance of an animal soul turned against itself . . . something so new, deep, unheard of, enigmatic, contradictory, *and full of future* had come into being that the appearance of the earth was thereby essentially changed" (*GM* 2.16–18).

So much for the origin of bad conscience as merely a "piece of animal psychology" (*GM* 3.20). But Nietzsche is interested in what was made of this concept by religion and especially Christianity. Returning to the primeval understanding of guilt in terms of debt, he points out that the original clan associations felt indebted to their founders and ancestors, and with time this sense of indebtedness grew to the point that the founders and ancestors were transfigured into gods. This imposed heavy burdens on the living debtors, sometimes even involving the sacrifice of human beings; but the debt was at least in principle payable. All this changed when guilt came to be entangled with bad conscience and God became an instrument of torture. Then all of man's natural instincts were interpreted as sources of guilt before God for which no payment or punishment could suffice. Christianity brought this psychic cruelty to its highest pitch in its symbol of God on the cross: "God sacrificing himself for the guilt of man," atoning for the sins that man cannot atone for himself. As usual, Nietzsche contrasts this Christian use of religion for self-crucifixion with the Greeks' nobler use of it for self-justification and self-deification (*GM* 2.19–23; see also *BGE* 46, 49).

In the third essay of *Genealogy* on the meaning of ascetic ideals, Nietzsche offers a somewhat more sympathetic interpretation of the exploitation of guilt and bad conscience by Judaism and especially Christianity. The hostility toward nature and life found in these religions, he argues, did not spring from a merely arbitrary decision but from a "necessity of the first rank" (*GM* 3.11). Once human beings came to be enclosed within civil society and the walls of peace, they became disconnected from their instincts and began to suffer from the "greatest and most uncanny of sicknesses." Man is "*the* sick animal"—also the most undetermined, interesting, courageous, and adventurous—and therefore in need of a physician (*GM* 2.16, 3.13; see also *BGE* 62; *A* 14). The ascetic priest supplies this need. The ascetic priest, "this strange shepherd," ministers to the sick by providing them with a reason for their suffering—indeed, by identifying who is to blame for their suffering: namely, themselves. The sick themselves are guilty for their suffering, which is now interpreted as punishment for their sinfulness. In this way, the ascetic priest "changes the direction of ressentiment," and his denial of life becomes a means of preserving life (*GM* 3.15).

Nietzsche calls the ascetic priest's invention of "sin" here "the greatest event in the history of the sick soul." In keeping with his general symptomological approach to morality, he insists that " 'sinfulness' in humans is not a factual state but rather only the interpretation of a factual state; namely, of being physiologically out of sorts." It is an interpretation designed to alleviate suffering by paradoxically intensifying it, producing orgies of feeling in which the sinner is "shattered, toppled, crushed, entranced, enraptured." No religion, according to Nietzsche, has proved to be more adept at producing such orgies of feeling than Christianity, which represents "a great treasury of the most ingenious means for comforting" those who suffer from life. Of course, the medicine Christianity offers to the sick and suffering does not ultimately make them better but leaves them worse off than they were before; and for that reason, Nietzsche calls it "*the true doom* in the history of European health" (*GM* 3.16–17, 20–21).

In the modern world, however, Christianity no longer takes this rapturous form, except perhaps in romantic art or Wagnerian opera; rather, it has adapted to bourgeois secularity and turned into a "gentle moralism" that prizes "benevolence and decency of disposition" above all—a far cry from the gruesome self-laceration described above, not to mention Pascal's tortured suicide of reason. Nietzsche calls this the "*euthanasia* of Christianity" (*D* 92), but the values of pity and love of neighbor that it elevates remain at the heart of nineteenth-century European morality, receiving their consummate expression in democracy. The "democratic movement is the heir of the Christian movement," Nietzsche states (*BGE* 202); and "the French Revolution is the daughter and continuation of Christianity" (*WP* 184; see also 94; *BGE* 46). The slave revolt against the noble lords that began with the Jews and was carried forward by Christianity is brought to completion by democracy and even more by socialism. The church is no longer necessary to guarantee the triumph of herd values. Indeed, Nietzsche claims it now gets in the way of the progress of equality and the morality of pity; "it alienates more than it seduces" (*GM* 1.9). In this way, democracy can be said to be a more natural and honest version of the antinatural values of Christianity: "Democracy is Christianity made natural" (*WP* 215). But this "naturalness" of democracy conceals the violence of the Jewish–Christian revaluation of values on which it rests. To expose this violence—or at least the historical contingency by which herd animal morality became the only recognized morality—is one of the central purposes of Nietzsche's genealogy.

This brings us back to the denaturalizing function that Nietzsche's genealogy shares with Rousseau's. As in Rousseau's genealogy, Nietzsche's denaturalization of Christian morality, herd morality, the morality of pity and altruism is critical to his evaluative (as opposed to his merely explanatory) aim. In some ways, the link between the explanatory and evaluative dimensions is even closer in Nietzsche's genealogy than in Rousseau's. Whereas Rousseau's genealogy focuses more on the evil consequences than on the base psychological motivations of social inequality, Nietzsche's genealogy shows that herd morality and the Christian exaltation of it have their source in ressentiment.[13] This sometimes gives rise to a note of incredulity in his genealogical account that we do not find in Rousseau's. Thus, when describing the way Christianity exploited the illness of bad conscience and cultivated its propensity for self-torture, Nietzsche stresses the unnaturalness of this development, claiming that in the "psychical cruelty" of Christianity "there resides a madness of the will that is absolutely unexampled." "Oh this insane, pathetic beast man!" he exclaims. "What ideas he has, what unnaturalness, what paroxysms of nonsense, what *bestiality of thought* erupts as soon as he is prevented just a little from being a *beast in deed*" (*GM* 2.22).

As to whether Nietzsche's genealogy goes beyond or supersedes Rousseau's, this is a difficult question—the answer to which depends, as I stated at the outset, on how one evaluates their respective diagnoses of our current predicament. There are two considerations that perhaps speak in favor of Nietzsche's genealogy. First, it goes further in its historical excavation of human nature than Rousseau's genealogy does. While Rousseau's conception of the natural goodness of man is not as naïve or sentimental as Nietzsche sometimes suggests, it is undeniable that Nietzsche goes considerably further than Rousseau in uncovering the nonmoral and animalistic bases of human nature. In this regard, he is right to see himself as sharing in the greater realism, historical sense, and intellectual honesty of the nineteenth century, which has discovered a *"truer image* of 'man'" than the natural man of Rousseau (*WP* 95, 1017). Second, Nietzsche's genealogy arguably shows a deeper understanding of the moral sources of our current discontent than Rousseau's. While social inequality and the pathologies that spring from it are no doubt serious problems in today's world, one wonders whether the loss of direction, purpose, and meaning and consequent lack of passion, individuality, and aspiration—in a word, nihilism—that Nietzsche highlights does not represent a more profound reading of our current moral situation.[14] This is a question to which we will return when we come to consider Rousseau's and Nietzsche's respective political philosophies.

3

The Self

Next to being two of the most trenchant critics of modern society, Rousseau and Nietzsche are probably best known for being two of the most profound theorists of the modern self. Their concern with the latter, of course, stems directly from their critique of the former. Both deplore the way modern society compromises the integrity of the self and promotes hypocrisy, conformity, and inauthenticity. Rousseau articulates this concern as early as the *First Discourse*, declaring that in modern society, "one no longer dares to appear what one is," conforming instead to the conventions of the "herd that is called society." "How sweet it would be to live among us," he muses, "if the outward countenance were always the image of the heart's dispositions" (*FD* 7–8). Nietzsche articulates the same concern at the beginning of his early essay "Schopenhauer as Educator." In the modern world, the individual hides "behind customs and opinions" and thinks and acts "like a member of a herd," despite being "a unique miracle" who knows that "no imaginable chance will for a second time bring into a unity so strangely variegated an assortment as he is." Therefore, Nietzsche urges the individual to listen to his conscience, which tells him: " 'Be yourself! All you are now doing, thinking, desiring, is not you yourself' " (SE 1:127).

The demand to "be yourself" that both Rousseau and Nietzsche express contains the core of what is often referred to as the ideal of sincerity or authenticity.[1] It must be admitted that these terms are not always the most perspicuous and can mislead by providing a single label for ideas and doctrines that are importantly different. These terms have also been debased, trivialized, and commercialized in our time, but as I stated in the introduction, that is no reason to completely abandon what they stand for. This is the tack taken by culturally conservative writers like Allan Bloom and Daniel Bell, who argue that the ideal of sincerity or authenticity that Rousseau and Nietz-sche articulate has led to a shallow culture of narcissism and solipsism and to a kind of cult of nonconformity and creativity.[2] In this chapter, in contrast to such "knockers" of the modern ideal of authenticity, I follow the alternative approach of Charles Taylor, who (as already noted in the introduction) main-tains that while the modern ideal of authenticity "has degraded," it is never-theless "very worthwhile in itself, and indeed . . . unrepudiable by moderns. So what we need is neither root-and-branch condemnation nor uncritical praise. . . . What we need is a work of retrieval, through which this ideal can help us restore our practice."[3]

As part of this work of retrieval, it is important to bring out not only the similarities but also the fundamental differences between Rousseau's and Nietz-sche's conceptions of being true to oneself, or authenticity. In what follows, I argue that the differences in their conceptions stem largely from the funda-mentally different way in which they conceive of the relationship between au-thenticity and morality. In the case of Rousseau, authenticity and morality are profoundly connected.[4] For this reason, his teaching about authentic selfhood culminates in an image of the virtuous individual who, no longer a slave to his appetites, exercises rational control over his irrational passions. (Though there are certainly important differences between Rousseau and Kant, Nietz-sche is not altogether wrong to see the latter as having been profoundly influ-enced by the "moral tarantula" Rousseau [*D*, preface, 3]). In the case of Nietz-sche, authenticity and morality are completely opposed. As he succinctly puts it in *Genealogy*: "'Autonomous' and 'moral' are mutually exclusive" (*GM* 2.2). For Nietzsche, authenticity involves the creation of a unique self out of the chaos of drives, desires, and values that it comprises. The universal-ity of morality can only get in the way of this endeavor to become who you are and create a unique self.

Rousseau's Conception of Happiness

As I have already indicated, Rousseau's reflections on the self and its fulfill-ment follow directly from his critique of modern society. As we have seen, the fundamental problem with modern society, according to Rousseau, is that it makes human beings insincere hypocrites who give the appearance of being virtuous and concerned for the welfare of others while all the time secretly harboring black inclinations to take advantage of their fellow human beings in order to achieve preeminence. There is a total disconnect between appearance and reality, word and deed, the outer countenance and the inner inclinations of the heart. In short, the modern self is divided, disunited. This is the problem of the bourgeois, as Rousseau articulates it at the beginning of *Emile*: "Always in contradiction with himself, always floating between his inclinations and his duties, he will never be a man or a citizen. He will be good neither for himself nor for others. He will be one of these men of our days: a Frenchman, an Englishman, a bourgeois. He will be nothing" (*E* 40).[5]

After stating the problem of the bourgeois in *Emile*, Rousseau goes on to outline two different paths to overcoming the division of the self and restoring it to wholeness. One is political and involves the denaturing of human beings so that there is no conflict between their particular inclinations and their public, citizen duties. This political solution will be the subject of the fifth chapter. The other solution to the problem of the self-divided bourgeois is individual and involves raising a child in such a way that it never comes into contradiction with itself. This, of course, is the project of *Emile*, and it is with this work that we will be primarily concerned in this chapter. In this section, I examine the conception of happiness Rousseau develops in *Emile* and to a lesser extent *The Reveries*. In the next section, I connect Rousseau's conception of happiness to his moral philosophy and the ideas of virtue and conscience that receive their fullest expression in "The Profession of Faith of the Savoyard Vicar." I will postpone consideration of Rousseau's romantic project in *Emile* until the next chapter.

If one were to ask why unity or harmony of self is important for human beings, Rousseau's answer would be that such unity is necessary for human happiness. Happiness is the key ethical consideration for Rousseau; it is the sovereign good for human beings. As he puts it one place, "The object of human life is the felicity of man, but who among us knows how to attain it?" (ML 179; see also *E* 442).[6] The primacy of happiness in Rousseau's ethical thought is, of course, what chiefly differentiates it from Kant's deontological ethics.[7] We will see in the next section that there are certainly important connections between Rousseau's ethical thought and that of Kant, but this should not obscure that Rousseau's ethics contain a strong eudaemonistic element that Kant ultimately rejects.

Rousseau gives an initial indication of his thinking about happiness in his treatment of the natural human being in the *Second Discourse*. In the pure state of nature, man is happy because his "desires do not exceed his physical needs," and these needs are simple—food, a female, and rest—and easily satisfied. One of the things that ensures that the natural human being does not become unhappy is that he is totally devoid of imagination and foresight. It is imagination that gives rise to desires that exceed our needs and our capacity to satisfy them, leading to unhappiness. The natural human being is also devoid of *amour propre*, the passion that leads civilized humans to constantly compare themselves with others and worry about their relative position in society. The natural human being is driven solely by *amour de soi-même* and is therefore indifferent to what others think of him. In his indifference to others and the future, the savage human being lives entirely "within himself"; and his "soul, which nothing stirs, yields itself to the sole sentiment of existence." The civilized human being, on the other hand, "always outside himself, is capable of living only in the opinion of others and, so to speak, derives the sentiment of his own existence solely from their judgment" (*SD* 142–43, 187, 218).

Rousseau develops his reflections on human happiness more fully in *Emile*. Relevant to the comparison with Nietzsche, he begins by defining happiness in terms of the reduction of pain and suffering: the happiest human being "is he who suffers the least pain. . . . Man's felicity on Earth is, hence, only a negative condition; the smallest number of ills he can suffer ought to constitute its measure" (*E* 80). This rather Epicurean conception of happiness contrasts sharply with Nietzsche's conception, which sees suffering as an essential component of human creativity and happiness. Indeed, it has more in common with the hedonistic conception of happiness of Nietzsche's great antagonist, Schopenhauer, who called Rousseau the "greatest moralist of modern times."[8] It is precisely Schopenhauer's identification of happiness with the absence of suffering that led him to pessimistically conclude that human existence was so miserable.

Again like Schopenhauer, Rousseau associates desire with privation and pain; therefore, the inability to satisfy our desires leads to unhappiness. From this, Rousseau concludes that "our unhappiness consists . . . in the disproportion between our desires and our faculties." Echoing the point he made in the *Second Discourse*, he states that the reason human beings are not unhappy in the state of nature is that their desires do not exceed their faculties. It does not follow, however, that in order to achieve happiness we must simply diminish our desires; for if our desires were to fall below our faculties, the latter "would remain idle, and we would not enjoy our whole being." An important part of our happiness lies in exercising our faculties. As Rousseau puts it in another part of *Emile*: "To live is not to breathe; it is to act; it is to make use of our organs, our senses, our faculties, of all the parts of ourselves which give us the sentiment of our existence." Therefore, the key to happiness lies not in eliminating our desires but in bringing them into equilibrium with our faculties (*E* 80, 42).

Again echoing the *Second Discourse*, Rousseau places much of the blame for our unhappiness on imagination. It is imagination that multiplies our desires and exacerbates our fears. With respect to the latter, it is the fear of death that most prevents us from living our lives to the fullest. Because the savage human being utterly lacks foresight and has no conception of death, he can yield himself up to the sentiment of his present existence. This is not the case with the civilized human being, who is filled with anxiety about all the bad things that can happen to him in the future. It is foresight, Rousseau says, that "takes us ceaselessly beyond ourselves and often places us where we shall never arrive. This is the true source of all of our miseries." From this he draws the following advice: "O man, draw your existence up within yourself, and you will no longer be miserable" (*E* 80–83).

Rousseau goes on to connect his conception of happiness with freedom; indeed, unlike in Kant, they seem to amount to practically the same thing. As we have seen, happiness consists in the equilibrium between our desires and the capacity to satisfy them. When our needs or desires exceed our strength to satisfy them, then we are weak and depend on others to do for us what we cannot do ourselves. In such a situation, we are not only unhappy, according to Rousseau, but also unfree. "The only one who does his own will," he writes, "is he who, in order to do it, has no need to put another's arms at the end of his own. . . . The truly free man wants only what he can do and does what he pleases." One could say the same about the truly happy man. The key to both happiness and freedom is self-sufficiency or self-dependence. The human being living in the state of nature exemplifies this sort of self-sufficiency, freedom, and happiness, while the human being in society, who is weak and dependent on others, is utterly miserable and unfree (*E* 84–85).

This brings Rousseau's initial discussion of happiness in *Emile* to a conclusion. But our examination of his conception of happiness would not be complete without considering his reflections on happiness and the sentiment of existence in the *Reveries*. We have seen that in both the *Second Discourse* and *Emile*, happiness for Rousseau is very much bound up with the sentiment of existence—the simple feeling of being alive, undistracted by regret for the past and anxiety for the future. He elaborates on this crucial concept in the *Reveries*, a work that in many ways is completely different from anything else that Rousseau wrote but that nevertheless discloses the same basic conception of happiness that is found in the *Second Discourse* and *Emile*.[9]

The key discussion of the sentiment of existence appears in the "Fifth Walk" of the *Reveries*, where Rousseau recounts his two-month stay on St. Peter's Island, "the happiest time of my life." He relates how he would spend his mornings studying the plants of the island—he was then in his "first botanical fervor"—and then in the afternoon he would row a boat into the middle of the lake and there spend several hours drifting back and forth in the water, "plunged in a thousand confused, but delightful, reveries that . . . were in my opinion a hundred times preferable to the sweetest things I had found in what are called the pleasures of life." Toward evening, he would sometimes sit on a beach at the edge of the lake, where the noise of the lapping water would chase away "all other disturbance from my soul," and again give himself up to "delightful reverie." Here, too, Rousseau emphasizes how the rhythmic ebb and flow of the water would provide just enough stimulation to allow him to "feel my existence with pleasure and without taking the trouble to think" (R 64–67).

When Rousseau comes to reflect on these experiences of perfect happiness, he stresses their temporal duration in contrast to the fleetingness of intense moments of passion and pleasure. These latter, he claims, "are too rare and too rapid to constitute a state of being; and the happiness for which my heart longs is in no way made up of fleeting instants, but rather a simple and permanent state which has nothing intense in itself but whose duration increases its charm to the point that I finally find supreme felicity in it." Intense moments of passion and enjoyment are necessarily transitory and therefore evoke anxiety for their future demise and sadness when they are past. How can we call such fleeting states happiness, Rousseau asks—again sounding an Epicurean note—when they "leave our heart still worried and empty"? We must seek instead for

> a state in which the soul finds a solid enough base to rest itself on entirely and to gather its whole being into, without needing to recall the past or encroach upon the future; in which time is nothing for it; in which the present lasts forever . . . without any other sentiment of deprivation or enjoyment, pleasure or pain, desire or fear, except that alone of our existence . . . ; as long as this state lasts, he who finds himself in it can call himself happy, not with an imperfect, poor, and relative happiness such as one finds in the pleasures of life, but with a sufficient, perfect, and full happiness which leaves in the soul no emptiness it might feel a need to fill. (R 68–69)

Such a vision of happiness could not be further from Nietzsche's Dionysian vision of life as involving constant self-overcoming, suffering, and creativity.

As in the Second Discourse and Emile, Rousseau connects this perfect happiness in which we feel only the sentiment of our own present existence to self-sufficiency. When we enjoy the sentiment of our own existence, we experience "nothing external to ourselves. . . . We are sufficient unto ourselves, like God." And again as in the Second Discourse and Emile, what prevents us from enjoying this sentiment and experiencing complete happiness are the social passions (R 69, 71). In the "Eighth Walk" of the Reveries, Rousseau traces the unhappiness he felt at a certain point in his life to his preoccupation with the opinions of others and the desire for their esteem. The source of his unhappiness was *amour propre*: "It is only because of *amour propre* that we are constantly unhappy." And he regained his happiness only once he detached himself from the social passions that took him away from himself and replaced his *amour propre* with *amour de soi*. This leads Rousseau to the realization that "I have savored the sweetness of existence more, that I have really lived more, when my sentiments—drawn back around my heart, so to speak, by my fate—were not being wasted on all the objects of men's esteem which are of so little merit in themselves, but which are the sole concern of the people we believe to be happy" (*R* 110–19).

Of course, the happiness Rousseau talks about in the *Reveries* is the happiness of the solitary dreamer. Though at times he speaks of it as the supreme happiness, he also indicates that it is the only happiness available to him, given his ostracism from society. At one point in the "Fifth Walk," he suggests that the solitary happiness he has described would not be good for most men, who might "become disgusted with the active life their ever-recurring needs prescribe to them as a duty," but it is all that can be hoped for by the "unfortunate person who has been cut off from human society and who can no longer do anything here below useful and good for another or himself" (*R* 69). In the "Sixth Walk," he continues in this vein: "I know and feel that to do good is the truest happiness the human heart can savor; but it is a long time now since this happiness has been put out of my reach, and it is not in such a wretched lot as mine that one can hope to perform wisely and fruitfully a really good action" (*R* 75). He follows this up by saying that though he possesses a certain natural goodness, he is incapable of virtue, which requires that one overcome one's inclinations in order to do what duty prescribes (*R* 75–77; see also *RJ* 126–28, 150–51, 154, 157–58). Whether Rousseau regards this as entirely a defect is certainly a question.[10] Nevertheless, he goes on to develop the moral dimension of the self in *Emile*, and it is to this crucial aspect of his teaching that we now turn.

Rousseau on Virtue and Conscience

The first three books of *Emile* are concerned with the early education of Emile, up to about the age of fifteen. This early education, Rousseau tells us, is entirely negative. It seeks merely to prevent the corruption of the child's natural goodness; "it consists not at all in teaching virtue or truth but in securing the heart from vice and the mind from error" (*E* 93). The happiness produced by this negative education is not altogether different from that of the savage human being. Emile's needs are simple and do not exceed his capacity to satisfy them. He is motivated almost exclusively by *amour de soi*; he regards only himself and does not compare himself to others: "*Amour propre*, the first and most natural of all the passions, is still hardly aroused in him" (*E* 208, 213–14). Rousseau makes clear that this happiness of the child and of the natural human being is quite different from that of the mature, moral human being, which involves an effortful overcoming of oneself and subordination of one's desires to duty (*E* 177, 193). At this stage of Emile's life, he is merely good but not yet virtuous. As the governor tells his pupil late in the book: "I have made you good rather than virtuous. But he who is only good remains so only as long as he takes pleasure in being so. Goodness is broken and perishes under the impact of the human passions. The man who is only good is good only for himself" (*E* 444).

The human passions Rousseau is talking about are specifically the sexual passions. With the onset of puberty, Emile begins to extend his relations beyond himself. Attracted to the opposite sex, he begins to have preferences and make comparisons. And the preference he grants to others he seeks to obtain for himself. But in order to have his love reciprocated, he needs to make himself lovable, and specifically more lovable than his fellows. This leads him to compare himself with others and see them as potential rivals. Competition, emulation, and jealousy soon follow, and *amour de soi* turns into *amour propre*. Rousseau regards this development as inevitable. Though *amour propre* is not natural insofar as it is not found in the savage human being or the child, it is natural in that it cannot be avoided once human beings begin to live with one another and arrive at the age of sexual maturity: "Whatever we may do, these passions will be born in spite of us." It is for this reason that Rousseau can call *amour propre* "the first and most natural of all the passions" (*E* 211–15, 235, 208).

What Rousseau says about the "naturalness" of *amour propre* in *Emile* forces us to reconsider his apparent thesis in the *Second Discourse* that human beings are not naturally sociable. I say "apparent thesis" because even in the *Second Discourse* the idea that human beings are not naturally sociable is complicated by the fact that Rousseau considers the first phase of social existence to be the "happiest and most lasting epoch" and the "best [state] for man" (*SD* 167). In *Emile*, the natural sociability of human beings becomes even less ambiguous. In several places, Rousseau refers to the natural tendency of human beings to "extend our being" (*E* 169, 219, 223, 235n; see also *RJ* 112). He also states explicitly that it "cannot be doubted" that "man is by his nature sociable, or at least made to become so" (*E* 290; see also *ML* 196; *LB* 54). Perhaps the strongest evidence for Rousseau's belief that human beings are naturally sociable comes in *Dialogues*, wherein he claims that "absolute solitude is a state that is sad and contrary to nature: affectionate feelings nourish the soul, communication of ideas enlivens the mind. Our sweetest existence is relative and collective, and our true *self* is not entirely within us" (*RJ* 118). This passage finds an echo in *Emile*, where Rousseau maintains that only God can find absolute happiness in being solitary; for human beings, such self-sufficient solitude leads to misery and loneliness: "I do not conceive how someone who needs nothing can love anything. I do not conceive how someone who loves nothing can be happy" (*E* 221).

As I have indicated, though, once we extend our relations to others and *amour propre* and the passions that depend on it come into play, natural goodness will no longer suffice to make us happy; we need virtue. The governor explains the vital connection between virtue and happiness when Emile's love for Sophie threatens to make him a slave of his desires and utterly dependent on fortune. In many ways, the problem of happiness here remains the same as it was for the younger Emile: to be happy requires that our desires not exceed our strength; the two must be in kept in some sort of equilibrium. The emergence of sexual passion and *amour propre*, however, makes this problem more difficult to resolve: "Our desires are extended; our strength is almost nil." We must compensate for our weakness here by strengthening our will. This is what virtue accomplishes. Rousseau emphasizes the etymological connection between "virtue" and manly "strength." Virtue involves conquering our passions, mastering our desires; only then can we be truly happy and free. "'Do you want, then, to live happily and wisely?'" the governor asks Emile:

> Attach your heart to imperishable beauty. Let your condition limit your desires; let your duties come before your inclinations; extend the law of necessity to moral things. Learn to lose what can be taken from you; learn to abandon everything when virtue decrees it, to put yourself above events and to detach your heart lest it be lacerated by them; to be courageous in adversity, so as never to be miserable; to be firm in your duty, so as never to be criminal. Then you will be happy in spite of fortune and wise in spite of the passions. (*E* 442–46)

Based on passages like this, where duty and inclination seem locked in mortal combat, it is not surprising that many scholars have assimilated Rousseau to Kant.[11] Nor are such passages rare in Rousseau's oeuvre. In *Julie*, for example, Rousseau emphasizes that virtue involves the strength to battle one's passions and the ability to sacrifice one's dearest desires (*J* 97, 431). And in his "Letter to Franquières," he once again distinguishes virtue from goodness: "This word virtue means *force*. There is no virtue without struggle, there is none without victory. Virtue consists not only in being just, but in being so by triumphing over one's passions, by ruling over one's heart." He follows this up by citing one of his favorite examples of virtue, Lucius Junius Brutus, who had his sons put to death for rebelling against the republic: "Brutus was a tender father; to do his duty he tore up his insides, and Brutus was virtuous" (LF 281; see also LR 64n, 78). Of course, despite his pitting of duty against inclination, Rousseau still differs from Kant in making happiness the supreme object of moral endeavor. But even here he sometimes anticipates the Kantian position, such as when he explains that the bitterness of his invectives against the vices of modern society springs from "my intense desire to see men happier, and especially worthier of being so" (LR 85).

Emile's path to virtue in the strenuous sense just described begins with pity. This is not merely the natural pity of the savage human being described in the *Second Discourse*. Unlike the savage human being, Emile possesses nascent imagination, which allows him to identify with his fellow human beings. In the first instance, this imaginative identification is directed at the species in general and not just the female sex. The first sentiment of which Emile is capable is not love but friendship. He feels himself in his friends, and he is particularly affected by their sufferings. Rousseau claims that human beings are moved much more by the sufferings than the pleasures of their fellows: "It is man's weakness which makes him sociable; it is our common miseries which turn our hearts to humanity." For this reason, he asserts that pity is the "first relative sentiment which touches the human heart according to nature" (*E* 220–22).

Rousseau's emphasis on the role of pity or compassion in the moral development of human beings is of obvious importance for our comparison with Nietzsche, given that the latter thinker is above all concerned to attack the morality of pity that he identifies with Schopenhauer (who, again, considered Rousseau the "greatest moralist of modern times") and that he believes is reducing modern humanity to herd-like mediocrity (*GM*, preface, 5). Because this is so, it is important to stress that Rousseau's discussion of pity in *Emile* is by no means overly sentimental. The very choice to cultivate pity as Emile's first relative sentiment is dictated by a realistic assessment of the nascent role of *amour propre* at this stage in his development. Comparing ourselves to those who are happier than we are, Rousseau argues, only makes us envious and unhappy, whereas comparing ourselves to those who are less fortunate arouses pity, which "is sweet because, in putting ourselves in the place of the one who suffers, we nevertheless feel the pleasure of not suffering as he does" (*E* 221–23, 229). Rousseau also grounds pity in self-love: "When the strength of an expansive soul makes me identify myself with my fellow, and I feel that I am, so to speak, in him, it is in order not to suffer that I do not want him to suffer. I am interested in him for love of myself. . . . Love of men derived from love of self is the principle of human justice" (*E* 235n). Finally, similar to Nietzsche (see, e.g., *D* 174; *GS* 56), Rousseau warns against becoming excessively preoccupied with the sufferings of others. The point in cultivating pity in Emile is to make him sensitive to the sufferings of others and to nourish a feeling for humanity; it is not to make him "a male nurse or a brother of charity, not to afflict his sight with constant objects of pain and suffering, not to march from sick person to sick person, from hospital to hospital, and from the Grève to the prisons" (*E* 231; compare 250).[12]

Rousseau also warns about the subjectivity of pity, which leads us to care more for our friends and neighbors than for mankind as a whole. Pity must be "generalized and extended to the whole of mankind" so that it accords with justice (*E* 253). This requires that Emile develop his reason so he can judge his fellows and his own place in society more impartially. He must learn to know the human heart, and Rousseau believes that history is crucial for this task because it allows the individual to "read the hearts of men" as a "simple spectator, disinterested and without passion" (*E* 236–37). Rousseau goes into some detail with respect to this education of Emile's judgment so that it accords with justice and reason (*E* 235–53). For our purposes, it is enough to know that he accords an important place to reason in the moral education of Emile. Subjective feeling, including the sentiment of pity—and, as we shall see, conscience—is not enough; it must be accompanied by a rational assessment of the genuine needs and interests of humanity and of what justice requires. At the end of this process by which Emile's moral reason and judgment is developed, Rousseau exclaims:

> What great views I see settling little by little in his head! . . . What judicial clarity, what accuracy of reason I see forming in him. . . . The true principles of the just, the true models of the beautiful, all the moral relations of beings, all the ideas of order are imprinted on his understanding. He sees the place of each thing and the cause which removes it from its place; he sees what can do good and what stands in its way. Without having experienced the human passions, he knows their illusions and their effects. (*E* 253)

But for Rousseau, reason alone is never enough. "In vain does tranquil reason make us approve or criticize," he writes in a line that sums up his lifelong opposition to abstract rationalism; "it is only passion which makes us act" (*E* 183; see also *J* 405). He makes a similar point in the crucial transitional paragraph that marks Emile's entrance into the moral order, stating that, were he writing a metaphysical treatise rather than a work of educational philosophy, he would show that *justice* and *goodness* are not merely abstract words—pure moral beings formed by the understanding—but are true affections of the soul enlightened by reason, are hence only an ordered development of our primitive affections; that by reason alone, independent of conscience, no natural law can be established; and that the entire right of nature is only a chimera if it is not founded on a natural need in the human heart. (*E* 235)

Here Rousseau introduces the key notion of conscience that will serve to mediate between individual desire and abstract duty. It is a notion that is not without difficulties. Indeed, many scholars find it to be deeply inconsistent with the morally neutral conception of nature and nonsocial conception of human nature found in Rousseau's other writings, especially the *Second Discourse*, and therefore consider it to be at best a morally edifying doctrine, a "salutary untruth."[13] That the doctrine appears as part of the "Profession of Faith of the Savoyard Vicar," which many of these scholars deny reflects Rousseau's own religious beliefs, only adds to its dubiousness in their eyes.[14]

Despite these doubts and without entering into the fraught question as to whether the "Profession of Faith of the Savoyard Vicar" represents Rousseau's own profession of faith,[15] I think it is hard to see its teaching about conscience as anything but a deeply felt truth on his part. There are simply too many places in Rousseau's writings where conscience is sincerely invoked—beginning with the *First Discourse*, and especially in the "Moral Letters"—for it to be dismissed as merely a salutary untruth (see, e.g., *FD* 28; *LD* 23; *ML* 189–201; *J* 183–85; *LO* 261–64; *LB* 28–29; *RJ* 242).[16] As to the incompatibility of conscience with Rousseau's conceptions of nature and human nature, we have seen that these latter cannot be reduced to what is found in the primitive state of nature. Nature is not simply what we begin with but is whatever accords with the "ordered development of our primitive affections" (*E* 235; see also 39). On this view, conscience constitutes the crowning insight of Rousseau's entire moral psychology.

What exactly does Rousseau understand by the term *conscience*? The definition he gives in the "Profession of Faith" is that it is an "innate principle of justice and virtue" (*E* 289; see also *ML* 195). And he begins his discussion of it by adducing a variety of examples of how it operates in everyday life. Thus, he points out that people generally take more pleasure in doing a beneficent act than a wicked one. In the theater, we sympathize more with the good man who suffers than with the wicked man who prospers. When we read history, it is the virtuous actions of Regulus and Cato that we admire rather than the tyrannical actions of Caesar and Nero. "If there is nothing moral in the heart of man," Rousseau asks, "what is the source of these transports of admiration for heroic actions, these raptures of love for great souls?" (*E* 287; see also *ML* 193–94; *J* 183–84). In his "Letter to D'Offreville," Rousseau gives the example of the English juror who stubbornly refused to convict another man of the crime he himself committed to show that there is something more than self-interest that motivates human beings (LO 263–64).

Rousseau anticipates that those who deny the existence of an innate principle or love of justice and virtue will dismiss his examples as merely the products of societal custom and education. He counters this by pointing to the universality of certain notions of morality and justice: "Cast your eyes on all the nations of the world. . . . Among so many and bizarre cults, among the prodigious diversity of morals and characters, you will find everywhere the same ideas of justice and decency, the same notions of good and bad." Of course, there will always be skeptics—here Montaigne comes in for special criticism—who try to find some bizarre custom in some remote corner of the world that contradicts this moral consensus of mankind; but Rousseau rejects such anthropological ingenuity. "O Montaigne," he writes, "tell me whether there is some country on earth where it is a crime to keep one's faith, to be clement, beneficent, and generous, where the good man is contemptible and the perfidious one honored" (E 288–89; see also ML 194–95). We will see later that Nietzsche supplies an answer in Montaigne's stead.

But beyond adducing examples of the innate principle of conscience, Rousseau also tries to provide a more theoretical basis for it. He claims that love of virtue—or as he often (and significantly) puts it, love of the morally beautiful—is as natural as self-love (*amour de soi*) (E 290; ML 196; LD 23). Indeed, he goes so far as to say that love of virtue is a species of self-love, albeit a self-love that belongs to our intelligent being rather than our merely sensitive being. The love that belongs to the latter is sensible and conduces to the well-being of the body, while the love of order that characterizes our intelligent being conduces to the well-being of the soul. "The latter love, developed and made active, bears the name of conscience." Rousseau goes on to make the important point that conscience in this sense is not to be found in the human being in the state of nature, for "conscience develops and acts only with man's understanding. It is only through this understanding that he attains a knowledge of order, and it is only when he knows order that his conscience brings him to love it. Conscience is therefore null in the man who has compared nothing and who has not seen his relationships" (LB 28; see also LO 261–62). This reinforces the point above about the inseparability of conscience and reason, but it also clarifies the relationship between them. Conscience provides the motivating love of the moral order disclosed by reason: "To know the good is not to love it; man does not have innate knowledge of it, but as soon as his reason makes him know it, his conscience leads him to love it. It is this sentiment which is innate" (E 290; see also 294; J 561).[17]

It is precisely because love of virtue is an innate sentiment in the human heart that there is an intimate connection between virtue and human happiness for Rousseau. The happiness we enjoy when we do a good deed, he argues, consists in the "good witness of oneself" (*E* 291; see also 281, 284; *J* 184). When we listen to our conscience, we discover the charm that comes from "tasting the internal peace of a soul satisfied with itself" (ML 194; see also 200–201). Against Kant, Rousseau maintains that we never do good simply for its own sake.[18] We also do it for own sake, "out of self-interest, since it gives the soul an internal satisfaction, a contentment with itself without which there is no true happiness" (LO 264).[19] Performing virtuous actions also provides the psychic unity that constitutes the essence of Rousseau's conception of happiness. When one fails to do what is virtuous, while loving the good, one is "always in contradiction with [oneself]." This leads the Savoyard vicar, who has still not entirely escaped the seductions of bodily pleasures, to say: "I aspire to the moment when, after being delivered from the shackles of the body, I shall be *me* without contraction or division and shall need only myself in order to be happy" (*E* 291, 293).

The ideal of sincerity or authenticity that is sounded in this passage can also be heard in Rousseau's response to the question of why, if conscience is innate and its dictates lead to happiness, so few people listen to it. As with the natural sentiment of pity, Rousseau argues that the false goods of the world, public opinion, and *amour propre* stifle the natural voice of conscience in us (*E* 291). Therefore, he counsels the recipient of his "Moral Letters," Sophie d'Houdetot, to escape the noise of Paris from time to time and seek out the solitude of the country in order to commune with her true self (ML 198–202). In this context, he invokes the ideal of sincerity and makes clear its connection to his teaching about conscience:

> Let us begin by becoming ourselves again, by centering ourselves in ourselves, by circumscribing our soul with the same limits that nature has given our being; in a word, let us begin by gathering ourselves together where we are, so that when we are seeking to know ourselves, everything that composes us comes to present itself to us at the same time. As for me, I think that the one who knows best what the human self consists in is the closest to wisdom and that, just as the first stroke of a drawing is formed by lines that make up its boundaries, the first idea of man is to separate him from everything that is not himself. (ML 198)

Though Rousseau advocates here a certain withdrawal from society and its prejudices in order to commune more effectively with one's inner self, it would be a mistake to see him as defending a radical sincerity in which the true self is understood to be "emphatically private," without connection to morality or what one has in common with others.[20] The true self for Rousseau is the moral self, the self that heeds the inner voice of conscience.[21] It is this identification of the authentic self with the moral self that Nietzsche questions.

Nietzsche: From the True Self to the Aesthetic Self

When Rousseau says, "Let us begin by becoming ourselves again," it sounds very similar to the paradoxical formula Nietzsche uses to encapsulate his ethical teaching about authenticity: "*What does your conscience say?*—'You should become who you are'" (GS 270). But beneath the superficial similarity of their formulations, there are fundamental differences between Rousseau's and Nietzsche's conceptions of the genuine or authentic self. For Rousseau, as we have seen, becoming oneself involves preventing one's desires from exceeding one's capacity to satisfy them and thus avoiding dependence on others. In the state of nature, this self-sufficiency and independence are achieved without effort. But once human beings enter into social relations and *amour propre* comes into play, virtue and conscience become necessary. For Nietzsche, on the other hand, becoming who you are involves what he calls "self-creation."[22] He connects the two ideas explicitly in an aphorism from *The Gay Science*: "We, however, want to *become who we are*—human beings who are new, unique, incomparable, who give themselves laws, who create themselves" (GS 335). The emphasis on the uniqueness and incomparability of the authentic self here contrasts sharply with Rousseau's emphasis on the universality of virtue and conscience in the authentic self.

In this and the following sections, I try to clarify what Nietzsche means by self-creation and how it relates to becoming who you are. In this section, I trace the emergence of Nietzsche's doctrine of self-creation in his early and middle writings, showing how he moves from the notion of a true self to an aesthetic conception of the self. In the next section, I examine his overcoming of the aesthetic model of the self in *The Gay Science*. And in the final section, I consider his fully developed doctrine of self-creation in his later writings, from *Thus Spoke Zarathustra* to *Ecce Homo*. Throughout I bring forward the similarities and, more important, the differences between Nietzsche's doctrine of self-creation and Rousseau's doctrine of moral self-determination.

In the first paragraph of "Schopenhauer as Educator," Nietzsche makes clear his concern with the question of how to become a genuine or authentic self. As in the passage from *The Gay Science* quoted above, Nietzsche asks what your conscience tells you. And much less paradoxically than in *The Gay*

Science, he answers: "Be yourself! All you are now doing, thinking, desiring, is not yourself." He elaborates on this theme in a way that has more in common with the nineteenth-century preoccupation with the uniqueness of the individual than with Rousseau's and Kant's identification of authenticity with moral autonomy. "Every man," Nietzsche writes, "is a unique miracle"; and "no imaginable chance will for a second time bring into unity so strangely variegated an assortment as he is."[23] What is it that prevents human beings from thinking and acting in accordance with their unique individuality? Again, Nietzsche joins a host of nineteenth-century thinkers, from Goethe to Emerson and Mill, in answering that it is laziness that makes men so conventional and herd-like and that leads them to "hide themselves behind customs and opinions" (SE 1:127).

A deeper answer to this question of why modern human beings are so conventional and herd-like is found in "The Uses and Disadvantages of History for Life." Here Nietzsche claims that historical consciousness has created a chaotic inner subjectivity in modern human beings that leads them to defer completely to convention. Far from encouraging honesty or sincerity (*Ehrlichkeit*), historical education produces people who wear "the identical bourgeois coat" (UDH 4–5:84). To overcome this inauthentic disjunction between inner subjectivity and outer appearance, the sincere or authentic individual must "rebel against a state of things in which he only repeats what he has heard, learns what is already known, [and] imitates what already exists" (UDH 10:123). Similar to Rousseau, Nietzsche here exhibits a concern for the loss of wholeness and self-division in modern human beings. But whereas for Rousseau it is modern commercial society that causes the contradiction between our inner and outer selves, for Nietzsche the problem lies in our disordered subjectivity, the "feeble many-sidedness of modern life" (RWB 2:201).

The question to which "Schopenhauer as Educator" addresses itself is how, under these alienating circumstances, we can gain access to our authentic self. After once again urging the individual to liberate himself from public opinion and convention and live according to his "own laws and standards," Nietzsche stresses how difficult it is to find or know oneself, for man "is a thing dark and veiled," and "it is a painful and dangerous undertaking to tunnel into oneself and force one's way down into the shaft of one's being" (SE 1:129). Nevertheless, he goes on to lay out a method by which the individual can achieve self-knowledge; and what is interesting about it is that it seems to point in a direction quite different from the one suggested by the tunneling metaphor:

> Let the youthful soul look back on life with the question: what have you truly loved up to now, what has drawn your soul aloft, what has mastered it and

at the same time blessed it? Set up these revered objects before you and perhaps their nature and their sequence will give you a law, the fundamental law
of your own true self. Compare these objects one with another, see how one
completes, expands, surpasses, transfigures another, how they constitute a
stepladder upon which you have clambered up to yourself as you are now;
for your true nature lies, not concealed deep within you, but immeasurably
high above you, or at least above that which you usually take yourself to be.
(SE 1:129)

Nietzsche's point here is somewhat ambiguous. On the one hand, he seems
to reject the idea of a fixed, antecedently given self buried within us, waiting
to be uncovered; somehow the self is constituted and transformed by what
it loves and reveres. On the other hand, he refers to a "true self" that is ultimately revealed by what we love and revere; such a self is somehow there and
not simply created. It is this latter, essentialist aspect that comes to the fore
when Nietzsche goes on to speak of education as liberation: "Your true educators and formative teachers reveal to you what the true basic material of your
being is, something in itself ineducable and in any case difficult of access,
bound and paralyzed: your educators are your liberators" (SE 1:129).

In the rest of "Schopenhauer as Educator," Nietzsche goes on to elaborate
on the liberating education he has in mind. Because modern human beings
are many-sided, complex, and devoid of wholeness, harmony, and honesty,
what is needed to counteract this condition of spiritual restlessness and chaos
is "an exalted and transfiguring goal," an overall image of man that will inspire individuals "to a transfiguration of their own lives" (SE 2:132–33; 4:150).
As we have seen, one of the images Nietzsche mentions here is that of the
Rousseauian man; but the one he is mainly concerned with in the essay is, of
course, the Schopenhauerian man, who is characterized above all by truthful-
ness (*Wahrhaftigkeit*). Having identified this image as the ideal that will orient, inspire, and give meaning to the lives of modern individuals, Nietzsche
goes on to extrapolate the fundamental duty that follows from it: namely, "to
promote the production of the philosopher, artist, and the saint within us
and without us" for the purpose of enlightening ourselves about the nature
of existence (SE 5:160). "How can your life . . . receive the highest value, the
deepest significance?" Nietzsche asks. "Certainly only by your living for the
good of the rarest and most valuable exemplars" (SE 6:162).[24]

This advice may seem to sit oddly with respect to Nietzsche's earlier ex-
hortations to "be yourself" and "live according to your own laws and standards," but he does not seem to see this living for the highest exemplars as
utterly divorced from living for oneself. The philosopher, artist, and saint are
exemplars precisely in the sense that they model a more vital, authentic, and

self-aware way of living; they inspire others to break out of their lazy conformity and transfigure their own lives. It is love for and devotion to some
great man, Nietzsche writes, that alone "can bestow on the soul . . . the desire
to look beyond itself and to seek with all its might for a higher self as yet
concealed from it" (SE 6:163). Here again we see how Nietzsche is complicat-
ing a common understanding of self-realization (not, however, Rousseau's)
as fidelity to one's unique or authentic self. Our unique self is not something
buried deep within us, waiting to be uncovered through introspection; rather,
it is something that can be disclosed only by attaching ourselves to great human beings who make us ashamed of our lazy conformity to convention and
public opinion and inspire us to transfigure our lives in accordance with our
higher selves. The reference to a "higher self," however, still seems to invoke
the model of fidelity to self; we do not yet have a doctrine of full-fledged
self-creation.

For the development of the latter, we must turn to Nietzsche's middle
works. In the first of these works, *Human, All Too Human* (along with its
sequels, *Assorted Opinions and Maxims* and *The Wanderer and His Shadow*),
Nietzsche's understanding of the self undergoes a radical shift, placing new
emphasis on the egoistic and self-interested basis of all human action. Breaking with his predecessor Schopenhauer, who identified morality with nonegoistic action and the motive of compassion, Nietzsche denies that there is
any such thing as a nonegoistic action: "No man has ever done anything that
was done wholly for others with no personal motivation whatever" (*HH* 133).
As for compassion or pity, it generally masks a desire for power over others. It
is driven by a "thirst for self-enjoyment" at the expense of one's fellow human
beings, and "it displays man in the whole ruthlessness of his own dear self"
(*HH* 50, 103). Justice, too, shares in this egoistic character of all action. Originally based on the idea of requital between parties of approximately equal
power, justice was not something independent of self-interest but, rather,
was grounded entirely on "enlightened self-preservation." Gradually, though,
through habit, education, and emulation, this utilitarian origin of justice was
forgotten, and it came to be associated with what is nonegoistic (*HH* 92; see
also 45).

Nietzsche draws two rather large conclusions from this doctrine of psychological egoism. First, insofar as "evil" actions share the same prudential motivation with "good" ones, they do not deserve to be simply condemned: "All 'evil'
acts are motivated by the drive to self-preservation or, more exactly, by the individual's intention of procuring pleasure and avoiding displeasure; so motivated,
however, they are not evil" (*HH* 99). In the end, "between good and evil actions
there is no difference in kind, but at most one of degree." From this, Nietzsche

draws the further conclusion that human beings are completely unaccountable for their deeds and natures. Human beings are composites of passions and desires that have been inherited from the past and modified in the present. There is no way to get beyond these desires and passions, no way to escape into a realm of transcendental freedom or nonegoistic action: "It is the individual's sole desire for self-enjoyment . . . which gratifies itself in every instance, let a man act as he can, that is to say as he must" (*HH* 107; see also *HH* 39; *AOM* 33).

From this doctrine of unaccountability, however, Nietzsche does not conclude that human beings are incapable of changing their lives in meaningful ways. The belief in fate grounded in psychological analysis does not dictate our particular response to it; it can be met with either "cowardice, resignation, or frankness and magnanimity. . . . Out of this [belief] anything and everything can grow" (*AOM* 363). This allows Nietzsche to continue to stress, as he did in "Schopenhauer as Educator," the importance of actualizing one's unique individuality, as opposed to conforming to public opinion, societal convention, or general utility. He complains bitterly about how mankind "mercilessly employs every individual as material for heating its great machines," degrading him to a mere "instrument of general utility" (*HH* 585, 593). Instead of clothing themselves in "general convictions and public opinions," human beings should create "their own costume" (*AOM* 325). This is not an easy task, especially for the young, who are vulnerable to the influence of what is thought and praised by society and as a result become alienated from their true selves (*HH* 612–13). In his impatience to become something, a youth often adopts the picture of life provided by a philosopher or poet, and in doing so he forgets "what is most worth learning and knowing: himself . . . Alas, much boredom has to be overcome, much sweat expended, before we discover our own colors, our own brush, our own canvas!" (*WS* 266).

All of this is consistent with the view of the self that Nietzsche lays out in "Schopenhauer." Where *Human, All Too Human* departs from the earlier essay, however, is in its emphasis on the fluidity and multifariousness of the self. Instead of identifying the authentic self with a fixed and constant core, Nietzsche now celebrates the figure of the free-spirited wanderer who does not "let his heart adhere too firmly to any individual thing" but, rather, "takes pleasure in change and transience" (*HH* 638). In order to acquire self-knowledge, we must constantly abandon our deepest convictions—"we *have* to become traitors, be unfaithful, again and again abandon our ideals" (*HH* 629; see also 483, 511, 630–37). This emphasis on the mutability and multifariousness of the self also suggests a somewhat different model of self-actualization from the one found in "Schopenhauer." No longer does Nietzsche see self-actualization in terms of fidelity to an already existing authentic self; rather, he sees it as bringing something new into being. "Active and successful natures," he writes in one aphorism, "act, not according to the dictum 'know thyself,'" but according to the commandment "*will a self* and thou shalt *become* a self" (*AOM* 366).

The idea of self-creation that is intimated here is much more fully developed in Nietzsche's second middle-period work, *Daybreak*. *Daybreak* is in many ways a breakthrough book with respect to Nietzsche's conception of the self. Whereas in *Human, All Too Human* he was concerned to point out the egoistic basis of all action, in *Daybreak* he questions the very notion of the ego, arguing that what it designates as a simple unity turns out to be in actuality a complex mechanism of drives and desires whose ultimate law we cannot know. He illustrates this point in an aphorism on self-mastery and the various methods by which the vehemence of a drive can be combated. These methods include avoiding opportunities for gratification of the drive, imposing strict regulations on its satisfaction, directing one's energy to satisfaction of another drive, and so forth. All of this is compatible with the traditional picture of self-mastery. But where Nietzsche departs from this picture is in denying that the very desire to combat a drive lies within our power or emanates from some unified self or reason: "In this entire procedure our intellect is only the blind instrument of *another drive* which is a *rival* of the drive whose vehemence is tormenting us." It is not a matter of reason supervening on passion but of one drive complaining about another. The self does not conflict with the drives but is merely the site where the drives themselves conflict (*D* 109).

Suddenly the prospect opens up that we neither control what we are doing nor even know exactly what we are doing. Nietzsche develops this humbling insight in an aphorism entitled "The Unknown World of the 'Subject.'" The most difficult thing for human beings to understand and accept has been their unavoidable ignorance of themselves. Ever since primeval times, human beings have suffered from the delusion that they know "quite precisely in every case *how human action is brought about*." Even the great doubters Socrates and Plato showed themselves to be "innocently credulous" in this regard by subscribing to "that most fateful of prejudices, that profoundest of errors, that 'right knowledge *must be followed* by right action.'" But Nietzsche denies that this is ever the case. All our actions remain "essentially unknown" to us, and therefore the gulf between knowledge and action can never be bridged (*D* 116). In addition to the conscious motives and reasons that we think determine our actions, there is a whole host of unconscious motives that exert an enormous influence on what we do. They, too, probably struggle with one another—as in the case of self-mastery above—but the struggle remains largely invisible to us (*D* 129). Nietzsche concludes that "our moral judgments and evaluations too are only images and fantasies based on a physiological process unknown to us," and "all our so-called consciousness is a more or less fantastic commentary on an unknown, perhaps unknowable, but felt text" (D 119).

Nietzsche's portrayal of human action as determined by unconscious drives and struggles between drives clearly undermines conventional notions of freedom of the will. What we call "will" is merely a shallow interpretation of a complicated process that goes on beneath the level of consciousness (D 130). In this way, Nietzsche arrives at the same conclusion about the innocence and unaccountability of human actions that he did in *Human, All Too Human*. But whereas in the earlier work he denied freedom of the will on the basis of the unavoidably egoistic character of human action, in *Daybreak* he does so on the basis of our ultimate ignorance of ourselves and the deepest wellsprings of our actions. In the same way, he denies the possibility of altruism—not on the basis that all our actions are egoistic, but on the basis that the complicated mechanism of our drives makes the distinction between egoistic and altruistic actions nonsensical. There is no single unified ego that can either assert or deny itself; there is only a multiplicity of drives that seek satisfaction in ways of which we have only the vaguest notion (D 133).

It is precisely because he conceives of the self as a multiplicity that Nietzsche now begins to deploy the metaphors of art and gardening to describe the process of cultivating the self. As Alexander Nehamas points out, by conceiving of the subject as a multiplicity, Nietzsche makes the "unity of the self . . . not something given but achieved, not a beginning but a goal."[25] A passage from his notebooks nicely captures this point about the self as something artistically made, not found: "It is mythology to believe that we will find our authentic selves. . . . Rather, making ourselves, shaping a form out of all the elements—that is the task! Always that of a sculptor, a productive man!" (*KSA* 9:7 [213]). Nietzsche illustrates this process of aesthetic self-fashioning in the aphorism "To Deploy One's Weaknesses Like an Artist," where he claims that while we all unavoidably have certain weaknesses, we also have "sufficient artistic power" to arrange these weaknesses in such a way as to create a desire for our virtues. Great composers like Beethoven, Mozart, and Wagner have possessed artistic power in abundance. All intersperse their music with passages of dry recitative, cloying sweetness, or restless dissonance that produce in us "a ravenous hunger for their virtues and a ten times more sensitive palate for every drop of musical spirit, musical beauty, and musical goodness" (D 218).

In another aphorism, "What We Are at Liberty to Do," Nietzsche uses the metaphor of gardening to capture his conception of the aesthetic self. Because this aphorism raises a number of important issues, I quote it in full:

One can dispose of one's drives like a gardener and, though few know it, cultivate the shoots of anger, pity, curiosity, vanity as productively and profitably as a beautiful fruit tree on a trellis; one can do it with the good or bad taste of a gardener and, as it were, in the French or English or Dutch or Chinese fashion; one can also let nature rule and only attend to a little embellishment and tidying-up here and there; one can, finally, without paying any attention to them at all, let the plants grow up and fight their fight out among themselves— indeed, one can take delight in such a wilderness, and desire precisely this delight, though it gives one some trouble, too. All this we are at liberty to do: but how many know we are at liberty to do it? Do the majority not *believe in themselves* as in complete *fully developed facts*? Have the great philosophers not put their seal on this prejudice with the doctrine of the unchangeability of character? (*D* 560)

One is immediately struck by the voluntarism of this aphorism and how it jars with Nietzsche's frequent denials of free will. By appealing to the liberty to dispose of one's drives like a gardener—or the power to deploy one's weaknesses like an artist—does he smuggle something like free will in through the back door?[26] Not necessarily. In several places in *Daybreak*, Nietzsche insists that the way we think about things and evaluate them has a profound effect on our feelings and actions (see *D*, 35, 76, 103, 104, 148). This does not mean, however, that there is not much about ourselves that is given or natural or even undeniable. This is precisely the point of the gardening and artistic metaphors. They put the emphasis not on denying or exterminating our drives or other natural aspects of ourselves, but on working with and arranging what is given. It is not a matter of something above the drives—reason, spirit, or the like—combating or suppressing them. Rather, our liberty extends only to arranging, cultivating, and nourishing what is already there. This creative activity is powerfully circumscribed by the natural facts that make up our being, but we are still far from being "fully developed facts" prior to this activity.

With respect to our circumstances, too, Nietzsche believes we have far more control than we often suppose. He insists that we should not live in an environment that makes us grow dissatisfied with ourselves, for then we will not achieve the best of which we are capable: "But who gives thought to such things, to possessing a *choice* in such things! One speaks of one's 'destiny,' spreads one's broad back, and sighs: 'what an unhappy Atlas I am!'" (*D* 364). Nietzsche provides numerous examples of how our environment can make us vengeful as well as magnify or diminish our power, concluding that "one should regard oneself as a variable quantity whose capacity for achievement can under favorable circumstances perhaps equal the greatest ever known: one should thus reflect on one's circumstances and spare no effort in

observing them" (*D* 326; see also 227, 323, 435). He dispenses the same advice
in his final book, importantly subtitled *How One Becomes What One Is* (*EH*,
"Clever," 1–8).

Overcoming the Aesthetic Self

The culmination of Nietzsche's reflections on the self and its cultivation or
creation in his middle works occurs in *The Gay Science*. We have already seen
that it is in this book—specifically, in the aphorism "Long Live Physics"—that
Nietzsche explicitly refers to self-creation and connects it with the notion of
becoming who you are. In this aphorism, Nietzsche also critiques the notion
of moral conscience that bears some resemblance to Rousseau's. The subject of the aphorism is self-knowledge, which Nietzsche regards as the most
elusive knowledge of all. "Each is farthest from himself," he writes, using a
phrase that he will repeat in the preface to the *Genealogy of Morality*; and yet
it is precisely on the subject of self-knowledge that everyone considers himself to be most expert. This can be seen in the confidence with which people
make moral judgments about right and wrong, and especially in the way they
appeal to conscience as the infallible basis for those judgments. This moral
conscience, Nietzsche maintains, must itself be made a matter of conscience,
of "intellectual conscience." It is not some God-given voice of nature but has
a "pre-history in your instincts, likes, dislikes, experiences, and lack of experiences." More often than not, weakness and stupidity impel one to listen
to one's conscience, and the firmness of one's moral judgment has less to do
with moral strength than will personal abjectness, stubbornness, and lack of
imagination. The same goes for Kant's categorical imperative, which rests on
selfishness insofar as it makes one's personal judgment a universal law, and
on timidity insofar as it "betrays that you have not yet discovered for yourself
nor created for yourself an ideal of your own, your very own" (*GS* 335; see also
5, 319).

The greatest defect of the Kantian categorical imperative—and of any morality that is based on universal laws—is that it fails to recognize the uniqueness of all our actions, that "there neither are nor can be actions that are the
same; that every action that has ever been done was done in an altogether
unique and irretrievable way" (*GS* 335; see also 354). Nietzsche's claim here to
some extent rests on his analysis earlier on in *The Gay Science* of how judgments of sameness and equality rest on simplifications and falsifications of
the seamless flux of reality and on crude comparisons of what is unique and
incomparable. He makes this point about the logical categories of equality and
substance as well as about cause and effect (*GS* 111–12), but it his application of

it to morality that is most relevant here. In the case of morality, simplification and falsification take the form of herd judgment in contradistinction to what is ineffably individual. Echoing what he said about the morality of custom in *Daybreak*, Nietzsche argues that morality "trains the individual to be a function of the herd and to ascribe value to himself only as a function. . . . Morality is herd instinct in the individual" (*GS* 116). This subordination of the individual to the herd was greatest during the "longest and most remote periods of the human past," when "nothing was more terrible than to feel that one stood by oneself," when individuality, freedom of thought, and egoism were considered painful and the desire to live "according to one's own weight and measure" was considered "madness." But modern human beings have learned to think and feel differently about themselves, so much so that it is difficult for them to grasp the crudity of primitive morality: "Today one feels responsible only for one's will and actions, and one finds pride in oneself. All our teachers of law start from this sense of self and pleasure in the individual as if this had always been the fount of law" (*GS* 117; see also 143, 296; *D* 9).

Certainly, Nietzsche believes we can go much further in the direction of individual responsibility and self-cultivation. As in his other writings, in *The Gay Science* he rails against the way modern society reduces individuals to herd animals and factory products. In its praise of the virtues of obedience and industriousness, for example, society has its own advantage in mind, not that of the individual. While these virtues may benefit society, they harm the individual by transforming him into a "mere function of the whole" and depriving him of "his noblest selfishness and the strength for the highest care of the self" (*GS* 21). In addition to these virtues, which exist for society's sake and for all the world to see, Nietzsche claims that there are unconscious virtues for which no microscope has yet been invented: "*our* industry, *our* ambition, *our* acuteness" (*GS* 8). And he argues that the ancient medical-moral formulation "Virtue is the health of the soul" needs to be changed to "*Your* virtue is the health of *your* soul. For there is no health as such." We must allow the "unique and the incomparable to raise its head again" and attempt "to find the peculiar virtue and peculiar health that belong to each individual" (*GS* 120).

To gain access to the "unique and the incomparable" is, of course, a difficult task; for as we learned from "Schopenhauer as Educator," the human being "is a thing dark and veiled." In "Long Live Physics," Nietzsche repeats the point he made in *Daybreak* (*D* 116) that all our actions are essentially "unknowable." And though he concedes that "our opinions, valuations, and tables of what is good certainly belong among the most powerful levers in the involved mechanism of our actions," he nevertheless denies that "in any particular case the law of their mechanism" can be demonstrated (*GS* 335). He beautifully captures the fathomlessness and unknowability of the self in an aphorism titled "Parable": "Whoever looks into himself as into vast space and carries galaxies in himself, also knows how irregular all galaxies are; they lead into the chaos and labyrinth of existence" (*GS* 322).

Given our unavoidable ignorance about the complex mechanism of our actions, how can we help bring our unique and incomparable selves to light? Having acknowledged the important role of our opinions and valuations, it is perhaps not surprising that Nietzsche recommends that we "*limit* ourselves to the purification of our opinions and valuations and to the *creation of our own new tables of what is good*" (*GS* 335). The former task of purification involves getting rid of the errors on which moral judgments have hitherto rested. In *Daybreak*, such purification consists mainly in the exposure of the intellectual error involved in free will and altruism, thus depriving egoistic actions of their bad conscience (*D* 148). In "Long Live Physics," insight into the unknowability and uniqueness of actions leads to the overturning of the identification of moral value with universality: "Sitting in moral judgment should offend our taste" (*GS* 335). Eliminating the errors of altruism, free will, and universality thus clears the ground for the second task mentioned above, the "creation of our own new tables of what is good." Scientific knowledge alone will never be enough to enable us to become the persons we are; we must creatively fashion something out of the formless chaos disclosed by physics.[27] The self we become is ultimately made, not found.[28]

We are once again back at the notion of the aesthetic self that Nietzsche began to elaborate in *Daybreak*. In *The Gay Science*, especially book 4, this notion receives its fullest articulation. The two aphorisms that are most frequently quoted to flesh out the idea of the aesthetic self are the one on giving style to one's character (*GS* 290) and the one on what one should learn from artists (*GS* 299). In the former, Nietzsche once again puts the emphasis on working with and arranging the natural aspects of ourselves rather than simply suppressing them that was such a prominent part of his presentation of the aesthetic self in *Daybreak*. Giving style to one's character, he writes, involves surveying "all the strengths and weaknesses of [one's] nature and then [fitting] them into an artistic plan until every one of them appears as art and reason and even weaknesses delight the eye" (*GS* 290). In the aphorism on what one can learn from artists, Nietzsche again stresses how artists work with what they are given, even if it is ugly, transforming it rather than simply denying it. "How can we make things beautiful, attractive, and desirable for us when they are not?" he asks. The key lies in viewing those things from the right angle or at the proper distance, framing them so that they compose a harmonious or tension-filled picture. This is what artists excel at. The only problem with artists, Nietzsche observes, is that they restrict their use of these techniques to their art rather than applying them to their lives. This is where he insists we must go beyond them, for "we want to be the poets of our life" (*GS* 299).

The exact manner in which we give style to our character or become poets of our life, however, will vary from person to person, according to Nietzsche. "Strong and domineering natures," he claims, are generally drawn to the constraint of style and "demur at giving nature freedom"; for this reason, they favor highly stylized palaces and gardens. "Weak characters without power over themselves," on the other hand, "*hate* the constraint of style." They like to give nature free rein and therefore favor gardens that are "wild, arbitrary, fantastic, disorderly, and surprising." What is striking about the contrast Nietzsche draws here is that he is less interested in ranking the alternatives than in stressing that one should give pleasure to oneself in whatever way one can. This is the "one thing needful" alluded to in the title of the aphorism: "For one thing is needful: that a human being should *attain* satisfaction with himself, whether it be by means of this or that poetry or art; only then will a human being be tolerable to behold. Whoever is dissatisfied with himself is continually ready for revenge, and we others will be his victim" (*GS* 290).

It is with a view to attaining satisfaction with oneself, taking pleasure in oneself, having a good conscience toward oneself—and not the achievement of aesthetic unity for its own sake—that Nietzsche generally invokes the analogy of art for self-making. Thus he argues that while it is impossible "to turn a poor virtue into a rich and overflowing one," we can reinterpret it in such a way that "it no longer offends us when we see it and we no longer sulk at fate on its account. That is what a wise gardener does when he places the poor little stream in his garden in the arms of a nymph and thus finds a motive for its poverty" (*GS* 17). Again, it is artists who excel at this technique of transforming what is otherwise base or ordinary into something interesting, pleasurable, and even heroic. It is artists who "have given men eyes and ears to see and hear with some pleasure what each man *is* himself, experiences himself, desires himself; only they have taught us to esteem the hero that is concealed in everyday characters; only they have taught us the art of viewing ourselves as heroes—from a distance and, as it were, simplified and transfigured—the art of staging and watching ourselves" (*GS* 78). And as he did in the garden example above, Nietzsche insists that it is only through this art of transfiguration that we can "deal with some base details in ourselves" and prevent them from becoming the source of resentment or revenge (*GS* 78).

We are now in a position to specify more precisely the role that art plays in Nietzsche's conception of self-creation. Art allows us to accept and take pleasure in ourselves and to transfigure even the basest or ugliest aspects of our character so that they do not become sources of resentment or revenge. Art does not lead us away from ourselves but more deeply into ourselves, into the chaos and labyrinth of our complex and multifarious souls. Art is not an end in itself but a means to access more completely our unique individuality; it enables us to become who we *are*, or, as Nietzsche puts it in the passage above, "to see and hear with some pleasure what each man *is* himself." Another way of stating this point is that through the transfiguring power of art, human beings no longer feel ashamed before themselves. Not feeling ashamed of oneself emerges as a major theme in a series of aphorisms on which Nietzsche was working up until the last minute before the publication of *The Gay Science*.[29] In one of these aphorisms, after restating that "art furnishes us with the eyes and hands and above all the good conscience to turn ourselves into [an aesthetic] phenomenon," he writes: "And as long as you are in any way *ashamed* before yourselves, you do not yet belong with us" (*GS* 107). And at the end of book 3, after raising a series of questions, including the previously cited "*What does your conscience say?*—'You shall become who you are,'" he concludes with this one: "*What is the seal of liberation?*—No longer being ashamed in front of oneself" (*GS* 275).

Nietzsche's aesthetic model of the self, which allows us to take pleasure in all aspects of our being and no longer feel ashamed, contrasts sharply with the model of self-renunciation and self-mastery found in many moralities, including to some extent Rousseau's. Nietzsche condemns those moralists who make self-control the one thing needful and thereby afflict human beings with a "constant irritability in the face of all natural stirrings and inclinations," rendering them incapable of entrusting themselves to "any instinct or free wingbeat" (*GS* 305). By seeing our natural inclinations and passions as dirty and disfiguring, these moralists commit a "great injustice against our nature, against all nature" (*GS* 294). St. Paul—admittedly a far cry from Rousseau—is Nietzsche's prime example of such a moralist who has "an evil eye for the passions" and aims only at their annihilation. The Greeks, on the other hand, with their powerful artistic tendencies, "loved, elevated, gilded, and deified the passions" (*GS* 139). This is the mark of the noble human being, according to Nietzsche: to trust oneself, to "feel no fear of oneself," to not be ashamed of oneself (*GS* 294).

The aphorism that perhaps best sums up Nietzsche's aesthetic conception of self-creation in *The Gay Science* is the one titled "Embark." In this aphorism, Nietzsche's emphasis again falls on transfiguring, justifying, and redeeming the various aspects of our being rather than denying or annihilating them. In keeping with what he said earlier about the importance of our opinions and valuations as levers in the complex mechanism of our actions, he highlights here the profound effect an "overall philosophical justification" has on the individual. Such a philosophical justification appears as "a sun that shines especially for him and bestows warmth, blessings, and fertility on him; it makes him independent of praise and blame, self-sufficient, rich, liberal with happiness and good will." As in other aphorisms we have investigated, Nietzsche here emphasizes how such an overall philosophical justification transforms our baser qualities and prevents them from becoming sources of frustration or revenge: "Incessantly it refashions evil into good, leads all energies to bloom and ripen, and does not permit the petty weeds of grief and chagrin to come up at all." He also refuses to give priority to one individual over another with respect to the need for such a philosophical justification. The evil, the unhappy, and the exceptional human being all have an equal right to their own philosophy and sunshine. Again, the one thing needful is that everyone attain satisfaction with himself. Nietzsche refers to this as a "new justice," and he calls on "new philosophers" to create as many new suns as there are individuals (*GS* 285).

This aphorism brings us back to the one on the health of the soul, in which Nietzsche declares that there are "innumerable healths" and that the task of the physician is to find the peculiar virtue that conduces to the peculiar health of each individual. In this latter aphorism, however, Nietzsche adds a reflection that complicates the rather one-dimensional and static picture of the self he has constructed so far. Even if we succeed in finding the peculiar virtue or health that belongs to each individual, he writes, "the great question would still remain whether we can really dispense with illness . . . and whether our thirst for knowledge and self-knowledge in particular does not require the sick soul as much as the healthy, and whether, in brief, the will to health alone is not a prejudice [and] cowardice" (*GS* 120).[30] Here Nietzsche suggests that the kind of happiness and contentment provided by an overall philosophical justification—and by implication, an overall artistic plan—may not satisfy those who seek genuine self-knowledge. Such self-knowledge requires that one be willing to give up one's overall philosophical justifications or ideals from time to time, that one become sick and dissatisfied, that one lose oneself.

In book 4 of *The Gay Science*, the idea of losing oneself in order to learn more about oneself becomes a persistent theme. One of the principal criticisms Nietzsche makes of the rigid morality of self-control, for example, is that it cuts the individual off from "the most beautiful fortuities of his soul" as well as from "all further *instruction*. For one must be able to lose oneself occasionally if one wants to learn something from things different from oneself" (*GS* 305). He praises "brief habits" for the same reason: they are "inestimable means for getting to know *many* things and states." Enduring habits, on the other hand, close off the path to self-knowledge. Interestingly, Nietzsche mentions "unique good health" as one of the circumstances that gives rise to enduring habits, and he expresses gratitude for "all my misery and bouts of sickness," which allow him to escape from them (*GS* 295).

Though Nietzsche here endorses a certain openness to change and ability to lose oneself or shed one's skin, it is important to point out that he is not advocating the sort of shallow experimentalism and role playing he associates particularly with Americans (see *GS* 356). As bad as enduring habits are for learning as much as we can about ourselves, even worse is a "life entirely devoid of habits, a life that would demand perpetual improvisation." In order to acquire self-knowledge, we need to fully commit to a particular ideal, perspective, or practice, albeit temporarily. In every brief habit, Nietzsche writes, there is a faith in eternity that belongs to all passion. There is also a certain pathos; we cannot simply adopt or shed a habit at will: "One day its time is up; the good thing departs from me, not as something that has come to nauseate me but peacefully and sated with me as I am with it" (*GS* 295). Such pathos, in contrast to the self-conscious role playing of the actor, is a prominent feature of Nietzsche's account of self-knowledge throughout book 4 of *The Gay Science* (see, e.g., *GS* 307, 309, 317).

In all of this, we recognize the idea of self-overcoming that Nietzsche will not systematically explicate until *Zarathustra*, and of course in conjunction with the will to power. What is of particular interest to us here is that this idea seems to stand in some tension with the aesthetic model of selfhood that Nietzsche develops elsewhere in *The Gay Science*. Aesthetic unity or coherence alone does not seem to be enough to become the persons we are; change, disruption, illness, and dissatisfaction seem to be necessary too.[31] Nietzsche beautifully illustrates the tension between these two models of selfhood in the aphorism "Two Who Are Happy." The first person described in the aphorism is said to be a "great improviser of life" who never seems to make a mistake not because he never does so, but because whenever he does make a mistake, he incorporates it into a larger thematic order that endows it with beauty and necessity. This seems to correspond fairly closely to the aesthetic model of the self that we have discussed. But Nietzsche goes on to depict another kind of person who is altogether different from the great improvisatory artist of life, a person whose desires and plans always go wrong but who does not feel unhappy on that account. Rather, he is grateful for his failures because he learns more about life through them: "I know more about life because I have so often been on the verge of losing it; and precisely for that reason I get more out of life than any of you" (*GS* 303).

Nietzsche does not indicate that one of these alternatives is better than the other, but the aphorisms that follow "Two Who Are Happy" tend to emphasize pain, suffering, loss, conflict, and self-overcoming rather than aesthetic unity, harmony, and permanent satisfaction (see GS 304, 305, 307, 309, 311, 312, 316, 317, 318, 325, 326). This clearly contrasts with Rousseau's (and Schopenhauer's) Epicurean emphasis on the avoidance of suffering in his conception of happiness.[32] In addition, there are several aphorisms that celebrate knowledge-seeking experimentation over aesthetic consummation (GS 319. 324). None of this implies that Nietzsche abandons his aesthetic model of the self, but it does suggest that he does not see it as the end or goal of self-creation. As I argued earlier, Nietzsche sees the aesthetic management of the self not as end in itself but as a means to access our unique individuality. Art allows us to accept and take pleasure in ourselves and to transfigure even the worst aspects of our character so that they do not becomes sources of resentment or revenge. No longer feeling ashamed in front ourselves is not the end of the process of becoming who we are but the beginning. Indeed, there is no end to this process—only a constant overcoming that discloses ever more aspects of our multifarious and labyrinthine selves.

Self-Creation and *Amor Fati*

The doctrine of self-creation that Nietzsche articulates in *The Gay Science* continues to inform his later writings, from *Zarathustra* to *Ecce Homo*, but it is couched in the more familiar—and to some extent more systematic—terms of his mature philosophy. In this section I want to connect the earlier doctrine to the later conceptual vocabulary, which does not merely translate the earlier doctrine but draws out its deepest grounds and most far-reaching implications. I will use the three fundamental ideas of *Zarathustra*—the will to power, the eternal return, and the *Übermensch*—to organize my discussion. Needless to say, I will not offer anything like an exhaustive analysis of any of these elusive and much-written-about concepts. Rather, my intention is merely to sketch Nietzsche's mature conception of the authentic self for the purpose of comparing it to Rousseau's conception.

We have seen that Nietzsche's model of authentic selfhood involves self-overcoming and the suffering that goes along with it. In *Thus Spoke Zarathustra*, he theorizes such self-overcoming in terms of the concept of the will to power. The section "On Self-Overcoming" contains seven references to the will to power, by far the most of any section in the book. In it, Nietzsche states plainly that the will to power is the will of life—not, however, the will *to* life, for we often sacrifice our lives for the sake of power. Here he rejects

Schopenhauer's claim that the will to existence or self-preservation is the fundamental aim of human beings (*Z* 2, "Self-Overcoming"; see also *BGE* 13). In his first reference to the will to power in *Zarathustra*, Nietzsche connects it to the act of valuing or esteeming. "No people," he writes, "could live without esteeming. . . . A table of good hangs over every people. Behold, it is the tablet of their overcomings; behold, it is the voice of their will to power" (*Z* 1, "Thousand and One Goals"). In "On Self-Overcoming," he repeats this equation of will to power with esteeming and draws the conclusion that "good and evil that are not transitory, do not exist. Driven on by themselves, they must overcome themselves again and again." It follows from this that the creator of good and evil must also be an annihilator of values and an advocate and justifier of all impermanence and of the suffering that goes along with it (*Z* 2, "Self-Overcoming" and "Blessed Isles").

The claim that "life simply *is* will to power" (*BGE* 259) involves a complete rethinking of the nature of human happiness and a revaluation of the role of suffering in it. Contrary to Schopenhauer's (and Rousseau's) identification of happiness with the absence of pain and a permanent contentment that escapes the dissatisfaction inherent in constant striving, Nietzsche sees pain, suffering, loss, and conflict as absolutely essential to human happiness. As he puts it in *The Antichrist*: "What is happiness?—The feeling that power *increases*—that a resistance is overcome. *Not* contentment, but more power; *not* peace at all, but war" (*A* 2). Happiness as the feeling of power requires resistance and the displeasure that comes with it. Man does not seek pleasure and avoid displeasure. Pleasure is merely the consequence of our gaining what we really want—namely, power; and displeasure as the resistance or obstacle we must overcome in order to gain power is a necessary ingredient of the whole process (*WP* 688, 696, 702, 704).[33] As for the happiness that consists in a struggle-free and comfortable contentment, Nietzsche is fond of saying that man as such does not seek it, only the Englishman (*TI*, "Maxims," 12; see also *TI*, "Expeditions," 38; *BGE* 228; *WP* 930).

The revaluation of the role of suffering in human existence that Nietzsche's concept of the will to power requires also leads to a revaluation of pity or compassion. This points to another fundamental difference with Rousseau. Given that suffering is crucial to human creativity, flourishing, and happiness, Nietzsche cannot have much sympathy for the pity that seeks to abolish it. To the exponents of this sort of pity, including Rousseau and his disciple Schopenhauer, Nietzsche addresses the following question: "The discipline of suffering, of *great suffering*—do you not see that only *this* discipline has created all enhancements of man so far?" The pity that seeks to abolish this discipline of suffering concerns itself only with the *creature* in man, to the neglect of the *creator*. Nietzsche's pity is for the latter. The fundamental conflict, therefore, is not between pity and hardheartedness but between two different kinds of pity (*BGE* 225). And the one that is directed to the creator in man must take precedence, for exclusive pity for the creature ultimately leads to nihilism.

Let us now turn to the second fundamental idea of *Zarathustra*—indeed, Nietzsche calls it the "fundamental conception" of the work (*EH*, "Books: *Z*," 1): the idea of the eternal recurrence. Nietzsche introduces this idea at the end of book 4 of *The Gay Science*, which suggests that it is intimately connected to the doctrine of self-creation developed there.[34] In a note written during the planning stages of *The Gay Science*, he remarks: "Only at the end will the *doctrine* be presented of the repetition of everything that has been, once the tendency has been implanted to *create* something that can *flourish* a hundred times more strongly in the sunshine of this doctrine" (*KSA* 9:11 [165]). It is precisely the notion of self-creation as constant self-overcoming— which involves a positive revaluation of pain, dissatisfaction, suffering, impermanence, and becoming—that flourishes in the light of the doctrine of the eternal recurrence. This doctrine does not pick out a final aim, purpose, or state of being to affirm, but rather affirms every moment in the process by which things come to be and pass away. This means affirming both the positive aspects of existence and the aspects that have hitherto been denied or disvalued: not only creation, but destruction; not only good, but evil; not only pleasure, but pain and suffering (*GS* 370; *TI*, "Ancients," 4–5; *EH*, "Books: BT*," 3; *WP* 1041, 1049–50).[35]

Nietzsche refers to the affirmation involved in the idea of the eternal recurrence as a "Dionysian affirmation of the world," and he connects it to the formula of *amor fati*—a formula he first introduced at the beginning of book 4 of *The Gay Science* (*WP* 1041; *GS* 276). This formula serves as a link to the third fundamental idea of *Zarathustra*, the *Übermensch*, which I will treat here generically as a term for Nietzsche's conception of the highest human type. In *Ecce Homo*, he states: "My formula for greatness in a human being is *amor fati*: that one wants nothing to be different, not forward, not backward, not in all eternity. Not merely bear what is necessary . . . but *love* it" (*EH*, "Clever," 10). But what exactly does this mean, and how does it relate to the idea of authentic selfhood and self-creation we have been following?

In order to clarify Nietzsche's meaning here, it is helpful to consider another one of his definitions of human greatness. In an age of specialization such as ours, he writes in *Beyond Good and Evil*, the "greatness of man, the concept of 'greatness,'" is to be found "precisely in his range and multiplicity, in his wholeness in manifoldness" (*BGE* 212). For Nietzsche, the great human being is the one who is richest in contradictions (*TI*, "Morality," 3), who contains within himself the greatest number of contradictory valuations and drives (*WP* 259), who can give the widest scope to his desires and passions (*WP* 933), and yet whose self does not fall into anarchy or incoherence; he adduces Shakespeare as an example (*WP* 966). This is also Nietzsche's conception of the free human being: "The freest human being has the greatest feeling of power over himself, the greatest knowledge of himself, the greatest order in the necessary struggle of his forces, the relatively greatest independence of his individual forces, [and] the relatively greatest struggle in himself" (*KSA* 9:11 [130]). In some places, Nietzsche refers to such a human being as the "synthetic" or "complementary" man (*WP* 866, 881, 883; *BGE* 207), and in *Zarathustra* as the "most comprehensive soul": "the soul that has the longest ladder and reaches down deepest . . . [that] can run and stray and roam farthest within itself; the most necessary soul, which out of sheer joy plunges itself into chance; the soul which, having being, dives into becoming; the soul which *has*, but *wants* to want and will; the soul which flees itself and catches up with itself in the widest circle" (*Z* 3, "Tablets," 19).

Zarathustra himself embodies this many-sidedness of strength—in contrast to the "feeble many-sidedness" of which earlier Nietzsche complained in his *Untimely Meditations*. Nietzsche makes this clear in *Ecce Homo* when he refers to Zarathustra as the "*supreme type of all beings*" who contains within himself a tremendous "width of space" and "accessibility for what is contradictory" and then goes on to quote the passage in *Zarathustra* on the most comprehensive soul quoted above (*EH*, "Books: *Z*," 6). In *Ecce Homo*, Nietzsche also describes Zarathustra in terms of what he calls the "great health"—the title of the penultimate aphorism of book 5 of *The Gay Science*, which he goes on to quote in full. This aphorism once again highlights the importance of multiplicity, contradiction, struggle, and self-overcoming in his conception of selfhood. Great health is distinguished from ordinary health in that it incorporates illness and suffering as a means to self-knowledge; it is "stronger, more seasoned, tougher, more audacious, and gayer than any previous health." And it is just this sort of great health that the free spirit requires as he gives himself up to the dangerous and often painful adventure of experiencing the "whole range of values and desiderata to date" (*EH*, "Books: *Z*," 2; *GS* 382; see also *HH* 1, preface,4).

The other figure who embodies the "wholeness in manifoldness" that Nietzsche identifies with human greatness is Goethe. Interestingly, Nietzsche speaks of Goethe in relation to the Rousseauian "return to nature," but he clarifies that Goethe attempted less a "going-back" than a "going-up" to nature, "up into a high, free, even frightful nature and naturalness," the "naturalness of the Renaissance" as opposed to the sentimental naturalness of the eighteenth century. The frightfulness of this nature seems to consist precisely in its manifoldness, the wealth of contradictory passions, drives, and values. Like the "synthetic man" Nietzsche speaks of elsewhere, Goethe aspired to "totality; he strove against the separation of reason, sensuality, feeling, will (preached in the most horrible scholasticism by Kant, the antipodes of Goethe); he disciplined himself to a whole, he *created* himself." The idea of self-creation referenced here recalls what Nietzsche says elsewhere about accessing as many parts of the self as possible while shaping those disparate and often contradictory elements into a coherent whole. The Goethean human being has "reverence for himself" and "dares to allow himself the whole compass and wealth of naturalness"; he is a "man of tolerance, not out of weakness, but out of strength, because he knows how to employ to his advantage what would destroy an average human being." Nietzsche concludes this remarkable aphorism on Goethe by returning to the idea of *amor fati* with which we began our consideration of the great human being: "A spirit thus *emancipated* stands in the midst of the universe with a joyful and trusting fatalism, in the faith that . . . in the totality everything is redeemed and affirmed—*he no longer denies*" (*TI*, "Expeditions," 48–49; see also *WP* 95).

This aphorism brings us back to our comparison with Rousseau. Nietzsche's conception of the authentic self certainly shares with Rousseau's a concern with wholeness. But where it diverges is in its valuing of the manifoldness of our drives, desires, and values and the suffering and struggle that come with it. For Rousseau, the key to happiness and authentic selfhood is ensuring that our desires do not exceed our capacity to satisfy them. As our desires increase, especially with the growth of *amour propre*, it becomes necessary to develop virtue in order to combat them. Though Rousseau differs from Kant in his eudaemonism, he nevertheless shares a certain moralism with Kant that warrants Nietzsche's charge that he is a "moral tarantula." It is this moralism that Nietzsche's conception of authenticity in terms of self-creation completely rejects. To become yourself through self-creation means constantly overcoming yourself as you open yourself up to more parts of your being; it is to accept and affirm the multifarious drives, desires, and values that make up the self because you are strong enough to do so; in short, *amor fati*.

4

Woman and Family

Between the time of Rousseau and that of Nietzsche, no question stirred up more controversy and passion than the question of the legal, economic, and political status of women and their role in the family. Rousseau, of course, was a central interlocutor in this debate over the so-called "woman question." His reflections in *Emile* on the nature, education, and moral role of women were vigorously attacked by Mary Wollstonecraft in her seminal feminist tract, *A Vindication of the Rights of Woman*, published in 1792.[1] They also exerted a profound influence on the discussions of women and the family found in such major nineteenth-century thinkers as Hegel and Tocqueville.[2] In comparison with Rousseau's, Nietzsche's reflections on the "woman question" occupy a much smaller place in his philosophy as a whole, and they certainly exerted less of an influence on his contemporaries. Nevertheless, he did see the question as a defining feature of the age and would no doubt have agreed with his contemporary Henry James, who, when planning his novel *The Bostonians*, asked himself "what was the most salient and peculiar point in our social life. The answer was, the situation of women, the decline of the sentiment of sex, the agitation on their behalf."[3]

There are many similarities between Rousseau's and Nietzsche's views on women, not least that they are controversial, reactionary, and by today's standards sexist. Both thinkers hold that there are fundamental differences between the natures of men and women and that these differences should be preserved. For Rousseau, this does not imply inequality between the sexes; for Nietzsche it does, but such inequality hardly constitutes an objection for him. Because of the controversial nature of Rousseau's and Nietzsche's views, the scholarly response to them has generally taken one of two tacks. Some scholars have simply dismissed their views as misogynistic.[4] Others have defended them against this charge by arguing that they contain at least elements of a more woman-friendly outlook.[5] My own approach in this chapter goes in a slightly different direction, aiming to be neither condemnatory nor apologetic. I am ultimately less interested in whether Rousseau's and Nietzsche's views can or cannot be labeled misogynistic and more interested in elucidating what exactly those views are, how they stand in relation to one another, and the place they occupy in the two thinkers' moral and political philosophies as a whole.

To this end, it is important to recognize not only the striking similarities between Rousseau's and Nietzsche's views on women but also the fundamental differences, which can ultimately be traced back to the differences in their larger critiques of modern bourgeois society. In the case of Rousseau, women play a crucial role in overcoming the individualistic, self-interested, and calculating character of such a society. The desire for women's approval inspires men to transcend the "baseness of the human *I*" and strive to be as virtuous as possible (*E* 391). For Nietzsche, on the other hand, it is precisely Rousseau's according women such an enormous role in the moralization of men that he takes issue with. He claims that Rousseau's sentimental and romantic philosophy is thoroughly informed by the feminine principle; and in this, it is reflective of the eighteenth century in general, which is "dominated by woman" and "given to enthusiasm" (*WP* 95).[6] In contrast to Rousseau, Nietzsche worries about the softening and feminization of modern bourgeois society, its excessive valorization of sympathy and compassion, and its reduction of fundamental differences between human beings in the name of equality. His emphasis on strength, struggle, aggression, conflict, war, and the will to power is in many ways intrinsically antifeminist. And yet he, too, finds an important place for women in his philosophy of the future. In exactly what way and with what implications for the comparison with Rousseau will become apparent in the analysis that follows.

Rousseau on the Nature and Education of Woman

Rousseau's distinctive views on women and their role in society emerge quite early in his philosophical career. Though there is an early protofeminist writing in which Rousseau decries the "tyranny of men" that has deprived women of their freedom and claims there would many more female heroines in history if "women had had as great share as [men] do in the handling of business and in the governing of empires" (OW 245–46), the stance that was to characterize his mature outlook on women was already clearly articulated in his first major writing. In the *First Discourse*, Rousseau complains about authors like Voltaire who, in order to satisfy their desire for applause, write works to please and flatter women, thus sacrificing their taste to the "tyrants of their freedom." In a footnote, he adds that he is "far from thinking that this ascendancy of women is in itself an evil." If it were "better directed, it would produce as much good as it nowadays does harm. We are not sufficiently sensible to the benefits that would accrue to society if the half of mankind which governs the other were given a better education. Men will always be what it pleases women that they be: so that if you want them to become great and virtuous, teach women what greatness of soul and virtue is" (FD 19; see also LR 66).

Rousseau develops these views on the relation between the sexes in the *Letter to D'Alembert*. There he repeats that men conform to the expectations women have of them: "Do you want to know men? Study women." He then goes on to declare that "there are no good morals for women outside of a withdrawn and domestic life . . . and that the dignity of their sex consists in modesty," shame, and chastity. Rousseau is perfectly aware that he is challenging the enlightened views on women of his day. He anticipates that those who hold such views will protest that chastity is merely a social construction designed to prop up the rights of fathers and husbands; also, that there is no reason why women should deny themselves more than men when their sexual desires are the same. But he responds by pointing out that although the sexual desires of the two sexes may be equal, the ability to satisfy them is not. Men need to be aroused in order to perform, and modesty on the part of women is far more effective in this regard than "boring freedom." Women also have to confine their sexual desires so that men can be assured that a child is their own. All of this is dictated by nature, according to Rousseau, and he even adduces examples of sexual shame and playing hard-to-get among the animals. But even if modesty and chastity were not simply natural but social constructions, he insists that it would still be in the interest of society for women to observe them. Whether it comes from nature or education, there is still no "sight so touching, so respectable, as that of a mother surrounded by her children, directing the work of her domestics, procuring a happy life for her husband and prudently governing the home" (LD 82–88).

Rousseau reiterates many of these views in the fifth book of *Emile*, which contains his most complete discussion of the nature of women and their relation to men. Before taking up that discussion, however, it is important not to overlook Rousseau's statement at the beginning of *Emile* that the prime addressees of his treatise are mothers: "The first education is the most important, and this first education belongs incontestably to women." He goes on to say that the laws "do not give enough authority to mothers" in this regard, and that any child who lacks respect for its mother should be strangled "as a monster unworthy of seeing the light of day" (*E* 37n). Such respect is owed partly because, in addition to carrying the child in her womb and caring for its interests more than her own, a mother nurses the child with her own milk; and Rousseau famously decries the practice of farming out this important maternal responsibility to nurses. "There is no substitute for maternal solicitude," he writes, and its neglect leads to the erosion of family life and general moral corruption: "Do you wish to bring everyone back to his first duties? Begin with mothers. You will be surprised by the changes you produce. Everything follows successively from this first depravity. The whole moral order degenerates, naturalness is extinguished in all hearts" (*E* 44–46).

Despite this early emphasis on their importance, we do not hear a great deal more about women until book 5 of *Emile*, where Rousseau discusses the education of Sophie and her romantic relationship with Emile. He begins this discussion with some observations about the general differences between men and women, the first of which is that men are "active and strong" and women are "passive and weak" (*E* 358). This natural difference seems to have been the basis of the sexual division of labor in the first families. In the *Second Discourse*, Rousseau describes the establishment of the family as the product of the first revolution in the life of human beings after they left the pure state of nature. Once men, women, and children began to live together in a common dwelling, there arose among them the "sweetest sentiments known to man, conjugal love and paternal love." At the same time, "the first difference was established in the ways of living of the two sexes, which until then had been one. Women became more sedentary and grew accustomed to looking after the hut and children, while the man went in quest of a common subsistence" (*SD* 164). It is clear that this development is natural for Rousseau, not in the sense that it belongs to the original state of nature, but in the sense that it grows directly out of it.[7]

From the natural difference in physical strength between men and women flows the difference that has provoked the most criticism of Rousseau's sexual politics: namely, that "woman is made specially to please man." Because she is weak, woman must earn the protection of man by pleasing him and making herself desirable to him. And as Rousseau did in the *Letter to D'Alembert*, he argues that the surest way for a woman to make herself desirable to men is to withhold her sexual favors. Through modesty and shame, a woman gains all the power she lacks because of her physical weakness. Indeed, it is through her control of sex that woman gains empire over man and the strong is made to serve the weak (*E* 358–61). This, of course, is the point that Rousseau made as far back as the *First Discourse*. And it is also the point that lies behind

Nietzsche's charge that Rousseau and the eighteenth century in general elevated woman to a dominant position and thereby feminized Europe.

Because women differ from men in the ways specified above, Rousseau concludes that their educations should differ correspondingly from men's.[8] He criticizes Plato for giving women the same exercises as men in the *Republic*. If women are educated in the same way as men, they will simply turn out to be inferior men and lose that empire that derives from their distinctive qualities. If you decide to raise women like men, Rousseau writes, the "men will gladly consent to it! The more women want to resemble them, the less women will govern them, and then men will truly be masters" (*E* 362–64). Because woman's power derives from her attractiveness and ability to please, Rousseau argues that her natural penchant for adornment—a penchant revealed in girls' love of playing with dolls—should be cultivated. In the same vein, he recommends that women should learn to be successful coquettes: "To be a woman means to be coquettish" (*E* 365–67).

This aspect of Rousseau's education for women has, of course, been roundly criticized by feminists, beginning with Wollstonecraft,[9] but we need to pay attention to the qualifications with which Rousseau hedges it. He is careful to distinguish between decent and degrading forms of adornment and coquetry: the former is designed to please "the man of merit, the truly lovable man," rather than those who are enamored of ostentatious fashion. Though Rousseau claims that "to be a woman means to be coquettish," he adds significantly that "her coquetry changes its form and its object according to her views. Let us regulate her views according to those of nature, and woman will have the education which suits her." Taking nature as a guide, girls should be encouraged to dress simply and not to regard adornment as anything more than "a supplement to the graces of her person." Rousseau insists that "true coquetry is sometimes elaborate, but it is never showy"; and "true care for adornment requires little time at the dressing table." Nor does the cultivation of attractiveness in girls require excessive softness or preclude the strengthening of their bodies through exercise. Women should be robust so that their children are robust, and therefore girls should engage in "many sports, races, and games outdoors in gardens" (*E* 365–66, 372–73).

After considering the physical aspects of women's education, Rousseau turns to the more intellectual aspects; and he makes it clear that women should not "be raised in ignorance of everything and limited to housekeeping functions alone." Rather, "nature wants them to think, to judge, to love, to know, to cultivate their minds as well as their looks." Nevertheless, he goes on to say that women should not know all the things that men know "but only those things that are suitable for them to know." Because women are dependent on men, they are "at the mercy of men's judgments" and must be particularly attentive to the opinions men have of them. In this regard, women's education differs radically from men's: "Opinion is the grave of virtue among men and its throne among women" (*E* 364–65). This is another notorious aspect of Rousseau's education for women, and he goes on to illustrate it in connection with religion. With respect to Emile's religious education, Rousseau advised that it be postponed until Emile's mind was in a condition to understand the abstract concepts of God and other articles of faith (*E* 254–59). But with women he suggests the opposite strategy: they must learn at an early age the religious dogmas that support morality, and therefore these dogmas must be imparted through authority rather than reason, because "in her conduct woman is enslaved by public opinion, in her belief she is enslaved by authority" (*E* 377–82).

Fortunately, Rousseau does not leave it at that. There comes a time, he says, when women must judge things not by the opinion of others but by themselves. As with men, there exists a "rule prior to opinion" for women that allows them to judge prejudice. This rule is conscience, and women need to cultivate the faculty of reason to serve as an arbiter between conscience and opinion, preventing the former from going astray and purging the latter of the errors of prejudice. The cultivation of reason in women is especially important in the present age when public opinion is so corrupt and unreliable as a guide. A woman must therefore become the "judge of her judges," deciding when to follow them and when to disobey them (*E* 382–83). This cultivation of reason is all the more important if women are expected to be the principal educators of their children. In the absence of reflection, how will a woman discern what is suitable for her children? "How will she incline them toward virtues she does not know, toward merit of which she has no idea?" If she relies solely on the prejudices of society, she "will make mannered monkeys or giddy rascals of them, never good minds or lovable children" (*E* 408–9).[10]

For all that Rousseau concedes to the cultivation of reason in women here, he still maintains that this cultivation will differ from that of men. The reason of women is practical, he argues, which "makes them very skillful at finding the means for getting to a known end, but not at finding that end itself" (*E* 377). It is the practical bent of their minds that makes women less adept at philosophical speculation and scientific inquiry. But they compensate for this deficiency with the subtlety and discernment of their emotional intelligence. When it comes to the passions and sentiments of human beings, a woman's "science of mechanics is more powerful than ours. . . . Men will philosophize about the human heart better than she does; but she will read in men's hearts better than they do" (*E* 386–87). Rousseau illustrates the superiority of women in reading men's hearts and discerning what is required at any given moment by considering the tact and delicacy of a hostess at a dinner party. Nothing "takes place that she does not notice"; she knows who to seat next to whom and divines when someone needs more food without their asking. After the guests have left, her observations turn out to be far more psychologically penetrating than her husband's (*E* 383–84).[11] All of this leads Rousseau to marvel at the complementarity of the sexes:

> This partnership produces a moral person of which the woman is the eye and the man is the arm, but they have such a dependence on one another that the woman learns from the man what must be seen and the man learns from the woman what must be done. If woman could ascend to general principles as well as man can, and if man had as good a mind for details as woman does, they would always be independent of one another, they would live in eternal discord, and their partnership could not exist. But in the harmony which reigns between them, everything tends to the common end; they do not know who contributes more. Each follows the prompting of the other; each obeys, and both are masters. (*E* 377)

This passage goes to the heart of why Rousseau puts such emphasis on the differentiation of the sexes. It is only through such differentiation that the sexes become dependent on each other and thereby overcome the radical individualism that reigned in the state of nature and that threatens modern bourgeois society. Rousseau states the danger clearly: if men and women were exactly the same, "they would always be independent of one another" and "live in eternal discord." It is precisely because he is so aware of the danger of individualism and competitiveness in bourgeois society that he sees the complementarity of the sexes as so necessary.[12] The partnership of man and woman by which they become a "moral person" and contribute to a "common end" is the first building block in the socialization of human beings that will eventually culminate in the political community created by the social contract. This is the crucial significance of the family for Rousseau, as it was for Burke, Hegel, and Tocqueville after him. It is what Plato overlooked when he gave the same education and employments to the male and female guardians in his republic and thereby abolished the family, "as though there were no need for a natural base on which to form conventional ties; as though the love of one's nearest were not the principle of the love one owes the state; as though it were not by means of the small fatherland which is the family that the heart attaches itself to the large one; as though it were not the good son, the good husband, and the good father who make the good citizen" (*E* 363).

There is no doubt something appealing about Rousseau's vision of the complementarity of the sexes as a means of combating the individualistic war of all against all in modern bourgeois society. The problem with it, as many commentators have pointed out, is that the social benefit conferred by the differentiation of the sexes comes at the expense of the freedom or autonomy of women.[13] Though Rousseau claims that each sex obeys the other and "both are masters," the indirect rule of men by women is precarious at best when legal, economic, and political power remains in the hands of men. Of course, Rousseau does not rely solely on the functionalist argument for the differentiation of the sexes; he also defends it on the basis that the differences between the sexes are natural. As we have seen, "natural" here does not refer to the pure state of nature, in which the differences between the sexes were largely nonexistent, but to the golden age, in which the sexual division of labor was established in the nascent family on the basis of the relative weakness of women and their physical dependence on men. Nevertheless, Rousseau still fails to account for changes in social conditions that make physical strength and childbearing less determining factors in the lives of men and women. And even more surprising, given his sensitivity to the distorting impact of social institutions on human nature, he fails to see how much of what he attributes to the nature of women is owing to artificial economic, legal, and political barriers.

These are weighty objections to Rousseau's sexual politics, but they do not provide an answer to the question of what, in the absence of the complementarity and interdependence of the sexes, will serve to get men and women to transcend the self-interest, individualism, competitiveness, and calculative reason that are so much a part of bourgeois society.[14] This question becomes even more pressing as we turn our attention to the concrete embodiments of Rousseau's generalizations about women in the figures of Sophie and Julie.

Sophie and Julie

After considering the nature of woman in general and the education appropriate to her, Rousseau goes on to illustrate his ideal of womanhood in the figure of Sophie and her romance with Emile. Of course, in 1761, the year before *Emile* appeared, he had published his bestselling novel *Julie, or The New Heloise*, in which the eponymous heroine embodies many of the qualities found in Sophie and in Rousseau's feminine ideal in general. *The New Heloise*, however, also complicates Rousseau's sexual politics insofar as Julie does not always live up to his ideal of feminine virtue. She succumbs to sexual passion in her premarital affair with St. Preux, and she never completely emancipates herself from that passion, even after her marriage to Wolmar. Her death at the end of the novel seems to represent the only possible solution

to the unresolved conflict in her soul. Sophie suffers a similar fall from feminine virtue in the unfinished sequel Rousseau wrote: *Emile and Sophie, or
The Solitaries*. To many commentators, the unhappy endings to Julie's and
Sophie's stories point to a fundamental problem with Rousseau's conception
and education of woman.[15] I hope to show that this is not necessarily the case.

Let us begin with Sophie. Rousseau endows her with all the qualities
we have considered above. Thus, though Sophie is not beautiful, she is said
to love adornment and to be "an expert at it." This does not mean that she
dresses in fancy or expensive apparel; rather, her clothes are characterized
by "simplicity joined with elegance." As Rousseau goes on to elaborate what
this involves, however, he does seem to fall into the "sensual fondness" of
which Wollstonecraft accuses him.[16] He declares that Sophie's "adornment
is very modest in appearance," but it is "very coquettish in fact." Though she
"does not display her charms . . . in covering them, she knows how to make
them imagined." Rousseau imagines the eyes of a man hungrily roaming over
Sophie's whole person and suggests that one might easily conclude that her
"simple attire was put on only to be taken off piece by piece by the imagination" (*E* 394).

Fortunately, Sophie's love of adornment is superseded by her love of virtue. It is this love, Rousseau claims, that becomes "her dominant passion. She
loves it because there is nothing so fine as virtue. . . . She loves it as the only
route to happiness." Here we come back to the moral idealism that forms the
core of Rousseau's romantic project and the object of Nietzsche's scorn. Love
of virtue, Rousseau declares, inspires in Sophie "an enthusiasm which lifts her
soul and keeps all her petty inclinations subjected to so noble a passion." As a
result, she "will be chaste and decent until her last breath," and this will make
her even more desirable to Emile. Rousseau insists that virtue and love go
hand in hand, for "there is no true love without enthusiasm, and no enthusiasm without an object of perfection, real or chimerical, but always existing in
the imagination. What will enflame lovers for whom this perfection no longer
exists and who see in what they love only the object of sensual pleasure?" It is
the moral perfection of the beloved that draws the lover upward, causing him
to detach himself from the "baseness of the human *I*" and even to sacrifice
his life for her. "We make fun of the paladins," Rousseau laments, but that is
because "they knew love, and we no longer know anything but debauchery"
(*E* 391).

Before Rousseau brings Sophie together with Emile, he has her father deliver a lengthy speech in which he gives Sophie the freedom to choose her
own husband. Even though she is only fifteen, Sophie's father trusts her reason and judgment and treats her as an adult, not a child. He tells her that

the mutual inclination of spouses, not birth or wealth or rank, should be the basis of marriage. Only on that basis will the marriage be a happy one (*E* 399–401). This was very progressive paternal advice in the eighteenth century and contrasts sharply with the more typical authoritarian position on marriage of Julie's father in *The New Heloise*. It is worth underlining Rousseau's progressivism here because it counters the common feminist criticism that he subjects Sophie to a completely infantilizing education. He is quite clear that "women's judgment is formed earlier than men's" (*E* 397) and that a girl of fifteen, if properly educated, has the maturity and rationality to make the most important decision of whom to marry on her own.

Sophie is now ready to meet Emile. We need not go through the details of their courtship, but there are a few items worth highlighting. First, Rousseau insists that a man of education should have a wife that is educated as well. It is a sad thing when a husband cannot think and converse with his wife. Also, as pointed out above, an uneducated mother cannot raise her children to be intelligent and virtuous individuals (*E* 408–9). Second, Rousseau emphasizes that, in subjecting himself to Sophie, Emile does not lose the virtues he acquired in his early education. Insofar as Sophie herself is characterized by love of virtue and decent things, she gives Emile "new reasons to be himself" (*E* 432–33). Rousseau illustrates Sophie's morally salutary influence on Emile with two examples. The first is when Sophie visits Emile at his workshop and commends him for not breaking his commitment to work in order to accompany Sophie and her mother home. The second is when Emile fails to keep an appointment with Sophie because he has to help a peasant with a broken leg and his wife who has just given birth to a baby. Emile tells Sophie: "You are the arbiter of my fate. . . . You can make me die of pain. But do not hope to make me forget the rights of humanity. They are more sacred to me than yours. I will never give them up for you." And Sophie responds by kissing Emile on the cheek and asking him to be her husband (*E* 439–41).

Emile concludes with the marriage of Sophie and Emile, and the governor gives the ardent couple his "recipe against the cooling off of love in marriage." He tells Emile that sex is never to be demanded as a right but enjoyed only when Sophie desires it as well: "Always remember that even in marriage pleasure is legitimate only when desire is shared." To Sophie the governor counsels that she should still play something of the coquette and make her sexual favors "rare and precious." In this way, she will maintain her empire over Emile and lead him to "give you his confidence, listen to your opinions, consult you about his business, and decide nothing without deliberating with you about it." This goes some distance toward an egalitarian ideal of marriage, but it is what the governor follows this advice with that is most striking.

He tells Sophie that even if she doles out her sexual favors judiciously, she cannot keep the flame of passion alive forever: "Whatever precautions anyone may take, enjoyment wears out pleasure, and love is worn out before all others." But this loss is compensated for by a different sort of intimacy that is no less sweet. In a way that anticipates Wollstonecraft's ideal of marriage, the governor indicates that as romantic passion wanes, it is replaced by deep friendship between husband and wife: "But when love has lasted a long time, a sweet habit fills the void it leaves behind, and the attraction of mutual confidence succeeds the transports of passion. Children form a relationship between those who have given them life that is no less sweet and is often stronger than love itself. When you stop being Emile's beloved, you will be his wife and friend" (E 475–79).[17]

Alas, conjugal happiness of the sort just depicted was not to be Emile and Sophie's fate, at least according to the unfinished sequel, *Emile and Sophie, or The Solitaries*. There we find out that the marriage of Emile and Sophie collapses after Sophie has an adulterous affair and becomes pregnant with another man's baby. As I have mentioned, many commentators take this unhappy turn of events as proof of the defectiveness of Sophie's education, but there are several reasons we should hesitate to draw such a conclusion. First, Sophie's infidelity is almost ridiculously overdetermined. Within the space of a few months, both of her parents and her daughter die. Then she and Emile move to the capital of vice, Paris, where Emile promptly succumbs to frivolous pleasure-seeking and utterly neglects his wife. At the same time, Sophie falls under the corrupting influence of a thoroughly cynical female friend. It's not clear that even the best education in the world would prepare a young woman to overcome this set of daunting circumstances. Second, even after she commits adultery, Sophie is still depicted as an honest, courageous, and utterly noble woman. Or at least that is how Emile depicts her, which constitutes the third reason we should not draw any hasty conclusions about Sophie on the basis of this fragmentary work: everything we know about Sophie in *The Solitaries* is refracted through Emile's consciousness. What we have of the novel presents Emile's story and only indirectly Sophie's; there simply is not enough there to conclude that her moral lapse is the result of her flawed education.

But if not Sophie in *The Solitaries*, perhaps the unhappy fate of Julie in *The New Heloise* points up the defects of Rousseau's conception of woman and marriage, as some commentators have suggested. Joel Schwartz has succinctly summed up *The New Heloise* as a "novel of romantic love and unromantic marriage."[18] It is the story of Julie's passionate love affair with her tutor, St. Preux; her eventual marriage to the hyperrational Wolmar; and her death, at which she confesses her unvanquished love for St. Preux. This sounds like the conventional formula for a romantic novel, and, indeed, *The New Heloise* served as the template for many romantic novels about the stifling effects of bourgeois marriage on passionate love. But this is not the message Rousseau means to convey in the novel. Though he evokes the love affair between Julie and St. Preux with all the throbbing excitement of a romantic novelist, his moral sympathies ultimately lie with the virtuous marriage between Julie and Wolmar. He makes his intention clear in the second preface to the novel. Responding to the criticism that the scandalous nature of the first half of the book contradicts the edifying purpose of the second half, he explains: "My means have changed, but not my purpose. When I tried to speak to men no one listened to me; perhaps by addressing children I shall be better listened to; and children do not relish the taste of naked reason any better than that of ill-disguised medicines. . . . It is only after deploring [my young people's] faults that you are able to appreciate their virtues" (*J* 12).

Julie speaks for Rousseau when she explains to St. Preux that she has made the right choice in marrying Wolmar. Even more emphatically than the governor does at the end of *Emile*, she makes the point that the ultimate basis of marriage is not romantic love but a kind of friendship: "The thing that long deluded me and perhaps still deludes you is the idea that love is essential to a happy marriage. My friend, this is an error; honesty, virtue, certain conformities, less of status and age than of character, suffice between husband and wife; that does not prevent a very tender attachment from emerging from this union which, without exactly being love, is nonetheless sweet and for that only the more lasting." Julie goes on to argue that the exclusivity of romantic love—the fact that lovers think only of each other, to the exclusion of the rest of the world (think Tristan and Isolde)—makes it unsuitable for spouses, who have many other duties, including the raising of children. Romantic love also rests to a large extent on illusion, which dooms it to transitoriness. Julie and Wolmar, on the other hand, have no illusions about each other: "We see each other such as we are; the sentiment that joins us is not the blind transport of passionate hearts, but the immutable and constant attachment of two honest and reasonable persons who, destined to spend the rest of their lives together, are content with their lot and try to make it pleasurable for one another." In addition, their personalities are completely complementary: she tender and loving, he tranquil and rational. "Each of us is precisely what the other requires; he enlightens me and I enliven him; we are enhanced by being together, and it seems we are destined to constitute but a single soul between us, of which he is the intellect and I the will" (*J* 306-7).

The end of the novel may seem to cast a different light on the marital happiness Julie describes here. On her deathbed, Julie writes a final letter to

St. Preux confessing that, despite her best efforts to stifle her love for him, she has not been able to do so. She seems to welcome death because she is not confident she could have resisted giving in to her passion for him in the future. Though this ending certainly adds a layer of complexity to Julie's character, it does not necessarily alter the moral message of the novel. She has already told us that the basis of marriage is not romantic love but a kind of friendship between two honest and reasonable persons who respect each other and fulfill their duties to their children. Therefore, a tension between marital affection and romantic passion is perfectly possible. That the virtue and happiness Julie has enjoyed with Wolmar have not come without effort would not dismay Rousseau. As he constantly reminds us, "There is no virtue without strength" (*J* 431; see also *E* 444). Julie has struggled against her passion for St. Preux and largely prevails. The mood at the end of the novel is not one of despair or world-weariness, as some commentators have maintained,[19] but rather of contentment, serenity, and acceptance. Julie thus embodies Rousseau's ideal of womanhood; she does not point up its limitations.

But that does not mean that the ideal does not have its limitations. We have seen that feminist scholars criticize Rousseau's ideal for reducing women to dependent beings whose main function is to moralize men. But there is another criticism of the "eternal feminine" that takes issue not simply with what it does to women but with what it does to men and to the cultivation of a higher humanity. This is where Nietzsche comes in.

Woman in Nietzsche's Middle-Period Writings

Woman and family certainly play a smaller role in Nietzsche's overall philosophy than they do in Rousseau's. For the latter thinker, as we have seen, woman and family constitute a crucial step in the overcoming of bourgeois individualism and the socializing of humanity that culminates in the political community created by the social contract. Nevertheless, woman and family occupy a not unimportant place in Nietzsche's reflections on modern bourgeois society, which is not surprising, given the increasing importance of the "woman question" in the nineteenth century. Nietzsche sees marriage properly understood and the bearing of children as vital—far more so than the state—for the cultivation of a higher humanity (see *KSA* 9:11 [179]). And he calls reproduction "the most holy of circumstances," in which a man and woman create in the child a "*monument to their oneness*" (*KSA* 10:1 [43]; see also 10:5 [1], 53). Nietzsche even boasts in his final work, *Ecce Homo*, that he "*know*[*s*] women" and is perhaps "the first psychologist of the eternal feminine" (*EH*, "Books," 5).

There is much that Nietzsche shares with Rousseau on the subject of women. They both insist on the fundamental difference between women and men, and for this they have both been attacked by feminist scholars for being misogynistic. In this regard, it must be said that Nietzsche far surpasses Rousseau in the offensiveness of his rhetoric. Everyone is familiar with his notorious comment that when you go to women, "do not forget the whip" (Z 1, "Women"). There are many such comments in Nietzsche's writings, especially the later ones. Needless to say, they need to be understood in context and in terms of the complex rhetorical strategies Nietzsche deploys; but even then, they do not cease to shock. In the next section, I take up Nietzsche's most controversial discussions of women in *Thus Spoke Zarathustra* and *Beyond Good and Evil*. In this one, I discuss the views of woman and family found in his middle writings, primarily *Human, All Too Human* and *The Gay Science*. Because there is no single, systematic discussion of woman and family in Nietzsche as there is in Rousseau, this chronological approach helps make sense of his dispersed and rhetorically complex statements.

Nietzsche's first sustained treatment of woman and family appears in the appositely titled chapter "Woman and Child" in *Human, All Too Human*. The first aphorism in this chapter suggests an image of woman that is far from misogynistic.[20] Nietzsche writes: "The perfect woman is a higher type of human being than the perfect man: also something much rarer.—The natural science of the animals offers a means of demonstrating the truth of this proposition" (*HH* 377). It is not clear what exactly Nietzsche has in mind when he says that the natural science of animals could demonstrate the superiority of women to men, so we have to look at what he says in the rest of the chapter to determine in what this superiority consists. What we find there discloses a more complex picture of the relative strengths and weaknesses of men and women.

A good place to start is with the aphorism "The Female Intellect." Here Nietzsche seems to take the opposite view from Rousseau when he argues that the "intellect of women reveals itself as complete presence of mind and the utilization of every advantage," whereas men contribute the "darker background of the will." Expressed differently, "Women possess reason, men temperament and passion." Nietzsche immediately complicates this distinction by adding that though women possess more reason than men, "men make better use of their reason: they possess deeper, more powerful drives; it is these that carry their reason, which is in itself something passive." (*HH* 411). In the immediately ensuing aphorisms, Nietzsche clarifies that the superior intellectual capacity of women consists chiefly in a kind of "shrewdness" or practical calculativeness; hence the characterization of the female intellect above in terms of the "utilization of every advantage." Nietzsche sees the shrewdness of women reflected most clearly in the fact that they have always known how to get men to take care of them: "Almost everywhere [women] have known how to get themselves fed, like drones in the beehive" (HH 412; see also 415).

In addition to seeing the intellect of women as largely practical or pruden-tial, Nietzsche also suggests that it is frequently disturbed by violent emotion. He claims that women are more subject to love and hate than men (which seems to jar with what he has already said about the more passionate nature of men), and this makes women less objective or just in their judgments. They tend to take sides for or against things instead of dispassionately assess-ing what is right or needed. For this reason, Nietzsche thinks women are un-suited to politics or sciences like history. "What could be rarer," he asks, "than a woman who really knew what science is? The best of them even harbor in their bosom a secret contempt for it" (HH 416; see also 414, 417, 419). In a later installment of Human, All Too Human, Nietzsche speaks in a similar vein of women's hostility to truth: "Women are so constituted that all truth regarding men, love, children, society, the aim of life, disgusts them" (AOM 286).

On what basis does Nietzsche attribute these qualities to women? Given his radically historical outlook (see HH 2), it would be inconsistent for him to see these qualities as belonging to some sort of essential and eternal femi-nine nature; and, indeed, he does not.[21] At the end of the aphorism in which he says that women are unsuited to science, he adds: "Perhaps all this may change, but for the present that is how things are" (HH 416). Nietzsche elabo-rates on the mutability of female nature in a later aphorism. "In the three or four civilized countries of Europe," he writes, "women can through a few centuries of education be made into anything, even into men. . . . Under such a regimen they will one day have acquired all the male strengths and virtues, though they will also of course have had to accept all their weaknesses and vices into the bargain" (HH 425). In addition to highlighting the historically or socially constructed nature of women, this aphorism is interesting because it holds out the possibility that women can aspire to the same virtues as men. This, of course, is what Rousseau denied—and what Wollstonecraft criticized him for denying.[22] We will see, however, that Nietzsche moves closer to the Rousseauian position in his later writings.

Given his belief that women will someday share the same virtues with men, including objectivity, justice, and scientific probity, it is not surprising that Nietzsche also envisages a new kind of marriage in the future—one that is based on a common purpose and shared understanding of virtue; a mar-riage that looks more like friendship than the asymmetrical relationship of traditional marriage. This is how Nietzsche evokes it: "Those noble and free-thinking women who set themselves the task of the education of the female sex ought not to overlook *one* consideration: the higher conception of marriage as the soul-friendship of two people of differing sex—a conception it is hoped the future will realize—contracted for the purpose of begetting and educating a new generation" (*HH* 424). Nietzsche's understanding of marriage in terms of soul friendship has some affinities with Rousseau's understanding in *Julie*, but he takes an even dimmer view of romantic love as a basis of marriage than Rousseau did (see *HH* 389, 399, 415). From this conception, Nietzsche draws a rather unusual consequence. Because a marriage based on soul friendship requires that a woman have time and freedom to cultivate her mind and converse with her husband, it would be too much to ask that she also satisfy her husband's sexual needs. A wife who is a soulmate cannot also be a sexual playmate. Therefore, Nietzsche suggests that men be allowed to avail themselves of concubines so that they can enjoy "head- and heart-satisfying companionship" with their wives (*HH* 424; see also 378, 406).

For the time being, though, the realization of such a conception of marriage seems to lie far in the future. Therefore, Nietzsche spends much of the chapter on woman in *Human, All Too Human* on how marriage as it currently exists is incompatible with the needs and aspirations of the male free spirit. As depicted in *Human, All Too Human*, the free spirit is someone who is constantly questioning and overcoming himself in his restless pursuit of knowledge. He is the enemy of habit and rules, of "everything enduring and definitive." He has to tear down what he formerly revered and love what he formerly hated. As a result, he suffers greatly in his heroic quest for knowledge. Is such a dissatisfied, suffering, questing spirit made for marriage? Nietzsche thinks not (*HH* 427). The reasons have as much to do with the complacent nature of women as the restlessness of the free spirit.

In a particularly revealing aphorism, Nietzsche writes: "The natural tendency of women towards a quiet, calm, happily harmonious existence, the way they pour soothing oil on the sea of life, unwittingly works against the heroic impulse in the heart of the free spirit." Women seek to remove obstacles from the paths of their husbands, while the free spirit seeks out just those obstacles in order to overcome them (*HH* 431). Nietzsche constantly compares wives to mothers who seek to alleviate the pain and suffering of their children. But again, suffering and dissatisfaction are indispensable to the growth of the free spirit: "Wives always secretly intrigue against the higher being of their husbands; they desire to deprive them of their future for the sake of a quiet, comfortable present" (*HH* 434). As he later does in the *Genealogy of Morality*, Nietzsche concludes that being a philosopher is incompatible with being married (*HH* 436; *GM* 3.7). In the final sentence of the chapter, he quotes Socrates from the *Phaedo*: "O Criton, do tell someone to take those women away!" (*HH* 437).

Nietzsche has traveled a long way from the opening aphorism of the chapter on woman and child, where he speaks of the "perfect woman [as] a higher type of human being than the perfect man." In the course of the chapter, he depicts the perfect woman as a kind of fellow free spirit with perhaps more "charm and intellectual flexibility" than her male counterpart (*HH* 424). Here one thinks of the women with whom Nietzsche cultivated intellectual friendships throughout his life, most famously Lou Salomé.[23] But social circumstances have hindered the emergence of such female free spirits, promoting instead women who are shrewd, prone to unjust love and hate, and concerned above all with peace, comfort, and the alleviation of spirit-enhancing suffering. For this reason, Nietzsche advises his male free spirits to steer clear of marriage, at least for the time being.

How does Nietzsche's conception of woman and marriage develop in his ensuing middle-period writings? In *Daybreak*, we find only scattered observations on women and marriage, and they do not depart radically from what Nietzsche has already said in *Human, All Too Human*. He describes women as having a highly developed capacity for empathy, partly as a result of fear (*D* 142); also as vengeful, largely as a result of having been "confined to a petty, dull environment" (*D* 227). He laments the role of chance in modern marriage, which "makes a grand rational progress of mankind impossible" (*D* 150), and he unfavorably compares the modern emphasis on "idealized sexual love" with the more profound ancient preoccupation with friendship (*D* 503). Finally, in an aphorism that belies the claim that Nietzsche is unambiguously antiwoman, he writes against misogynists, whose hatred of women springs from their hatred of their own immoderate lust (*D* 346; see also 294).

The Gay Science contains a much more substantial discussion of women, and accordingly it has received considerable scholarly attention.[24] Significantly, this discussion takes place in the context of a larger discussion of art. In *The Gay Science*, art plays a crucial role as the antidote to the disillusioning questioning of science. As Nietzsche puts it in an aphorism titled "Our Ultimate Gratitude to Art," without art and the "cult of the untrue . . . the realization of general untruth and mendaciousness that now comes to us through science—the realization that delusion and error are conditions of human knowledge and sensation—would be utterly unbearable. *Honesty* would lead to nausea and suicide" (*GS* 107). He makes this point more pithily in an oft-quoted later note: "We possess *art* lest we *perish of the truth*" (*WP* 822). Art and science thus have a complementary relationship—a fact

reflected in the very title of *The Gay Science*—and this suggests that by identifying women with art, Nietzsche sees the relationship between men and
women as complementary in a similar way. This marks a shift from his earlier
position, in which women at their best would share the same free-spirited
virtues with men. And, of course, it also marks a shift in the direction of
Rousseau's position.

Nietzsche begins his reflections on women in *The Gay Science* (59–75) by
connecting women with the idealizing tendencies of art. When a man loves a
woman, he declares, he ignores "all the repulsive natural functions to which
every woman is subject" and constructs an ideal image of his beloved. In the
past, worshipers of God did the same thing, ignoring the mechanical, disen-
chanted nature disclosed by natural science and choosing to live in a dream.
Nietzsche does not seem to see this antinatural dreaming as necessarily a bad
thing; indeed, he sees it as unavoidable. "Oh, these men of former times,"
he writes, "knew how to *dream* and did not find it necessary to go to sleep
first. And we men of today still master this art all too well." Whenever we
love, hate, or desire, we leave reality behind and enter a dream world: "With
our eyes open, coldly contemptuous of all danger, we climb up on the most
hazardous paths to scale the roofs and spires of fantasy—without any sense
of dizziness, as if we had been born to climb, we somnambulists of the day!
We artists!" (*GS* 59). This is the great lesson we can learn from both lovers
and artists: how to "make things beautiful, attractive, and desirable for us
when . . . in themselves they never are" (*GS* 299).

Nietzsche connects this idealizing function of art even more explicitly
with women in the poetic aphorism "Women and Their Action at a Distance."
Here he imagines himself in a tempestuous sea, with howling wind and loud
thunder all around him, when suddenly he sees a sailboat calmly gliding in
front of him. This is an image of the calming and enchanting effect women
can have on men when they are caught up in their own noise: "When a man
stands in the midst of his own noise, in the midst of his own surf of plans and
projects, then he is apt also to see quiet, magical beings gliding past him and
to long for their happiness and seclusion: *women*." As he does in the previous
aphorism, Nietzsche makes clear here that the happiness and quietness attributed to women is largely an illusion. There is actually a lot of noise on the sailboat, "and unfortunately much small and petty noise." That is why distance
is necessary for women to have the magical effect on men that is evoked here
(*GS* 60). But with the requisite distancing and aesthetic idealization, women
seem to play for Nietzsche a salutary and indispensable role in human life.

This role, however, is always understood to be auxiliary to the passionate
quest for knowledge of the free spirit. As I have already indicated, Nietzsche

sees art as an antidote to the rigors of the free-spirited quest for knowledge. We need art as a respite from those rigors (see *GS* 107). But Nietzsche also makes clear that artists and women are not quite up to those rigors. "We know very well," he writes, "how science strikes those who merely glance at it in passing, as if they were walking by, as women do and unfortunately also many artists: the severity of its service, its inexorability in small as in great matters, and the speed of weighing and judging matters and passing judgment makes them feel dizzy and afraid." Artists and women cannot live in the "*virile* air" that is the element of the free spirit (*GS* 293). So on the one side we have the severity of science that Nietzsche associates with men, and on the other we have the "cult of the untrue" and the "good will to appearance" that Nietzsche associates with art and women. Both are necessary, both are complementary.

Based on the aphorisms I have discussed so far, one might wonder whether, in *The Gay Science*, woman functions simply as a metaphor for one side of Nietzsche's grand polarity of art and science rather than as a flesh-and-blood human being. One's suspicion in this regard is not allayed by statements such as "truth is a woman" (*GS*, preface, 4) and "life is a woman" (*GS* 339). Nevertheless, Nietzsche does have things to say about women in a more concrete sense. Some of his observations are not terribly profound: for example, that women are more interesting to men when they are changeable, unpredictable, and unfathomable (*GS* 67; see also 74; *HH* 400); or that women exaggerate their weaknesses in order to gain power over men (*GS* 66; see also *HH* 412). There are two aphorisms, however, that treat women more sympathetically and merit closer attention.

The first is an aphorism that tells the story of a youth who is brought to a sage with the complaint that he is being corrupted by women. The sage replies that it is men who corrupt women, not the other way around, "for it is man who creates for himself the image of woman, and woman forms herself according to this image." (This recalls what Nietzsche says about misogynists in *Daybreak* [346]: that their image of women is the product of their own immoderate lust.) When the sage is accused of being too kindhearted to women, he continues: "Will is the manner of men; willingness that of women. That is the law of the sexes—truly, a hard law for women. All of humanity is innocent of its existence; but women are doubly innocent. Who could have oil and kindness enough for them." Here Nietzsche reformulates the difference between men and women in terms of will and willingness as opposed to science and art. Women conform themselves to the image men create of them. Nietzsche does not suggest that this inequality can ever be changed: it is the "law of the sexes"—a hard law for women, but a law nonetheless.[25] When someone shouts, " 'Damn kindness . . . women need to be educated better,' " the sage once again objects that it is men, not women, who need to be educated better (*GS* 68). The implication is that men need to be educated better in order to create a better image for women to conform to. Despite the sage's sympathy for the plight of women, he is hardly a feminist.

The second aphorism is devoted to female chastity and has a less fatalistic message than the previous one. It begins on a note of indignation: "There is something quite amazing and monstrous about the education of upper-class women." Such women are brought up in total ignorance of erotic matters. Then, suddenly, they are "hurled, as by a gruesome lightning bolt, into reality and knowledge, by marriage—precisely by the man they love and esteem most!" Feelings of love, shame, delight, horror, pity, and terror all vie in the young bride's heart, forming a "psychic knot" that has no equal. In order to cope, she closes her eyes to herself and affects superficiality and impertinence. She experiences her husband as a question mark concerning her honor and regards her children as a kind of apology or atonement. Nietzsche spares no pains in his exposure of the psychological trauma that the sexually inexperienced bride undergoes. Returning to the point about the need for kindness in the previous aphorism, he concludes that "one cannot be too kind about women" (*GS* 71). But unlike in the previous aphorism, the problem here seems to have a remedy: more sexual education for women. Nietzsche is not, like Rousseau, a champion of female chastity. This becomes even more evident in his teaching about sex in his later writings.

And what of the perfect woman who was envisaged at the beginning of Nietzsche's reflections on women in *Human, All Too Human*? There is only one aphorism in *The Gay Science* that touches on this theme, "Women Who Master the Masters" (*Die Herrinnen der Herren*). Nietzsche observes that sometimes one hears in the opera house a deep contralto voice that makes one believe that "somewhere in the world there could be women with lofty, heroic, and royal souls, capable of and ready for grandiose responses, resolutions, and sacrifices, capable of and ready for rule over men because in them the best elements of man apart from his sex have become an incarnate ideal" (*GS* 70). Here Nietzsche appears to return to his earlier position in *Human, All Too Human*, that the perfect woman possesses the same virtues as the perfect man. But he complicates it by saying that what makes the perfect woman superior to the perfect man and capable of rule over him is that in her, his best qualities have become an "incarnate ideal." This brings in the idealized, artistic element of woman. The eternal imperfection and ceaseless wandering of the heroic male free spirit becomes embodied perfection in the female free spirit.

This aphorism reflects the still-unsettled state of Nietzsche's conception of women in his middle works. Though in other aphorisms in *The Gay Science* he stresses how women are different from but complementary to men, in this one he returns to his earlier conception of the perfect woman as similar to the perfect man, albeit in a more ideal, complete, and embodied form. What is perhaps most striking about Nietzsche's reflections on women in the middle works is the absence of any sustained discussion of the much-debated woman question—the question of the legal, political, and economic equality of women. This question becomes much more prominent in Nietzsche's later writings, as does his assertion of the differences between and complementarity of the sexes. It is to these writings that we now turn.

The Most Abysmal Antagonism

In his later writings, beginning with *Zarathustra*, Nietzsche's portrayal of women and their relation to men takes on a more extreme and intentionally provocative character. He describes woman, for example, as the "most dangerous plaything" for men and counsels the latter, when going to women, not to "forget the whip" (Z I: "Women"). Despite the greater offensiveness of his rhetoric, however, Nietzsche continues to build on the idea of the differentiation and complementarity of the sexes that emerged in *The Gay Science*. Indeed, this idea takes on even greater urgency in the light of Nietzsche's deepening critique of democratic equality and homogenization in his later writings. As has already been remarked, by stressing the differences between the sexes, Nietzsche seems to move closer to Rousseau's position on women. But for Nietzsche, these differences do not ultimately lead to harmonious interdependence between men and women, but, rather, to the "most abysmal antagonism" between them, an "eternally hostile tension" that serves as the basis of human enhancement and creativity (*BGE* 238).

Nietzsche's later views on the subject of woman receive their most notorious expression in Zarathustra's speech "On Little Old and Young Women," which contains the sentence about not forgetting the whip. As many commentators have noted, this sentence is not uttered by Zarathustra himself but by a little old woman.[26] This is but one example of the rhetorical complexity and indirection that pervade the speech. It begins with Zarathustra's disciple asking him what he carries concealed under his coat as he steals furtively through the twilight. Zarathustra responds that "it is a little truth I carry" and that he has to hold his hand over its mouth lest it "cry overloudly." He then relates that, earlier in the day, he met a little old woman, who asked him to speak about woman (Z 1, "Women"). In the speech that follows, Zarathustra lays out the fundamental differences between men and women.

He begins by saying, "Everything about woman is a riddle, and everything about woman has one solution: that is pregnancy. Man is for woman a means: the end is always a child." (*Z* 1, "Women"). That man is regarded as a mere means for woman obviously complicates our views of Nietzsche's supposed subordination of women to men. Of course, Zarathustra goes on to say that woman is also a means for man. Man is a warrior—in the context of *Zarathustra*, a free-spirited warrior of knowledge (*Z* 1, "War and Warriors"; see also *GS* 283)—and woman is for him a recreation, a "dangerous plaything." Zarathustra also claims that it belongs to woman to love more than she is loved. But this unconditional devotion of a woman carries some risk for a man; for if he is not strong enough to merit it, he then earns her contempt and hatred. Zarathustra concludes his speech with some remarks that recall *The Gay Science*. First, he says the "happiness of man is: I will" and the "happiness of woman is: he wills." Then he goes on to identify woman with artistic surface and man with depth (*Z* 1, "Women"; see also *GS* 363).

It is at this point that the little old woman gives Zarathustra her little truth, which she warns him to wrap up and cover its mouth lest it cry overloudly: "You are going to women? Do not forget the whip!" (*Z* 1, "Women"; see also *BGE* 147). By putting this little truth in the mouth of the old woman, does Nietzsche mean to distance himself from it? In a way, yes. The old woman certainly expresses the relationship between the sexes in the baldest, most cynical way possible. That is what old women do. As Nietzsche puts it elsewhere: "I am afraid that old women are more skeptical in their most secret heart of hearts than any man" (*GS* 64). And both the old woman and Zarathustra are aware that this little truth does not accord with current egalitarian orthodoxy—hence the need to wrap it up and cover its mouth. But it would be a mistake to deny that the old woman's little truth expresses, albeit crudely, what Nietzsche sees as an essential truth about men and women. After all, it is perfectly congruent with what Zarathustra says about men and women in the speech immediately preceding it. Zarathustra's later reference to the whip as something with which to tame life and keep time as she dances makes clear that he is not advocating physical violence against women (*Z* 3, "Other Dancing Song"), but it does not deny the element of mastery and will that Nietzsche sees as inherent in the relationship of men and women.

Besides elaborating on the differences between men and women, *Zarathustra* also contains a teaching about marriage and children. Nietzsche exhibits a serious interest in the institution of marriage throughout his philosophical career. In his middle writings, as we have seen, he articulates an ideal of marriage as the "soul-friendship of two people of differing sex" (*HH* 424).

But more frequently he complains about the irrationality of modern marriage, especially insofar as it is based on the transitory feelings of romantic love (see, e.g., *HH* 389; *D* 150). Zarathustra spends much of his speech titled "On Child and Marriage" making many of the same complaints. That which is called marriage today is really "poverty of the soul in pair," "filth of the soul in pair," "wretched contentment in pair." Many marriages seem utterly senseless: heroic men marry unworthy women, saints mate with gooses. Again, the idealization of romantic love seems to be the culprit: "Many brief follies— that is what you call love. And your marriage concludes many brief follies, as a long stupidity" (*Z* 1, "Child and Marriage"; see also *TI*, "Expeditions," 39; *WP* 732).

Nietzsche does not, however, give up on marriage. For him, though, it involves more than the happiness of the two parties or their reproduction; it must seek to produce something higher: "Marriage: thus I name the will of two to create the one that is more than those who created it. Reverence for each other, as for those willing with such a will, is what I name marriage" (*Z* 1, "Child and Marriage"; see also *Z* 3, "Old and New Tablets," 24). Though Nietzsche has abandoned his earlier ideal of marriage as soul friendship between two people who share the same virtues, he continues to see marriage as primarily concerned with "begetting and educating a new generation" (*HH* 424). And though he ascribes very different virtues and roles to men and women in marriage, he does not see the relationship as essentially one of domination or subjugation. Husband and wife share a goal that transcends them both, and it is in the light of this higher goal that they have reverence for each other. Not altogether unlike Rousseau, Nietzsche sees marriage as an ethical institution in which sexual difference ultimately issues in a higher commonality.

Not at all similar to Rousseau is Nietzsche's teaching on sex in *Zarathustra*. Here he broadens the assault on chastity begun in *The Gay Science*. He concedes that for a few people chastity is a virtue, but for most it is closer to a vice. For these latter, chastity is a desperate attempt to suppress the immoderate lust that burns within them, and it is rarely entirely successful: "They abstain, but the bitch, sensuality, leers enviously out of everything they do. Even to the heights of their virtue and to the cold regions of the spirit this beast follows them with her lack of peace" (*Z* 1, "Chastity"). As we saw in *Daybreak*, the same lack of control over their sensuality leads some men to misogyny (*D* 346; see also 294). More positively, Nietzsche includes sex among the three traditional evils that need to be revalued. To all "hair-shirted despisers of the body," sex is "their thorn and stake," he writes; but for free and innocent hearts, sex is the "garden happiness of the earth, the future's exuberant gratitude to the present." This happiness is the "great parable of a higher happiness and the highest hope. For to many marriage is promised, and more than marriage—to many who are stranger to each other than man and woman. And who can wholly comprehend *how* strange man and woman are to each other?" (*Z* 3, "Three Evils," 2).

In keeping with the constructive nature of the book, Nietzsche's discussion of woman and marriage in *Zarathustra* focuses on the ideal case. It is only in *Beyond Good and Evil*, a book that is "in all essentials a *critique of modernity*" (*EH*, "Books: *BGE*," 2), that he fully and critically engages with the "woman question" of the nineteenth century, the movement toward women's equality and emancipation. He does so in a series of aphorisms at the end of the chapter devoted to "Our Virtues." Some of these aphorisms are, on the surface, every bit as misogynistic as the little truth about not forgetting the whip. To take just one egregious example, Nietzsche writes that a man of true depth "must always think about woman as *Orientals* do: he must conceive of woman as a possession, as property that can be locked, as something predestined for service and achieving her perfection in that" (*BGE* 238). As with the little truth in *Zarathustra*, however, the aphorisms devoted to women in *Beyond Good and Evil* are far from straightforward. Nietzsche embeds them in a complex rhetorical framework that requires careful unpacking.

The place to start is with the question of why Nietzsche places his discussion of women in the chapter devoted to "Our Virtues."[27] He makes clear that the quintessential virtue of "we free spirits" is intellectual honesty, the fearless questioning of all comforting beliefs, the courageous striving for what is forbidden (*BGE* 227). In the two aphorisms that precede the ones devoted to women, he brings out that this intellectual honesty of the knowledge-seeking free spirit involves a kind of self-cruelty, a desire to hurt what Nietzsche calls the "basic will of the spirit." This latter, basic will seeks to appropriate what is foreign by assimilating it to what is already known and familiar; it "files new things in old files." Sometimes this requires shutting one's windows to what is new; sometimes it even involves letting oneself be deceived; but the overall goal is to remain in control of one's environment, to master it. It is this "will to mere appearance, to simplification, to masks, to cloaks, in short, to the surface" that the free-spirited seeker after knowledge thwarts by insisting on "profundity, multiplicity, and thoroughness, with a will which is a kind of cruelty of the intellectual conscience" (*BGE* 229–30).

So why does Nietzsche follow this evocation of the self-cruelty of the knowledge-seeking free spirit with his reflections on woman? It does not seem accidental that the qualities he associates with the basic will of the spirit—the "will to mere appearance, to simplification, to masks, to cloaks, in short, to the surface"—are the very qualities he has ascribed to woman in his earlier writings. And in the reflections on woman that follow, it is these qualities that he emphasizes in contradistinction to the desire for scientific knowledge and truth. This suggests that at least one of the reasons Nietzsche concludes the chapter on "Our Virtues" with a series of aphorisms on woman is that he feels compelled to consider the dialectical opposite of and necessary complement to the heroic male free spirit, who cruelly seeks to penetrate surfaces and destroy appearances and illusions. This dialectical move whereby Nietzsche articulates the complementary relationship between science/man and art/woman is, of course, familiar to us from *The Gay Science*.

Between the aphorisms on the self-cruelty involved in the free spirit's quest for knowledge and the aphorisms on woman's predilection for appearance and deception, Nietzsche inserts a transitional aphorism that further complicates his overall argument. In this aphorism, he claims that a thinker's views on man and woman are not purely objective but relate to something "deep down" within him, "some granite of spiritual *fatum*, of predetermined decision and answer to predetermined selected questions." About man and woman, "a thinker cannot relearn but only finish learning—only discover ultimately how this is 'settled in him.'" Nietzsche does not exempt himself from this substantial limitation on a thinker's objectivity in relation to the question of man and woman. He declares that the truths he is about to state about "woman as such"—he puts this phrase in quotation marks, suggesting there is no such thing as "woman as such"—are only "*my* truths" (*BGE* 231).

This reveals another way in which the aphorisms on woman fit into the chapter on "Our Virtues." Nietzsche's reflections on "woman as such" are an expression of the intellectual honesty that is the quintessential virtue of the free spirit; they are "steps to self-knowledge, signposts to the problem we *are*—rather to the great stupidity we are, to our spiritual *fatum*, to what is *unteachable* very 'deep down'" (*BGE* 231).[28] But we must not mistake Nietzsche's honesty here for an admission of the purely arbitrary or subjective nature of the claims he is about to make about woman. Though he admits that these claims about woman are only *his* truths, he does not mean to diminish them or suggest they should not be taken seriously, any more than he means to diminish the truths of his new philosophers when he says their judgments are *their* judgments: no one else is entitled to them (*BGE* 43). In his reflections on "woman as such," Nietzsche discloses what woman must be for a man such as he, a courageous free spirit, a hard and severe warrior of knowledge, a man of tremendous spiritual depth.

In the first of these reflections, he criticizes the "clumsy attempts of women at scientific self-exposure," their attempts to "enlighten men about 'woman as such,'" going so far as to state "with medical explicitness what woman *wants* from man." He finds these attempts on the part of women to become scientific "in the worst taste." By losing her shame, woman allows her most undesirable qualities to come forth: superficiality, schoolmarmishness, pettiness, and so on—qualities that have hitherto been "kept under control by *fear* of man." She also unlearns her best qualities, "her prudence and art—of grace, of play, of chasing away worries, of lightening burdens and taking things lightly—and her subtle aptitude for agreeable desires." Nietzsche himself doubts whether woman, in the end, "really *wants* enlightenment about herself." Perhaps "she seeks a new adornment for herself"—like Rousseau, Nietzsche sees such adornment as part of the eternal feminine—but "she does not *want* truth: what is truth to a woman? From the beginning, nothing has been more alien, repugnant, and hostile to woman than truth—her great art is the lie, her highest concern is mere appearance" (*BGE* 232; see also 127).

It is interesting to note that these claims about woman's hostility to truth and lack of aptitude for science go all the way back to Nietzsche's earliest reflections on woman in *Human, All Too Human* (see *HH* 416; *AOM* 286). But there he held out the hope that this might change in the future, that women might become fellow free spirits united in soul friendship with their male counterparts. This no longer seems to be desirable to Nietzsche. It's not that he does not think women can change and become more like men; as we will see more clearly in a moment, this is precisely what he fears. Rather, he does not see this development as being good for men—especially men like himself—or women. It is noteworthy that, in the aphorism under consideration, Nietzsche identifies himself among the men who appreciate woman's art of lying and preoccupation with appearance and beauty: "Let us men confess it: we honor and love precisely *this* art and *this* instinct in woman—we who have a hard time and for our relief like to associate with beings under whose hands, eyes, and tender follies our seriousness, our gravity and profundity almost appear to us like folly." This passage is highly reminiscent of what Nietzsche says about art in relation to the knowledge-seeking free spirit in *The Gay Science* (107). A little later in the aphorism, he again speaks from the perspective of a man, underlining that he makes no pretense to disinterestedly describing "woman as such": "We men wish that woman should not go on compromising herself through enlightenment" (*BGE* 232).

In the concluding aphorism of the series devoted to woman, Nietzsche develops exactly how women have compromised themselves under modern democratic conditions. He argues that as women have become more equal to men, they have become correspondingly less powerful and influential. By unlearning her fear of man, woman has surrendered those womanly instincts described above. Aspiring to the "economic and legal self-reliance of a clerk," she has dulled and weakened those feminine instincts that gave her power over men. "Since the French Revolution," Nietzsche writes, "woman's influence in Europe has *decreased* proportionately as her rights and claims have increased." He can hardly contain his astonishment that woman would willingly surrender the very weapons that have given her dominion over men in the past. Once again, we are reminded of Rousseau and the empire he believes women exercise over men. But the qualities Nietzsche claims have inspired respect for woman as well as fear end up being quite different from the ones Rousseau emphasizes: "the genuine, cunning suppleness of a beast of prey, the tiger's claw under the glove, the naïveté of her egoism, her uneducability and inner wildness, the incomprehensibility, scope, and movement of her desires and virtues." In addition to fear, this "beautiful cat 'woman'" also elicits pity by appearing to "suffer more, to be more vulnerable, more in need of love, and more condemned to disappointment than any other animal." Nietzsche concludes by dramatically evoking man's manifest disadvantage in relation to woman: "Fear and pity: with these feelings man has so far confronted woman, always with one foot in tragedy which tears to pieces as it enchants" (*BGE* 239).

Again, though, woman has foolishly surrendered her advantage over man, and this has led to the "'borification' of woman" and the "*uglification* of Europe" (*BGE* 239, 232). Nietzsche's couching of his judgments in aesthetic terms in these aphorisms on woman—recall that he also criticized women's attempts to become scientific as being in bad taste—is significant. The claims he is making are not about the essence of "woman as such" but about the conditions of a higher, deeper, more interesting culture and the enhancement of humanity. Among the most important of these conditions is the maintenance and deepening of the differences between man and woman—differences that will enhance the manly in men and the womanly in women. Far from being incompatible with Nietzsche's more general philosophical principles, as some commentators have maintained,[29] this emphasis on the difference between men and women fits in with his more general reflections on the need for an order of rank and pathose of distance for the enhancement of the type "man" (see *BGE* 257).

As we have seen, it is this emphasis on the differences between the sexes and their complementarity that links Nietzsche to Rousseau. But as we have also seen, the two thinkers diverge sharply on the ends that these differences serve. For Rousseau, the differences create an interdependence between men and women that allows them to transcend the individualism that characterizes modern bourgeois society. The complementarity of the sexes plays a crucial role in the moralization and socialization of humanity. For Nietzsche, on the other hand, the differences between the sexes is first and foremost an expression of the dialectical relationship in his philosophy between science and art, truth and appearance, depth and surface, seriousness and play. Both sides are necessary and in that sense complementary. But unlike in Rousseau, this complementarity results not in a harmonious interdependence but in a creative antagonism that promotes the enhancement of the species. Nor does it serve the purpose of morality. As Nietzsche makes clear, there is something "harsh, terrible, enigmatic, and immoral" in the antagonism of man and woman; for "love, thought of in its entirety as great and full, is nature, and being nature it is in all eternity something 'immoral'" (GS 363).

It is, of course, their insistence on the differences between the sexes and their worry about women becoming too much like men that have made Rousseau and Nietzsche questionable thinkers in the eyes of many feminists. This is unfortunate because, however flawed and outdated these philosophers' views on women, marriage, and the family are, there is still something to learn from them. There are few subjects on which moral opinion has changed more dramatically in the last 150 years than on the subject of the nature and role of women in society. Rousseau and Nietzsche certainly fail to anticipate many aspects of this complex sociological sea change, but they show an acute awareness of the dangers involved in the complete erasure of the differences between the sexes—what James referred to as the "decline in the sentiment of sex." These dangers are not merely personal but go to the debilitating individualism of modern bourgeois society that confines human beings to the "abjectness of the human I" (E 312n) and prevents them from sacrificing themselves for a goal that transcends petty self-interest. In this respect, Rousseau's and Nietzsche's reflections on woman point to their reflections on politics.

5

Politics

There would seem to be no sharper difference between Rousseau and Nietzsche than in their respective political philosophies. Rousseau is the great democratic theorist for whom equality is of supreme importance for human flourishing. Nietzsche is the great antidemocratic theorist who supports some form of aristocracy and regards equality as the primary obstacle to human greatness. Nietzsche certainly views Rousseau as his great antagonist on political matters, identifying him with the French Revolution and its assertion of the equal rights of man (*HH* 463; *TI*, "Expeditions," 48). When in *Zarathustra* he refers to the preachers of equality as vengeful tarantulas, he seems to have the "moral tarantula Rousseau" primarily in mind (*Z* 2, "Tarantulas"; *D*, preface, 3). There he writes: "I do not wish to be mixed up and confused with these preachers of equality. For, to *me* justice speaks thus: 'Men are not equal.' Nor shall they become equal!" And he goes on to connect inequality with his doctrine of will to power and self-overcoming: "Life wants to build itself up into the heights with pillars and steps; it wants to look into vast distances and stirring beauties: therefore it requires height. And because it requires height, it requires steps and contradiction among the steps and the climbers. Life wants to climb and to overcome itself in climbing" (*Z* 2, "Tarantulas").

Perhaps just as important as their difference with respect to democracy and equality is the difference between Rousseau and Nietzsche on the importance of politics itself. Rousseau famously glorifies politics and the life of the virtuous citizen in many of his writings. As one scholar puts it, "Perhaps no modern writer and certainly no modern thinker has celebrated the nobility of political life as vividly as [Rousseau]."[1] Rousseau himself highlights the importance of politics in a well-known passage in the *Confessions*, where he states that he has come to realize that "everything depends radically on politics, and that, from whatever aspect one considers it, no people ever would be anything other than what it was made into by the nature of its government" (*C* 340; see also PN 101). Nietzsche, on the other hand, is famously ambivalent about politics. Given his primary concern with culture, he worries about the excessive growth of the state and even characterizes himself as the "last antipolitical German" (*EH*, "Wise," 3). In his later writings, however, he begins to speak approvingly of a "great politics" in the service of culture and human enhancement (*BGE* 208; *EH*, "Destiny," 1). What exactly Nietzsche means by "great politics" will be discussed later. For now, it is enough to indicate that he would not necessarily disagree with Rousseau that everything does depend radically on politics *in some sense*.

The one place Rousseau and Nietzsche indisputably converge is in their critical stance toward liberalism; and for this reason, they have both been treated with suspicion by liberal partisans, sometimes being accused of having authoritarian or even totalitarian tendencies.[2] I will argue that in both cases these charges are misguided. In the case of Rousseau, while it is no doubt true that he levels a profound critique of classical, Lockean, and Enlightenment liberalism, his critique is ultimately in the service of the quintessentially liberal values of individual liberty and equality. Nietzsche presents a much more difficult case because his critique of liberalism is so much more radical than Rousseau's, rejecting both liberal equality and liberty. Where liberal critics go wrong, however, is in supposing that Nietzsche's aristocratic politics involves an institutionalized political system in which the gifted few rule over, manipulate, oppress, enslave, and sometimes even exterminate the mediocre. In what follows, I will argue that Nietzsche's understanding of the relationship of the few to the many and of aristocracy to democracy is far more complex and ambiguous than this tyrannical picture suggests.

With these confusions cleared up, we can see more precisely the fundamental differences in Rousseau's and Nietzsche's political philosophies and what exactly is at stake in those differences. As I have already suggested, Rousseau criticizes the classical liberal tradition from within, arguing that the social inequality it promotes leads to personal dependence and the loss of individual liberty. His solution to this problem is the democratic ideal articulated in the *Social Contract*—an ideal that has individual liberty as its goal, political and economic equality as its condition, and law as its guarantee. Coming more than one hundred years later, Nietzsche's political outlook reflects the growing concern in the nineteenth century that democracy leads to cultural mediocrity and the loss of individuality and human greatness. This concern is shared by liberal thinkers like Tocqueville and Mill, but Nietzsche's diagnosis of the problem in terms of nihilism goes deeper than theirs and ultimately calls for a more radical solution.³ However we judge his achievement in relation to these latter two thinkers, I will argue that Nietzsche succeeds in identifying a real problem in Rousseau's highly individualistic and juridical vision of politics, and that his own perfectionist and aristocratic vision, while no doubt flawed, offers a more promising starting point for reflection on the politics of culture today.

Rousseau's Legitimate State

Rousseau's political philosophy can be seen as responding to two different questions: first, the theoretical question of what constitutes a legitimate political order; and second, the more practical question of how to preserve or maintain such a political order. In this section, I take up the first, theoretical question, drawing primarily on the *Social Contract*. In the next section, I take up the second, more practical question, drawing not only on the *Social Contract* but also on the *Discourse on Political Economy*, the *Letter to D'Alembert*, and *Considerations on the Government of Poland*.

Rousseau announces the theme of the *Social Contract* in the first sentence of the work: "I want to inquire whether in the civil order there can be some legitimate and sure rule of administration, taking men as they are, and the laws as they can be: In this inquiry I shall try always to combine what right permits with what interest prescribes, so that justice and utility may not be disjoined" (*SC* 1:41). Two related points come to the fore in this succinct statement of Rousseau's intention in the *Social Contract*: first, that the object of his inquiry is *legitimate* political order (legitimate meaning that the political order is one that is accepted as valid or justified by the members who belong to it); and second, that these members are not to be understood as idealized rational actors who naturally act in accordance with the common good but, rather, as real human beings—"men as they are"—who act in their self-interest and agree to rules of justice only if those rules can be squared with their own utility.

The master theme of legitimacy is sounded once again in the famous opening paragraph of book 1, chapter 1: "Man is born free, and everywhere he is in chains. . . . How did this change come about? I do not know. What can make it legitimate? I believe I can solve this question" (*SC* 1:1). Rousseau quickly rejects force as a possible basis for legitimate political authority: "To yield to force is an act of necessity, not of will," and therefore has nothing to do with moral duty (*SC* 1:1, 3). Rousseau also follows Locke in rejecting the natural authority of the father as a basis for legitimate political authority. Once a child reaches the age of reason, he no longer has a natural obligation to obey his father but "becomes his own master" and the "sole judge of the means proper to preserve himself" (*SC* 1:2). Having rejected both force and paternal authority, Rousseau concludes that only the agreement or consent of human beings can create legitimate political authority: "Since no man has a natural authority over his fellow-man, and since force produces no right, conventions remain as the basis of all legitimate authority among men" (*SC* 1:4; see also 1:1).

Rousseau is in firm agreement with his great predecessors Hobbes and Locke that the basis of the state is artificial or conventional. He makes his rejection of nature—and traditional natural law[4]—as the basis of the legitimate state especially clear in an earlier version of the *Social Contract*, the so-called *Geneva Manuscript*. There he argues that the need for political institutions arises once the needs of human beings in the state of nature increase to the point where they require the assistance of their fellows. Unfortunately, this dependence on others does not lead to cooperation but competition. The more we need others, the more we become their enemies; and "one man's happiness makes for another's misery." At this point, Rousseau declares, "the gentle voice of nature is no longer an infallible guide." Nor is natural law—or the "law of reason," as Rousseau prefers to call it—of much help, since it develops only with the growth of the passions, which in turn render "all of its precepts powerless." In the impure state of nature, reason does not incline us to contribute to the common good; we want others to adhere to social laws while exempting ourselves. And even if we were inclined to obey social laws, we could not be assured that others would observe those laws toward us (GenMS 1:2, pp. 153–57).

It is on the basis of such realistic considerations that Rousseau concludes—against Diderot and other natural-law theorists—that "there is no natural and general society among men" and that the "laws of justice and of equality are as naught to those who live at the same time in the freedom of the state of nature and subject to the needs of the social state." The latter phrase reminds us that Rousseau, unlike Hobbes, does not confuse this half-independent, half-social state with the original state of nature. Our ills do not come from nature but are of our own making; they are the product of human art, and it is through human art, not nature, that we must cure them. Rousseau formulates the general parameters of his solution to the problem of legitimate political authority in this way: "Let us endeavor to derive from the evil itself the remedy which will cure it. By means of new associations, let us correct, if possible, the lack of a general association." Let us find "in perfected art the redress of the evils which beginning art caused to nature" (GenMS 1:2, p. 159).

Having established that legitimate political authority rests on conventional agreement rather than natural obligation, Rousseau turns his attention to the nature of the original agreement or social contract that establishes the state. As we have seen, human beings have reached a point where they require the assistance of others, which also produces enmity between them. In order to preserve themselves, they must abandon their primitive independence and unite their forces. The question for each individual is how to do this "without harming himself, and without neglecting the care he owes to himself." Rousseau describes the task of the social contract in the most paradoxical way possible: "To find a form of association that will defend and protect the person and goods of each associate with the full common force, and by means of which each, uniting with all, nevertheless obeys only himself and remains as free as before" (SC 1:6).

We are immediately struck by the prominence of freedom in Rousseau's description of the task of the social contract. This is what distinguishes his conception of the social contract from the conceptions of Hobbes and Locke, both of whom accept a certain loss of freedom in exchange for security of life and property. For Rousseau, such a trade-off is unthinkable: "To renounce one's freedom is to renounce one's quality as a man, the rights of humanity, and even its duties" (SC 1:4; also SD 176–78). This is why Hegel credits Rousseau, and not Hobbes or Locke, with the crucial innovation in modern political philosophy of making will or freedom the principle of the state.[5] How does Rousseau understand this freedom? As we have seen in previous chapters, he tends to identify it with self-dependence or the absence of dependence on others. Thus, in Emile, he writes: "The only one who does his own will is he who, in order to do it, has no need to put another's arms at the end of his own" (E 84). He makes a similar point in the Second Discourse: "Since ties of servitude are formed solely by men's mutual dependence and the reciprocal needs that unite them, it is impossible to subjugate a man without first having placed him in a position of being unable to do without another" (SD 159). It is this essentially negative conception of liberty as the absence of personal dependence that continues to inform the Social Contract. Rousseau encapsulates it succinctly in his Letters Written from the Mountain: "Liberty consists less in doing one's own will than in not being subject to someone else's" (LWM 260; see also LMal 573).[6]

Of course, what makes Rousseau's task in the Social Contract so difficult is that human beings have come together precisely because they need one another and are mutually dependent. How can one retain one's freedom understood as self-dependence in these circumstances? Rousseau responds, again paradoxically, by everyone's totally alienating himself and all his rights "to the whole community." The key here lies in the equality of this alienation. Rousseau explains that "since each gives himself entirely, the condition is equal for all, and since the condition is equal for all, no one has any interest in making it burdensome to the rest." The complete reciprocity of the arrangement eliminates any possibility of personal dependence: "Each, by giving himself to all, gives himself to no one, and since there is no associate over whom one does not acquire the same right as one grants over oneself, one gains the equivalent of all one loses, and more force to preserve what one has" (SC 1:6). Political equality is the other foundational idea, besides freedom, that defines Rousseau's legitimate state. It is of crucial importance not so much for its own sake, but "because freedom cannot subsist without it" (SC 2:11).[7]

From the social contract there emerges a democratic sovereign—the collective body is "made up of as many members as the assembly has voices" (SC 1:6)—that is directed by the general will or common interest. With respect to the democratic sovereign, Rousseau has some startling things to say that have set liberals' teeth on edge. Declaring that the democratic sovereign is not bound by any fundamental law or constitution, he argues that because the sovereign is made up of all the individuals who have joined the social contract, it "cannot have any interests contrary to theirs." He goes on to explain this seemingly naïve belief in the infallibility of popular sovereignty in the following way: "The sovereign power has no need of a guarantor toward the subjects, because it is impossible for the body to want to harm all of its members, and . . . it cannot harm any one of them in particular." Because the laws emanate from and apply equally to all citizens, the democratic sovereign, "by the mere fact that it is, is always everything that it ought to be" (SC 1:7).

Of course, it is the way Rousseau concludes his chapter on the democratic sovereign that has caused the most controversy. Though subjects require no guarantees against a democratic sovereign who is directed by the general will and legislating in the genuinely common interest, the sovereign may require guarantees against the subjects, for the latter sometimes allow their selfish interests or particular wills to overrule the common interest or general will. In such cases, the state must be able to back up its laws with coercive power; otherwise it would end up being an empty institution. As Rousseau infamously puts it: "For the social compact not to be an empty formula, it tacitly includes the following engagement which alone can give force to the rest, that whoever refuses to obey the general will shall be constrained to do so by the entire body: which means nothing other than he shall be forced to be free." It is the latter phrase, juxtaposing force and freedom, that has given commentators the most difficulty; but Rousseau explains it in the sentence that follows. It is only the legitimate and effective authority created by the social contract that provides the individual with freedom and "guarantees him against all personal dependence" (SC 1:7).[8]

Rousseau goes on to elaborate on the freedom and personal independence provided by the state in the following chapter. He begins by describing the "remarkable change" produced by the transition from the state of nature to the civil state: no longer driven by instinct or appetite but by justice and moral duty, man's "faculties are exercised and developed, his ideas enlarged, his sentiments ennobled, his entire soul is elevated to such an extent, that . . . he should ceaselessly bless the happy moment which wrested him from [the state of nature] forever, and out of a stupid and limited animal made an intelligent being and a man." This is probably the clearest evidence that Rousseau is no romantic glorifier of the primitive state of nature. In terms of freedom, he admits that man loses his natural freedom by the social contract, but he gains instead "civil freedom and property in everything he possesses." Natural freedom is an unlimited right to all that one desires—in the state of nature, of course, one desires very little—and civil freedom is limited by the general will (*SC* 1:8).

Almost as an afterthought, Rousseau adds that there is another freedom associated with the civil state—namely, moral freedom, "which alone makes man truly master of himself, for the impulsion of mere appetite is slavery, and obedience to the law one has prescribed to oneself is freedom" (*SC* 1:8).[9] Anticipating Kant's notion of autonomy, this moral freedom certainly has a more positive connotation than the negative freedom we have encountered so far, but it has little to do with the Berlinian concept of positive freedom that justifies coercion in the name of some sort of "real self."[10] In *Emile*, moral freedom is equated with virtue and the triumph of duty over personal inclination and passion (*E* 444–45). In the *Social Contract*, it refers to the identification of the individual's will with the general will as opposed to his particular and selfish will. Such moral freedom is not in tension with the more negative freedom from personal dependence that the social contract guarantees; rather, it corresponds to the internal willing of the conditions necessary for that negative freedom. It does not lead to totalitarian coercion but describes the virtuous citizen of a liberal democracy who does not need to be forced to be free.

It is noteworthy that Rousseau includes the right of property as one of the key contributions of the civil state. Given that he claims that an individual alienates all his rights and goods when he enters the social contract—not to mention what he says about property in the *Second Discourse*—we would not necessarily expect Rousseau to be a huge defender of private property. Nevertheless, we find him arguing in the *Discourse on Political Economy* that the "right of property is the most sacred of the rights of citizens, and more important in some respects than freedom itself" (*PE* 230). In the *Social Contract*, he makes clear that the individual's alienation of his property to the political community only makes his right to it more secure: "What is remarkable about this alienation is that the community, far from despoiling individuals of their goods by accepting them, only secures to them their legitimate possession, changes usurpation into a genuine right, and use into property." In short, Rousseau is no socialist. It is true that he adds that the "right every individual has over his own land is always subordinate to the right the community has over everyone" (SC 1:9); Rousseau is not Locke either. But that he concedes a certain priority to the public good over the absolute right of the individual to his property should not obscure that he nevertheless gives considerable importance to this quintessentially liberal right.

Before we conclude too quickly that Rousseau is a liberal thinker, however, we need to consider his central and perhaps most controversial idea in the *Social Contract*—namely, the general will. Though Rousseau alludes to this idea at several points in book 1, it is only in book 2 that he begins to unpack it. Again, he identifies it with the common good or interest, and he assumes that such a common interest must exist; otherwise there would be no reason for people to enter the social contract in the first place: "While the opposition of particular interests made the establishment of societies necessary, it is the agreement of these same interests which made it possible. What these different interests have in common is what forms the social bond, and if there were not some point on which all interests agree, no society could exist" (SC 2:1). This common interest or general will is easy to see in a small society. For a group of peasants attending to political affairs under an oak tree, "the common good is everywhere fully evident and requires only good sense to be perceived." As society grows larger and particular interests assert themselves more forcefully, the general will becomes more difficult to discern. At a certain point, the state may become so corrupt that the general will is completely mute. Even then, though, Rousseau claims the general will is not extinguished: "It remains constant, unalterable, and pure; but it is subordinated to others that prevail over it." The selfish individual still apprehends the common good but subordinates it to his own exclusive good. Indeed, he wills the public good out of self-interest, provided he can exempt himself from bearing its cost (SC 4:2; see also LD 24–27).

In the latter scenario, Rousseau envisages the possibility that the democratic will of all no longer expresses the general will. As he puts it in a famously enigmatic passage:

> There is often a considerable difference between the will of all and the general will: the latter looks only to the common interest, the former looks to private interest, and is nothing but a sum of particular wills; but if, from these same wills, one takes away the pluses and minuses which cancel each other

out, what is left as the sum of the differences is the general will. If, when an adequately informed people deliberates, the citizens had no communication among themselves, the general will would always result from the large number of small differences, and the deliberation would always be good. (*SC* 2:3)

Rousseau's arithmetical formulation of the general will here does not necessarily render the concept more perspicuous. What he seems to have in mind is that every individual's rational (in the economic sense) particular will is to want the public good without bearing the cost himself: everyone else should pay a tax to build the road so that he can free-ride. When you add all such particular wills together, the self-exemptions create a "large number of small differences" that cancel each other out. Rousseau goes on to point out that when factions arise, the differences become correspondingly fewer and larger, creating majorities and minorities, which when added up "yield a less general result." No less than James Madison, Rousseau fears the influence of factions in politics; and if they cannot be completely eliminated, he agrees with Madison that their number should be multiplied (*SC* 2:3).

Once again, we see that equality and reciprocity are at the heart of Rousseau's conception of the general will. "Why is the general will always upright, and why do all consistently will each one's happiness," he asks, "if not because there is no one who does not appropriate the word *each* to himself, and think of himself as he votes for all." Rousseau does not demand that citizens sacrifice their self-interest when entering the social contract, only that they generalize it. It is through such generalization—again, it is hard not to think of Kant here—that the "admirable agreement between interest and justice" announced at the outset of the *Social Contract* can be achieved.[11] The power of Rousseau's democratic sovereign is not absolute; it is limited by the general will, which requires that the conditions imposed by the sovereign apply equally to all. This is the central nerve of his argument: "From whatever side one traces one's way back to the principle, one always reaches the same conclusion: namely, that the social pact establishes among the citizens an equality such that all commit themselves under the same conditions and must all enjoy the same rights" (*SC* 2:4; see also 1:9).

Rousseau has shown that a truly general will must be general not only in its source but in its object as well; and a statute that is general in its object as well as its enacting will is precisely what he means by law (*SC* 2:4, 6). It would be hard to overestimate the role—and rule—of law in the *Social Contract* and in Rousseau's political philosophy in general. This is made clear in the epigraph to the *Social Contract*, taken from Vergil's *Aeneid*—"Let us declare the fair laws of a compact"—as well as in Rousseau's definition of a republic as "any state ruled by laws: for then the public interest alone governs" (*SC* 2:6). It is through subjection to impersonal law that the individual is liberated from personal dependence.[12] The central place of law in Rousseau's political philosophy receives perhaps its most powerful expression in the *Discourse on Political Economy*, where he claims that the problem of reconciling governmental authority with individual freedom "was resolved . . . by the most sublime of all institutions, or rather by a celestial inspiration that taught men to imitate here below the immutable decrees of the divinity."

> By what inconceivable art were the means found to subjugate men in order to make them free? . . . How can it be that they obey and no one commands, that they serve yet have no master; all the freer in fact than in apparent subjection, no one loses any more of his freedom than might harm someone else's? These marvels are the work of law. It is to law alone that men owe justice and freedom. It is this salutary organ of the will of all that restores in [the realm of] right the natural equality among men. It is this celestial voice that dictates the precepts of public reason to every citizen, and teaches him to act in conformity with the maxims of his own judgment, and not to be in contradiction with himself. (*PE* 9–10; see also GenMS 1:7; *E*, 85; *GP* 179)

As crucial as generality in both the enacting will and enacted object is for law, Rousseau recognizes that it is not enough to make laws good or wise and in the best interest of all. The democratic people responsible for enacting the laws is not enlightened enough to know what is in its long-term self-interest. It certainly wants the good, "but by itself it does not always see it. The general will is always upright, but the judgment that guides it is not always enlightened." Rousseau is the greatest of all democrats, but he is not naïve, and he does not assume that the people possesses wisdom. "How will a blind multitude," he asks, "which often does not know what it wills because it rarely knows what is good for it, carry out an undertaking as great, as difficult as a system of legislation?" The short answer is, they will not; and this is what gives rise to the need for a wise and disinterested lawgiver (*SC* 2:6).

The figure of the lawgiver, of course, raises a whole set of other issues and has fueled the charge that Rousseau is an antiliberal or authoritarian thinker. To address these issues adequately would take us well beyond the scope of this chapter. The one thing that can be said in favor of the mythical figure of the lawgiver is that it represents a recognition on Rousseau's part that bare generality is not sufficient to guarantee that laws are good or in the common interest; intelligence or wisdom is needed. This does not undermine the central conclusion of this section: that in the *Social Contract* Rousseau defends a conception of legitimate government that has freedom from personal dependence as its primary aim and political equality and the rule of law as its necessary conditions. As theoretically appealing as such a republican or liberal democratic conception of government may be, it nevertheless faces many practical challenges as far as realization and preservation are concerned. It is to Rousseau's response to those practical challenges that we now turn.

Citizenship, Virtue, and Patriotism

For Rousseau, the practical question of how to bring about and preserve a just society or legitimate state is at least as important as the theoretical question of what defines such a society or state.[13] Among the various challenges confronting a republic of laws, there are three that especially occupy Rousseau's attention. The first is the threat posed by the body charged with executing the laws to the democratic sovereign responsible for making the laws. The second is the distorting effect on the general will that substantial economic inequality produces. And the third and most important is the difficulty of getting citizens to obey the laws and contribute to the common good.

With respect to the first, it is necessary to say something about what Rousseau understands by *government*, a term he reserves for the body charged with executing the laws of the democratic sovereign. Contrary to the accusation that he rejects the separation of powers in the *Social Contract*,[14] Rousseau sharply differentiates between sovereign legislative power and governmental executive power; the latter applies the general laws made by the former to particular cases. Unlike sovereign authority, which is "everywhere the same," there is no single best form of government. As the number of magistrates in government increases, its force diminishes; therefore, Rousseau believes the larger the population of a state is (resulting in a greater disconnect between the individual will and the general will) the smaller the number of magistrates there should be. In general, he favors an elective aristocracy because its magistrates are marked by "probity, enlightenment, [and] experience." He is withering in his criticism of monarchy, which elevates "petty bunglers, petty knaves, [and] petty schemers." And he is highly skeptical of democratic government—as distinguished from democratic sovereignty—not only because it is impractical to have the people constantly assembled for the purpose of executing the laws but because it is corrupting to turn the attention of the people away from general considerations to particular objects (*SC* 3:1–6).

Rousseau believes there is a natural tendency for the executive power to encroach on the power of the democratic sovereign (*SC* 3:10–11). He saw this happening in his native Geneva, where the sovereign General Council had been slowly deprived of its power by the twenty-five magistrates who made up the executive Small Council (see *LWM*, letters 7–9). The principal means by which to prevent such usurpation of the sovereign power by the executive power, he argues, is the frequent assembly of the democratic sovereign. He anticipates the obvious objection: "The people assembled, it will be said! What a chimera!" And he answers: "It is a chimera today, but it was not so two thousand years ago: Have men changed their nature? The bounds of the possible in moral matters are less narrow than we think: It is our weaknesses, our vices, our prejudices that constrict them. Base souls do not believe in great men: vile slaves smile mockingly at the word freedom" (*SC* 3:12). He goes on to give the example of the Roman republic and elaborates on it in the lengthy chapter on the Roman comitia (or assemblies) in book 4 (*SC* 4:4; see also *GP* 197–211).

This sets the stage for Rousseau's famous attack on representatives and his stirring defense of participatory democracy. "As soon as public service ceases to be the citizens' principal business," he writes, "and they prefer to serve with their purse rather than with their person, the state is already close to ruin." This happens when commerce and moneymaking become the primary activities of citizens. They would rather pay others to carry out their citizen duties than take precious time away from business and the stock exchange. In this way, the general will is silenced and freedom lost. "The better constituted the state," Rousseau argues, "the more public business takes precedence over private business in the minds of citizens." And for a law to be a valid expression of the general will, it must be ratified by the people in person. For this reason, he claims the English people is free only during the election of members of Parliament; at all other times, it is enslaved, "it is nothing." As he did in the *First Discourse*, he holds up the ancient republics of Greece and Rome as counterexamples. There the citizens were constantly assembled, and their chief business was to exercise and preserve their freedom. Rousseau does not overlook that having slaves do all the work made this possible, but he does not think slavery is necessary for such freedom to be exercised. What is necessary, however, is that the state be small (*SC* 3:15; *FD* 18).

Let us turn now to what Rousseau considers to be the second great obstacle to the maintenance of a free republic based on the rule of law: namely, substantial economic inequality. His concern with this issue goes all the way back to the *Second Discourse*, where the "historical" social contract is shown to be much more favorable to the rich than the poor and therefore not fully legitimate (*SD* 172–73). Rousseau makes a similar point in the *Social Contract*, contrasting the "moral and legitimate equality" produced by the genuine social contract with the formal and illusory equality of bad governments, which "serves only to maintain the poor in his misery and the rich in his usurpation. In fact the laws are always useful to those who possess something and harmful to those who have nothing. Whence it follows that the social state is advantageous for men only insofar as all have something and none has too much of anything" (*SC* 1:9). Later in the book, he makes clear he is not advocating that everyone should have the same amount of wealth, only that no citizen should "be so very rich that he can buy another, and none so poor that he is compelled to sell himself" (*SC* 2:11). Economic equality here is not an end in itself. The point is to prevent wealth from undermining the political equality and freedom from personal dependence that are pillars of the legitimate state. Extreme inequality of fortunes causes citizens to hate one another, makes them indifferent to the common good, and weakens the springs of government. Therefore, a wise government must prevent extreme economic inequality "in order to maintain, by means of good morals, respect for the laws, love of fatherland, and the vigor of the general will" (*PE* 19–20; see also 31–32).[15]

The references to "good morals" and "love of fatherland" bring us to the third challenge to legitimate republican rule that Rousseau addresses: namely, how to get citizens to obey the laws and contribute to the common good. This is in many ways the most important consideration for Rousseau, for he—like his successors Burke, Hegel, and Tocqueville—does not think laws alone accompanied by punishment are sufficient to maintain a liberal polity. Citizens must possess the appropriate ethical habits, customs, manners, dispositions, and sentiments (what Rousseau and Tocqueville both referred to as *mœurs*) to have the necessary motivation to carry out their duties. Here we encounter what might be called the "communitarian" dimension of Rousseau's political thought, a dimension that has again given rise to accusations that he is some sort of authoritarian or totalitarian thinker. It is important to remember, however, that this communitarian dimension of Rousseau's thought does not elevate the community or communal solidarity above individual freedom; rather, it is completely in the service of the latter and of the rule of law that is its most important condition.

In the *Social Contract*, Rousseau's conviction that his liberal democratic state requires the deliberate shaping or formation of the ethical dispositions of citizens appears most prominently in his discussion of the lawgiver. There he writes that anyone "who dares to institute a people must feel capable of, so to speak, changing human nature; of transforming each individual who by himself is a perfect and solitary whole into a part of a larger whole from which that individual would as it were receive his life and his being" (*SC* 2:7). And a little later, he elaborates on this educative aspect of the lawgiver's task, declaring that the most important of the latter's laws are not graven in marble or bronze, "but in the hearts of citizens," where they "imperceptibly substitute the force of habit for authority. I speak of morals (*mœurs*), customs, and above all of opinion; a part [of the laws] unknown to our politicians but on which the success of all the others depends" (*SC* 2:12; brackets in the original). It is this emphasis on the importance of morals, customs, and opinions, as opposed to statutory or even constitutional laws, that will become the linchpin of Tocqueville's theoretical outlook in *Democracy in America*.

Given the theoretical focus of the *Social Contract*, Rousseau's discussion of the ethical formation of citizens does not loom large in the book, though he comes back to it at the end in the chapters on censorship and civil religion. It is in the *Discourse on Political Economy* and the *Considerations on the Government of Poland* that he gives the most sustained attention to this topic. In *Political Economy*, after describing law as the "sublime institution" that reconciles political authority with individual liberty, Rousseau states that the most urgent task of civil magistrates is to make sure that the law is observed, and that this is most effectively accomplished not through harsh punishments but by making the laws loved. "This is all that the talent for ruling consists in," he writes. "With force in hand, there is no art to making everyone tremble," nor in simply punishing transgressions; "the genuine statesman knows how to prevent them; he exercises his respectable dominion over wills even more than actions" (*PE* 9–11). It is only through such shaping of the ethical dispositions of citizens that one can ensure their obedience to the laws and allegiance to the common good. In the *Confessions*, Rousseau reports that through historical study he learned that "everything depends radically on politics" (*C* 340). Here he shows how thoroughly he imbibed that lesson: "Certain it is that in the long run peoples are what government makes them be. . . . Therefore, form men if you want to command men; if you would have the laws obeyed, see to it that they are loved. . . . That was the great art of ancient governments" (*PE* 13).

Perhaps the greatest difficulty in maintaining legitimate political authority, Rousseau argues, is getting citizens to conform their particular wills to the general will. Such conformity is what he means by virtue, and therefore he insists that the fundamental practical task of politics is to "make virtue reign." How does one make citizens virtuous? Rousseau declares that it "is not enough to tell citizens, be good"; one must inspire them to love their duty (*PE* 13–15; see also *J* 14). The most effective means of bringing this about, he claims, is through love of fatherland or patriotism. Whereas cosmopolitanism only weakly motivates human beings to care for their fellows—"interest and commiseration must in some way be constricted and compressed in order to be activated"—love of fatherland has produced the "greatest marvels of virtue": "This gentle and lively sentiment which combines the force of *amour propre* with all the beauty of virtue, endows it with an energy which . . . makes it into the most heroic of all the passions" (*PE* 15–16; see also GenMS 1:2, p. 158).

Rousseau reserves his greatest praise for patriotism and its ability to promote civic virtue for the *Government of Poland*. Once again, he insists that "no constitution will ever be good and solid unless the law rules the citizens' hearts." To attach citizens' hearts to the fatherland, he suggests that one start early, with children's games. Beyond that, festivals, public games, spectacles, and ceremonies are effective ways of keeping the fatherland constantly before the citizen's eyes. One is reminded of the passage in the *Letter to D'Alembert* where Rousseau recalls the time he saw the regiment of Saint-Gervais dancing in the public square. Keeping citizens occupied with the fatherland is key for Rousseau, and sometimes he goes very far in expressing its importance: "Upon opening its eyes, a child should see the fatherland, and see only it until his dying day. . . . [Love of fatherland] makes up his whole existence; he sees only his fatherland, he lives only for it; when he is alone, he is nothing: when he no longer has a fatherland, he no longer is" (*GP* 179–89; *LD* 123–37). Here one has to concede that Rousseau's liberal critics may have a point; even an antiliberal critic like Nietzsche would find such hyperpatriotism hard to swallow.

Of course, it is Rousseau's chapter on civil religion in the *Social Contract* that comes in for the harshest criticism from liberals who accuse him of totalitarianism. But here they may be on shakier ground. In this chapter, Rousseau trenchantly brings out how the union of religion and politics in the ancient world encouraged love of the laws and fatherland and how Christianity destroyed that unity with disastrous consequences for the social bond. As a purely spiritual religion, Christianity inspires indifference to the things of this world and thus makes citizens apathetic soldiers and easy prey for tyrants. Nevertheless, Rousseau also recognizes the defects of ancient theocracy, which is "founded on error and lies" and makes citizens "credulous" and "superstitious" as well as "bloodthirsty and intolerant." Therefore, he constructs a watered-down version of civil religion that requires of citizens only that they have some religion that makes them love their duties but does not prescribe any specific dogmas, apart from those that are necessary for social unity. The positive dogmas of this minimalist civil religion include the "existence of the powerful, intelligent, beneficent, prescient, and provident Divinity, the life to come, the happiness of the just, the punishment of the wicked, [and] the sanctity of the social contract and the laws." The only negative doctrine is the prohibition of intolerance. "Beyond this everyone may hold whatever opinions he pleases, without its being up to the sovereign to know them" (*SC* 4:8; see also *LWM* 146–49; LU 265–68).

One wonders whether such a liberal civil religion can ultimately deliver the social unity the state requires. Like his successors Hegel and Tocqueville, Rousseau struggles to balance his recognition that the state needs religion for the sake of social unity and his hesitation to overstep the boundaries of liberal toleration. This tension between what one might call Rousseau's communitarianism and his liberalism pervades his political philosophy. I have argued that the latter doctrine constitutes the dominant note of the tension. Rousseau's political ideal is of a legitimate state in which the rule of law and political equality guarantee the freedom from personal dependence of individual citizens. Robust political participation and the ethical education of citizens through morals, patriotism, and ultimately civil religion are necessary as means to support this essentially liberal democratic ideal. This is important to underline because it is precisely Nietzsche's rejection of this liberal democratic ideal that lies at the heart of his political difference with Rousseau.

Nietzsche's Early Cultural Politics

Perhaps the most striking formal difference between Nietzsche's political philosophy and Rousseau's is the former's sheer elusiveness. While Rousseau's political philosophy is not without its obscurities and paradoxes, no one would deny that he has a political philosophy or that he does not belong in the canon of important political philosophers. This is not the case with Nietzsche. A number of scholars deny that he has a political philosophy in any meaningful sense. Walter Kaufmann originally gave currency to this antipolitical reading of Nietzsche, in an effort to save him from the imputation of fascism; and other scholars have followed suit.[16] Thus, Brian Leiter writes, "Nietzsche . . . has no political philosophy, in the conventional sense of a theory of the state and its legitimacy. He occasionally expresses views about political matters, but, read in context, they do not add up to a theoretical account of any of the questions of political philosophy."[17] Similarly, Bernard Williams claims that Nietzsche does not offer "a coherent politics. He himself provides no way of relating his ethical and psychological insights to an intelligible account of modern society—a failing only thinly concealed by the impression he gives of having thoughts about modern politics that are determinate but terrible."[18] Other scholars have rejected this antipolitical reading of Nietzsche, some arguing that he advocates an aristocratic political system in which the gifted few rule over, manipulate, oppress, enslave, and sometimes even exterminate the mediocre many,[19] while others insist that his philosophy contains intimations of a more democratic and agonistic politics.[20]

None of these interpretations of Nietzsche's political philosophy strike me as getting it quite right. While it is certainly true that Nietzsche does not have a political philosophy "in the conventional sense of a theory of the state and its legitimacy" (a rather loaded way of putting it) and that his reflections on politics are highly suggestive, experimental, and ambiguous,[21] it would be a mistake to dismiss them as incoherent, irrelevant to modern society, and unconcerned with any of the questions of traditional political philosophy. Nevertheless, neither the aristocratic radical nor the agonistic democratic interpretations capture what is distinctive and possibly valuable in Nietzsche's political philosophy. Against the latter, I argue that Nietzsche's politics are undeniably aristocratic. But against the former, I maintain that his aristocratic politics do not involve an actual set of political institutions through which the elite few exercise political power—or "ruthless political control"[22]—over the herd-like masses; rather, they consist of a set of beliefs, a system of valuation, that insists on an order of rank and difference in value between human beings. As Nietzsche says in several places, his principal concern lies with culture, not the state (see, e.g., *TI*, "Germans," 4). Such an aristocratic system of valuation is clearly at odds with the democratic—and Rousseauian—belief in equality, but it is not necessarily incompatible with democratic political institutions. A note from 1883 provides a revealing clue to how Nietzsche understands this peculiar opposition and coexistence of aristocracy and democracy: "The aim is *by no means* to conceive the [*Übermenschen*] as masters of the [last men]. Rather: the two types are to exist beside each other—separated as much as possible; *like the gods of Epicurus, the one not meddling with the other*" (*KSA* 10:7 [21]).

Because Nietzsche's political philosophy is not contained in a single treatise like the *Social Contract*, and because it shifts over time and is so elusive and ambiguous, it is best to proceed chronologically with his writings on politics, beginning with his early essay "The Greek State" (1871/72). It would be hard to find a political teaching more diametrically opposed to Rousseau's than the one presented in this essay, which begins with a stinging attack on the modern watchwords of the "dignity of man" and the "dignity of work." According to Nietzsche, there is nothing dignified about work, which merely serves the "drive to exist at any price," the pointless Schopenhauerian will to live. The Greeks suffered from no such illusions about work, regarding it as a disgrace, something suitable only for slaves. Nevertheless, they recognized that work and slavery were necessary conditions for culture. "In order for there to be a broad, deep, fertile soil for the development of art," Nietzsche

writes, "the overwhelming majority has to be slavishly subjected to life's necessity in the service of the minority." The latter, "privileged class is to be re-
moved from the struggle for existence, in order to produce and satisfy a new
world of necessities." Consequently, "the misery of men living a life of toil has
to be increased to make the production of the world of art possible for a small
number of Olympian men." Nietzsche does not shrink from encapsulating his
point in a shocking formula: "*Slavery belongs to the essence of a culture*" (GSt
176–79). What exactly he means by slavery here and what form he envisages
it as taking under modern conditions remain to be seen.

Nietzsche goes on to dismantle the modern—and Rousseauian—contrac-
tual understanding of the origin and meaning of the state. It is not the consent of egoistic individuals that creates the state; rather, it is the "iron clamp
of the state" that forces the masses into cohesion, creating a "pyramidal structure" with slaves as its base. Not contract but power "gives the first *right*, and
there is no right which is not fundamentally presumption, usurpation, and
violence." The aim of the state, Nietzsche argues, "lies far beyond the compre-
hension and egoism of the individual"; it consists of culture, the salvation of
nature "in appearance, in the mirror of genius." The state is absolutely necessary for art and culture because it puts an end to the *bellum omnium contra
omnes*. It is true that after states have been founded, they continue to fight
wars with one another. But there are still intervals between wars; and in these
intervals, Nietzsche writes, "the concentrated effect of that *bellum*, turned in-
wards, gives society time to germinate and turn green everywhere, so that it
can let the radiant blossoms of genius sprout forth as soon as warmer days
come" (GSt 180–82).

Nietzsche contrasts this "perfectionist" or "teleocratic" understanding
of the state[23] with the liberal understanding of the state as a means to self-
preservation and the personal freedom of the individual. On this latter,
"liberal-optimistic" understanding, which "has its roots in the teachings of
the French Enlightenment and Revolution," the state is seen as merely guar-
anteeing the "most undisturbed coexistence possible" so that everyone can
"pursue their own purposes without restriction." Instead of being seen as an
end for which individuals sacrifice themselves, the state is viewed as a mere
means for people to achieve their selfish aims. For such a state, peace is the ultimate goal and war above all something to be avoided. This allows the "truly
international, homeless, financial recluses"—here Nietzsche reflects the influence of his antisemitic mentor, Wagner—to "misuse politics as an instrument of the stock exchange." The antidote to this pacific and financial cosmopolitanism, Nietzsche declares, is "war and again war." Sounding almost like
Hegel, he claims it is only in war that the state ceases to be a mere "protective

measure for egoistic individuals, but instead produces from within itself an ethical momentum in the love of fatherland and prince, which indicates a much higher destination" (GSt 182–84).[24]

War and its hierarchical organization also provide Nietzsche with his model for society. Society should be organized in the shape of a pyramid, with a broad base consisting of a "slave-like" caste. While this caste remains largely unconscious of the purpose that it serves (namely, the creation of the genius), the higher castes make this purpose their explicit aim. Here is where the real dignity of man lies: "not as absolute man and non-genius but as a means to genius. . . . Every man, with his whole activity, is only dignified to the extent that he is a tool of genius, consciously or unconsciously." Nietzsche concludes by comparing his perfectionist conception of the state to Plato's republic, which had as its goal the rule of the philosopher. Though he criticizes Plato for "excluding the inspired artist from his state"—an error he attributes to the influence of the excessively rationalistic Socrates—he nevertheless endorses Plato's teleocratic understanding of the state as a means for the "creation and preparation of the genius" (GSt 184–85). Such an understanding of the state contrasts sharply with Rousseau's "nomocratic" conception of a republic of laws. While some of Nietzsche's criticisms of the liberal state do not apply to Rousseau's legitimate republic—for example, that it reduces politics to being an "instrument of the stock exchange"—his worry about a regime of neutral rules that serves no greater purpose than individual freedom from personal dependence definitely does.

Because it is such an early writing that Nietzsche never saw fit to publish, one would not want to put too much weight on "The Greek State." Nevertheless, it articulates some of the abiding themes of Nietzsche's political thought: first, that politics is not merely a neutral framework that guarantees individual rights and allows individuals to pursue their selfish interests but, rather, something that serves a higher, more substantial purpose; second, that that purpose is bound up with culture and human excellence; and third, that society is organized hierarchically in order to achieve that purpose. What becomes less prominent in Nietzsche's subsequent writings is the emphasis on the role of the state in this cultural project.

This is already evident in his 1874 essay "Schopenhauer as Educator." There, in a passage that echoes Tocqueville's diagnosis of the individualism, materialism, and restlessness of modern life, Nietzsche characterizes ours as "an age of atoms, an age of atomistic chaos." It is an age in which "haste and hurry" are universal and contemplativeness has disappeared. With the "waters of religion ebbing away" and skepticism spreading, the educated classes are increasingly "swept along by a hugely contemptible money economy," and they "grow daily more restless, thoughtless and loveless" (SE 4:148). How can this nihilistic situation be rectified? Once again, Nietzsche looks to culture for a solution. The goal of society must be the production of individual great men, geniuses—the philosopher, artist, and saint—who redeem the rest of humanity by providing insight into the metaphysical significances of existence (SE 5–6:161–63). But unlike in "The Greek State," Nietzsche here sharply distinguishes the realm of culture from that of the state. The "greed of the state" leads it to misappropriate culture for its own purposes: "However loudly the state may proclaim its service to culture, it furthers culture in order to further itself and cannot conceive of a goal higher than its own welfare and continued existence" (SE 6:165–66, 174). Therefore, Nietzsche advises potential philosophers to take their duties to the state lightly and avoid the "*furor politicus*" (SE 7:180–81).

The most sustained discussion of politics in Nietzsche's early and middle works appears in the chapter "A Glance at the State" in *Human, All Too Human* and the parallel sections in *Assorted Opinions and Maxims* (294–324) and *The Wanderer and His Shadow* (275–93). In this chapter and its sequels, Nietzsche continues to view politics through the lens of culture, though his understanding of the latter undergoes a significant change, no longer looking to art to resolve the aimlessness and fragmentation of modern culture but to the scientific spirit embodied in the Enlightenment: the knowledge-seeking free spirit replaces the Wagnerian genius as the linchpin of cultural renewal.[25] And as in "Schopenhauer as Educator," he worries about the growth of the state and the possibility of its overwhelming the realm of culture. Therefore, he speaks out vociferously against "great politics," which has a different meaning here from what it will have in his later writings.

It is in connection with his hostility toward great politics that Nietzsche levels his first explicit attack on Rousseau and his revolutionary followers. He derides those "political and social fantasists who with fiery eloquence invite a revolutionary overturning of all social orders in the belief that the proudest temple of humanity will then at once rise up as though of its own accord." These fantasies can all be traced back to Rousseau, who believed in the natural goodness of human beings and blamed society for its corruption. History shows that revolutions do not restore a pristine human nature but unleash the "most savage energies." For this reason, Nietzsche prefers "Voltaire's moderate nature, inclined as it was to ordering, purifying, and reconstructing," to the revolutionary optimism of Rousseau, which "has for a long time banished *the spirit of the Enlightenment and of progressive evolution*" (*HH* 463).

The two revolutionary political movements that Nietzsche aims his fiercest criticisms at are socialism and nationalism. In the former, people seek to "work as little as possible with their hands," and in the latter, they seek to work "as little as possible with their heads" (*HH* 480). Socialism, Nietzsche claims, is distinguished by its desire for an excess of state power and an almost complete absence of individual freedom. With considerable political astuteness, he writes: "Socialism is the fanciful younger brother of the almost expired despotism whose heir it wants to be; its endeavors are thus in the profoundest sense reactionary. For it desires an abundance of state power such as only despotism ever had." Most troublingly, socialism seeks to annihilate the individual, "who appears to it like an unauthorized luxury of nature destined to be improved into a useful *organ of the community*." It is only through its negative example, Nietzsche declares, that socialism can contribute to the higher culture of the future. It "can serve to teach, in a truly brutal and impressive fashion, what danger there lies in all accumulations of state power, and to that extent to implant mistrust of the state itself" (*HH* 473).

Nietzsche is no less critical of nationalism. Indeed, it is in *Human, All Too Human* that he first espouses the "good Europeanism" that will become a central feature of his mature political outlook. Developments in communication and trade are eroding national barriers, and it is only an "artificial nationalism" that seeks to reverse this inexorable trend. Therefore, "one should not be afraid to proclaim oneself simply a *good European* and actively to work for the amalgamation of nations." Nietzsche is particularly concerned about the hatred of the Jews being whipped up by nationalists, and he presciently warns that the scapegoating of Jews "for every public or private misfortune" is rapidly gaining ground (*HH* 475).

Related to his discussion of nationalism—and quite at odds with his "paean to war" in "The Greek State"—Nietzsche complains about the prosecution of costly wars in the pursuit of great politics. The problem with such Bismarckian great politics is that it sacrifices the talent and energy previously dedicated to culture on the "altar of the fatherland or of the national thirst for honor." The pursuit of great politics—and, with it, great wars—comes at tremendous spiritual and cultural cost: "The political emergence of a people almost necessarily draws after it spiritual impoverishment," sacrificing the "more spiritual plants and growths" to the "coarse and gaudy flower of the nation" (*HH* 481).

The aspect of Nietzsche's discussion of politics in *Human, All Too Human* and its sequels that has attracted the most attention is its treatment of democracy. Some scholars have seen this discussion as indicative of a more favorable attitude toward democracy on Nietzsche's part;[26] others have dismissed it as being anomalous with respect to the alleged "aristocratic radicalism" of his later works.[27] Neither of these views quite captures the nuance of his position. While Nietzsche certainly takes democracy seriously in *Human, All Too Human* as an undeniable feature of modernity, he never treats it as anything more than a means to a more aristocratic conception of culture. And far from being anomalous with respect to his later political outlook, his treatment of democracy in *Human, All Too Human* in many ways anticipates how he will envisage the coexistence of democracy and aristocracy in his later works.

He begins by acknowledging—in a manner similar to Tocqueville—that the "democratization of Europe is irresistible" (*WS* 275). And he even concedes that such democratization is a legitimate demand on the part of the many: "If the purpose of politics really is to make life endurable for as many as possible, then these as-many-as-possible are entitled to determine what they understand by an endurable life." Unlike Tocqueville, though, who saw equality of conditions as a "generative fact" that penetrates every aspect of democratic life, Nietzsche insists that the narrow-mindedness that belongs to democratic politics must not be allowed to infect all spheres of activity, especially higher activity.[28] The few must be allowed to "refrain from politics" and assume an "ironic posture" with respect to the happiness of the many" (*HH* 438). No matter how much Nietzsche concedes to the unavoidability of democracy in the modern world, he still maintains that a "higher culture can come into existence only where there are two different castes in society: that of the workers and that of the idle, of those capable of true leisure" (*HH* 439; see also 462). The former Nietzsche considers to be no different from slaves, by which he means anyone "who does not have two-thirds of his day to himself." But he insists that the idle few do not merely enjoy life at the expense of the workers; indeed, they suffer more, their "enjoyment of existence is less, [their] task heavier" (*HH* 283, 439, 462).

Nietzsche's analysis of the inevitable democratization of Europe shows that he does not regard it as incompatible with cultural aristocracy. Indeed, he suggests that this democratization may in fact serve as a secure and durable foundation for the "cyclopean building" of culture in the future; it may turn out to be the ultimate "prophylactic measure" that makes it "henceforth impossible for the fruitful fields of culture to be destroyed overnight by wild and senseless torrents." Nietzsche does not speak as a committed democrat here; he conceives of democracy merely as a means, providing the protective walls and trellises required by the "supreme artist of horticulture" to carry out his more spiritual task. Such is not the understanding of the present-day advocates of democracy, he comments, who "loudly decree that the wall and the trellis *are* the end and final goal" and do not yet see "the gardener or fruit trees *for whose sake* the trellis exists" (*WS* 275).[29]

That Nietzsche regards democracy as a form of government that cannot stand on its own is made clear in a lengthy aphorism titled "Religion and Government," a subject that obviously recalls Rousseau's reflections on civil religion. Like Rousseau, Nietzsche sees religion as indispensable for the stability and legitimacy of the state, promoting a "calm, patient, trusting disposition in the masses." But unlike Rousseau (and in this regard, his disciple Tocqueville), Nietzsche does not think this complementary relationship between religion and the state can be sustained in a democratic government, where religion "is regarded as nothing but the instrument of the popular will, not as an Above in relation to a Below." In a democracy, everyone is entitled to hold their own opinions on religion, which deprives it of its unifying social function. Religion comes to be treated as a purely private affair, which initially strengthens it (as Tocqueville hoped) but eventually weakens it through the proliferation of sects and religious controversy. Gradually the state loses its sacred aura and the individual's relationship becomes grounded in utilitarian self-interest. Nietzsche worries that this will lead democratic citizens to devote themselves exclusively to their momentary self-interest and cease to engage "in undertakings that require quiet tending for decades or centuries if their fruits are to mature." This is why he calls modern democracy "the historical form of the *decay of the state*" (*HH* 472).

One of the most interesting aspects of this aphorism—an aspect that reveals his wholly experimental approach to politics—is that Nietzsche does not regard the decay of the state and the "liberation of the private person (I take care not to say: of the individual)" that goes along with it as necessarily a bad thing. As a result of this development, he writes, "a new page will be turned in the storybook of humanity in which there will be many strange tales to read and perhaps some good ones." He puts his trust in human prudence, self-interest, and ingenuity to fill the void left by the state: "If the state is no longer equal to the demands of these forces, then the last thing that will ensue is chaos; an invention more suited to their purpose than the state will gain victory over the state." Many an organizing social power has died out in the past—for example, the racial clan and the family—only to be superseded by something better suited to the historical moment. It can happen again (*HH* 472).

Nietzsche's careful distinction between democracy's "liberation of the private person" and the liberation of the genuine individual in this aphorism is especially noteworthy and serves as a segue to his other two middle works, *Daybreak* and *The Gay Science*, both of which (as we saw in chapter 3) are very much concerned with the achievement of genuine individuality.[30] In *Daybreak*, he decries how the modern glorification of work and industriousness

reflects a "fear of everything individual," preventing the young from developing into mature human beings (D 173, 178). And he considers the whole idea
of commercial culture to be anti-individualistic insofar as it demands that the
individual appraise everything "*according to the needs of the consumer*, not
according to his own needs" (D 175). But it is his remarks on the modern "cult
of philanthropy," which he associates with Schopenhauer, Mill, and above all
Herbert Spencer, that are most relevant to our concern here. This cult, which
seeks to eliminate all danger and suffering from life, threatens to lead to the
"abolition of the individual" and to reduce humanity to "*sand* . . . small, soft,
round, unending sand" (D 132, 174).[31] In an important note from 1880, Nietzsche elaborates on this reduction of humanity to sand and dull uniformity,
connecting it more explicitly with democracy:

> The more the feeling of unity with one's fellow humans gains the upper hand,
> the more human beings are made uniform, the more they will perceive all
> diversity as immoral. In this way, the sand of humanity necessarily comes into
> being: all are very similar, very small, very round, very accommodating, very
> boring. Christianity and democracy have done the most to drive humanity
> along the path toward sand. (*KSA* 9:3 [98])[32]

Nietzsche's concern about democracy's tendency to promote uniformity
and undermine individuality, which he shares with other nineteenth-century
thinkers like Tocqueville and Mill, is also found in *The Gay Science*. It is in
this work that he begins to refer to "herd men" versus individuals (GS 23;
see also 50, 116, 117). And he points out that the virtues praised by modern
society—obedience and industriousness, for example—benefit society but
harm the individual by transforming him into a "mere function of the whole"
and depriving him of "his noblest selfishness and strength for the highest care
of the self" (GS 21). The concern for the individual that Nietzsche expresses
here and in *Daybreak* reminds us that the "culture" he wants politics to serve
is not to be understood merely or even mainly in terms of great art but, rather,
in terms of the human beings we want to become.[33] The problem with much
modern romantic art is that it reflects a distorted understanding of the relationship between art and life, using the former as a compensation or escape
from the impoverished character of the latter (see RWB 4–5; AOM 169; WS
170; GS 86). Nietzsche, on the other hand, does not want us to restrict our
power of making things beautiful to art alone. As he puts it: "We want to be
poets of our life—first of all in the smallest, most everyday matters (GS 299).

In *The Gay Science*, Nietzsche also returns to the idea of an aristocracy
within democracy that he sketched in *Human, All Too Human*. He begins by
distinguishing between noble and common types of human being, claiming

that the latter has a healthy sense of its own advantage, considering "all noble, magnanimous feelings inexpedient and therefore incredible," while the noble type is more "unreasonable," sacrificing its interest and possibly its life for a passion—the passion for knowledge, for example (*GS* 3; see also 2, 10, 20, 31, 42). Precisely because of their unreasonableness, Nietzsche realizes that society cannot be made up entirely of such noble spirits. Society—and this includes democratic society—requires the "universal binding force of a faith." The "most select spirits bristle at this universal faith—the explorers of *truth* above all." But Nietzsche urges them to do everything in their power "to make sure that the faithful of the great shared faith stay together and continue their dance." He concedes that the exception always needs to be defended in democratic society, but he adds that it ought never to want to become the rule (*GS* 76; see also 55). How exactly this dual strategy works becomes somewhat clearer in Nietzsche's later works.

A New Kind of Aristocracy

In his later works, beginning with *Zarathustra*, Nietzsche develops the notion of an aristocracy coexisting with democracy that he first sketched in his middle-period writings. But these later works also exhibit a deeper engagement with politics than anything found in the free-spirit trilogy. This is reflected in Nietzsche's new, positive invocation of "great politics"—by which he does not mean the nationalist, socialist, or revolutionary politics he decried in his earlier writings. He is still very much against "great politics" in the Bismarckian sense that seeks to aggrandize and glorify the state; he remains concerned above all with culture, the spiritual enhancement of humanity. Nevertheless, he now places more emphasis on the problem of how to create and cultivate an aristocracy. In contradistinction to the free spirit, who "refrains from politics" (*HH* 438) and "silently goes through the world and out of the world" (*HH* 291), Nietzsche now becomes concerned with the problem of "ruling."

Nietzsche's new, more political orientation is already evident in the opening section of *Thus Spoke Zarathustra* (which is also the concluding section of the 1882 edition of *The Gay Science*). Zarathustra has lived for ten years as a free spirit in the solitude of his mountain cave acquiring knowledge. He now declares that he is sick of his (gay) wisdom, "like a bee that has gathered too much honey; I need hands outstretched to receive it. I would give away and distribute, until the wise among men find joy once again in their folly, and the poor in their riches" (*Z* 1, prologue, 1). Zarathustra's desire to give to others here contrasts sharply with the birdlike aloofness of the free spirit;

and his beneficence is further amplified in the next section, when he tells the saint that he loves man and brings him a gift (*Z* 1, prologue, 2). Zarathustra is no longer content merely to pursue knowledge; he seeks to redeem humanity from the terrible illness that afflicts it.

This illness, of course, is the nihilism that results from the death of God. The latter event, which Nietzsche evoked in all its terrifying reality in the aphorism on the madman in *The Gay Science* (125), is mentioned in *Zarathustra* merely as an aside after the eponymous hero's encounter with the saint. The event's potential consequences, however, are clearly depicted in Zarathustra's portrait of the contemptible "last man," who has no ideals or goals to strive or die for, is without love or longing, and seeks only "wretched contentment" (*Z* 1, prologue, 3, 5). This nihilistic goallessness receives political expression in the modern liberal state, which Zarathustra describes as the "coldest of all cold monsters." Unlike a "people," which is animated by a faith, a love, a table of good and evil above them, the liberal state merely guarantees peace and allows individuals to pursue happiness in their own way. Coldly, it hangs "a sword and a hundred appetites" over a people, but it does not specify a goal, a love, a value to give their lives meaning. Instead of a singular table of good and evil, the state accommodates all such tables and thereby becomes a "confusion of tongues of good and evil" (*Z* 1, "Idol").

With his talk of "peoples," though, Zarathustra does not mean to induce a romantic longing for the warmth of premodern community as an escape from the rootlessness of atomistic modern society. After defining a people in terms of a collective esteeming and valuing based on what they find difficult and have overcome through their "will to power," he comments that whereas at first peoples were the creators of values, now it is individuals; and he adds that "the individual is himself the most recent creation." In the past, "peoples hung a tablet of good over themselves"—the good conscience was identified with the community or herd, and the bad conscience with the ego. As we have seen, this is what differentiates the premodern morality of custom from modern moral sensibility (see *D* 9; *GS* 117). Therefore, Zarathustra speaks of going beyond the parochial morality of peoples to an overarching goal for humanity: "A thousand goals have there been so far, for there have been a thousand peoples. Only the yoke for the thousand necks is still lacking: the one goal is lacking. Humanity still has no goal" (*Z* 1, "Goals").

It is just such an overarching goal or ideal that Zarathustra aims to provide with his teaching about the *Übermensch*. The term *Übermensch* has, of course, been a source of considerable confusion, conjuring up images of a biological master race, not to mention a comic-book superhero. But for Nietzsche it refers primarily to the great human being, the human being with the most comprehensive soul that contains the greatest amount of diversity, opposition, and struggle without falling into disunity. Such great human beings, or *Übermenschen*, have been produced in the past by accident—Goethe, for example—but it is only now, after the death of God, that their creation becomes the self-conscious goal of humanity. Hitherto the goal of humanity has been to preserve the species at the expense of the individual. Now, Nietzsche writes, "the goal can be set higher": no longer merely to preserve mankind but to overcome it (*KSA* 10:7 [21, 238]). This is what Zarathustra means when he says that "man is something that shall be overcome" (*Z* 1, prologue, 3). The goal is to produce the most manifold and therefore most powerful individual. Instead of serving merely as a means, the individual is now to be made the "*fruit* of the communal entity" (*KSA* 10:7 [258]; see also *WP* 269).[34]

When Zarathustra presents his gift of the *Übermensch* to the people, he is met with laughter and derision. By the end of the prologue, he resolves never again to speak to the people at large but only to companions. It is to the search for the right companions with which to pursue the goal of the *Übermensch* that the rest of *Zarathustra* is devoted. This again points to the political dimension of the book. After his initial failure to persuade the masses, Zarathustra searches for the appropriate audience for his teaching, the relevant political community that can join with him to produce the *Übermensch*. In the end, he does not find it and realizes that he must create such a community; he must, in other words, become a founder. The tool with which he creates this community—a "new nobility"—is his teaching of the eternal recurrence, which Nietzsche frequently refers to in his notes as the "hammer" (see *KSA* 10:15 [48], 17 [69], 21 [6]; 11:25 [249], 27 [80, 82], 34 [78, 190]).

Nietzsche calls the idea of the eternal recurrence the "fundamental conception" of *Zarathustra* (*EH*, "Books: *Z*," 1). While this fecund idea has many different meanings and implications in the work, its primary political function is to serve as a selective principle and breeding agent for Zarathustra's "new nobility." In his notes from the time of *Zarathustra*, Nietzsche repeatedly refers to this winnowing and cultivating function of the eternal recurrence— how it destroys the sick and the weak and strengthens the healthy and the strong (*KSA* 10:7 [238], 10 [3], 16 [41]; 11:25 [211, 227, 249, 335]). It is precisely the suffering which the idea of the eternal recurrence will impose on his friends and companions that causes Zarathustra's agony in part 3 of *Zarathustra* and makes him reluctant to rule. As Nietzsche describes it in a revealing note: "Z3: the *transition* from *freethinker* and hermit *to having to rule* . . . The *most profound suffering* is not for [Zarathustra's] own sake, but rather for the sake of those *dearest* to him who bleed to death on account of his doctrine"

(*KSA* 10:16 [51]; see also [52]; *Z* 2, "Stillest Hour"). Part 3 constitutes Zarathustra's definitive farewell to the Blessed Isles and the apolitical complacency of
the free spirit and his gay science (*KSA* 10:15 [17, 21], 16 [49, 86, 89], 17 [53]). He
accepts the responsibility to rule and with it the necessity to impose suffering
on himself and others. In order to bring about the *Übermensch*, he must become hardhearted in his compassion for humanity: "the Roman Caesar with
the soul of Christ" (see *KSA* 10:3 [1], 44; 10 [25, 47]; 22 [3]; p. 621; 11:27 [60]).

Out of the process of differentiation, education, and cultivation instigated
by the idea of the eternal recurrence there emerges a "new nobility," which
Zarathustra describes in the important chapter "On Old and New Tablets."
That he thinks of this new nobility primarily in cultural terms is evident
from the fact that he sees it as a necessary antidote to the democratic rabble's
obliviousness of history, its abandonment of the spiritual inheritance of the
past, and its reinterpretation of "all that has been as a bridge to itself." "A *new
nobility* is needed," Zarathustra declares, "to be the adversary of all rabble"
and its despotism over history, thought, and culture. Paradoxically, he sees
the new nobility's recuperation of the past as contingent on its orientation
toward the future. This future orientation is what ultimately differentiates the
new nobility from the old: "O my brothers, your nobility should not look
backward but ahead! . . . Your *children's land* shall you love: this love shall be
your new nobility—the undiscovered land in the most distant sea. . . . In your
children you shall make up for being the children of your fathers: thus shall
you redeem all that is past" (*Z* 3, "Old and New Tablets," 11–12).[35]

The sections on the new nobility in *Zarathustra* make clear that despite
its more political orientation, the "politics" of the book remain remote from
politics in any sort of mundane sense, largely serving the interests of culture
and human greatness.[36] What makes *Zarathustra* political in *some* sense is
that it seeks to establish a structure or institution for ruling, albeit outside
the parameters of the state. In many ways, the aristocracy Nietzsche defends
in *Zarathustra* comes close to what he elsewhere describes as a church. "A
church," he writes in the fifth book of *The Gay Science*, "is above all a structure for ruling that secures the highest rank for the more spiritual human
beings and that *believes* in the power of spirituality to the extent of forbid-
ding itself the use of all the cruder instruments of force; and on this score the
church is under all circumstances a *nobler* institution than the state" (*GS* 358).
We will see that this description fits the aristocratic great politics of *Beyond
Good and Evil* as well.

In *Beyond Good and Evil*, Nietzsche gives perhaps the clearest statement of
what he understands an aristocratic society to be and why he finds it desirable:

Every enhancement of the type "man" so far has been the work of an aristocratic society—and it will be so again and again—a society that believes
in the long ladder of an order of rank and differences in value between man
and man, and that needs slavery in some sense or other. Without that *pathos
of difference* which grows out of the ingrained difference between strata—
when the ruling caste constantly looks afar and looks down upon subjects
and instruments and just as constantly practices obedience and command,
keeping down and keeping at a distance—that other, more mysterious pathos
could not have grown up either—the craving for an ever new widening of
distances within the soul itself, the development of ever higher, rarer, more
remote, further-stretching, more comprehensive states—in brief, simply the
enhancement of the type "man," the continual "self-overcoming of man," to
use a moral formula in a supra-moral sense. (*BGE* 257)

There are several things to note in this remarkable paragraph. First, the
goal of Nietzsche's aristocratic great politics is the "enhancement of the type
'man,'" a phrase he repeats twice. His concern is not with the happiness of a
few individuals but with what Daniel Conway calls the "fundamental question of political legislation: *what ought humankind to become?*"[37] Second,
there is nothing in the paragraph to suggest that Nietzsche is concerned to
establish aristocratic political institutions. For him, an aristocratic society is
understood to be a "society that believes in the long ladder of an order of
rank and differences in value between man and man," one that is characterized by the "pathos of distance" between strata. He mentions a "ruling caste"
and "subjects," but he does not specify what "ruling" means here; we will see
that, as in *Zarathustra*, he often uses this term in a sense that is not strictly
political but spiritual or cultural. None of this is to suggest that Nietzsche is
not defending aristocracy in some sense, only that he associates it primarily
with a system of values, an ethical and cultural outlook, rather than a literal
set of political institutions.[38]

Finally, and perhaps most troublingly, Nietzsche asserts that the enhancement of the type man requires "slavery in some sense or other." He is
even more explicit in the aphorism that follows number 257, stating that in
a healthy aristocracy an untold number of human beings must be sacrificed,
"reduced to incomplete human beings, to slaves, to instruments," for the sake
of the higher, more spiritual human beings (*BGE* 258). But as we have seen,
Nietzsche frequently speaks of "slavery" in a broad, even metaphorical sense.
In *Human, All Too Human*, he defined a slave as anyone "who does not have
two-thirds of his day to himself." And in a note from 1884, he claims that
slavery exists in every society, "whether you want it or not: for example, the
Prussian civil servant, the scholar, the monk" (*KSA* 11:25 [225]).

It is slavery in just this sort of sense that Nietzsche sees as gaining ground in Europe as a result of democracy. As he pointed out in the note from the time of *Daybreak* on how human beings are becoming increasingly uniform and sand-like, he observes in *Beyond Good and Evil* that "Europeans are becoming more similar to each other." They are more and more losing their national and class differences and becoming "increasingly independent of any *determinate* milieu that would like to inscribe itself for centuries in body and soul with the same demands." The process of democratization has created a "supra-national and nomadic type of man" who is eminently trainable and adaptable: "a useful, industrious, handy, multi-purpose herd animal." Nietzsche even claims that this democratic herd animal is "highly intelligent" and therefore a slave "in the subtlest sense" (*BGE* 242; *WP* 128).[39]

Unlike the earlier note on the growing uniformity and sand-like character of modern human beings, Nietzsche here sees an opportunity in the leveling and "dwarfing" tendencies of democracy. Indeed, he argues that there is a way in which the democratization of Europe is inadvertently creating conditions for a new and even more refined aristocracy: "The very same new conditions that will on average lead to the leveling and mediocritization of man . . . are likely to give birth to exceptional human beings of a most dangerous and attractive quality." The process of democratization thus serves as a training ground for "*slavery* in the subtlest sense" and for the "cultivation of *tyrants*" in the most spiritual sense (*BGE* 242; see also *WP* 128). Nietzsche even goes so far as to suggest that the development of a new aristocracy out of the democratic movement that creates the industrious, intelligent, and adaptable herd animal of Europe might constitute something like a justification of that movement: "And would it not be a kind of goal, redemption, and justification of the democratic movement itself if someone arrived who could make use of it—by finally producing beside its new and sublime development of slavery . . . a higher kind of dominating and Caesarian spirits who would stand upon it, maintain themselves by it, and elevate themselves through it?" (*WP* 954).

Nietzsche's reference to "justification" here raises the question of the normative status of his aristocratic great politics. A common criticism of Nietzsche's political philosophy—and one that bears directly on the comparison with Rousseau's—is that it lacks a concept of legitimacy. We have seen that Leiter makes some such criticism; and Ansell-Pearson considers Nietzsche's failure to address the question of political legitimacy, which for Rousseau was the "most important question of politics in the modern age," the biggest failure of his political thought.[40] But this criticism needs to be unpacked. If by "legitimacy" one means justified according to the self-interest of every individual, then Nietzsche clearly rejects it as a normative standard, along with the whole social-contract tradition that invokes it. Nevertheless, he just as clearly sees that the reduction of the vast majority of human beings to handy, industrious herd animals—slaves in his sense—requires some sort of justification, and the production and maintenance of a higher, more spiritual class of human beings that enhances the human species as a whole provides exactly that (*WP* 866, 898, 997). Justification here means serving some objectively higher goal or purpose. For the highest class as well as the various grades of human beings leading up to it—the "second- and third-rate talents" Nietzsche refers to in "Schopenhauer as Educator" (6:176)—such justification will be part of their subjective consciousness. As for the many who remain unconscious of the higher goal they serve, they can still be satisfied by the lower form of legitimacy that continues to operate in democratic political institutions.

Nietzsche frequently uses the image of base and superstructure (not in the Marxian sense) to describe the relationship between the few and the many. In *Human, All Too Human*, he spoke of democracy as providing the protective walls and trellises required by the "supreme artist of horticulture" to carry out his more spiritual task. In his later writings, he speaks of high culture as a "pyramid" that requires a broad, sturdy base to support the lofty spiritual achievements of the few (*AC* 57). In a late note, he puts it this way: "A high culture can stand only upon a broad base, upon a strong and healthy consolidated mediocrity" (*WP* 864; see also 890, 903). Why is such a broad base necessary? As Nietzsche suggested in *The Gay Science*, society requires the "universal binding force of a faith" to avoid destruction. The "most select spirits bristle at this universal binding force" and even delight in unreason and madness. For this reason, they must remain exceptions and never seek to become the rule (*GS* 76). He repeats this point in a later note, declaring that struggle "against great men [is] justified on economic grounds" because they are "dangerous, accidents, exceptions, tempests" who threaten to blow up "things slowly built and established" (*WP* 896; see also 864; *TI*, "Expeditions," 44). Nietzsche also indicates that the great human being requires the "opposition of the masses . . . a feeling of distance from them! he stands on them, he lives off them" (*WP* 866).

The base-superstructure analogy suggests something else about the relationship of the few to the many—namely, that the former do not "rule" or "lead" the latter in any sort of conventional political sense. This was intimated in the note quoted earlier about the superman and the last man existing side by side, "the one not meddling with the other" (*KSA* 10:7 [21]). But it is made explicit in many of the notes from Nietzsche's later years. In one, he writes:

"Main consideration: not to see the task of the higher species in leading the lower . . . but the lower as a base upon which the higher species performs its *own* tasks" (*WP* 901; see also 876). In another, he says of the "master race" excoriated by so many of Nietzsche's critics that it is not a race "whose sole task is to rule, but a race with its own sphere of life, with an excess of strength for beauty, bravery, culture, manners . . . a hothouse for strange and choice plants" (*WP* 898). The "masters of the earth" do not seek to impose their values on the herd—what could their values have to do with the needs of the herd (*WP* 287, 904)?—rather, they exist far apart from the herd, creating and self-legislating in their own sphere, working artistically on themselves as a means of enhancing the type "man" (*WP* 960).[41]

But what of Nietzsche's frequent favorable references to explicitly political artists and sculptors of men like Caesar and Napoleon, who seem to engage in much more than self-legislation? While it might seem difficult and even naïvely apologetic to deny that Nietzsche means to recommend the specific actions and policies of these political figures, there is actually a great deal of ambiguity in his scattered references to them. More often than not, both Napoleon and Caesar seem to function for Nietzsche as examples of the qualities needed by his philosophical creators and self-legislators—objectivity, discipline, hardness, and self-mastery—rather than as models for actual political action. Thus, in one place, he uses Caesar as a model of someone who combats the most pitiless and dreadful instincts with the "maximum of authority and discipline" toward himself (*TI*, "Expeditions," 38). Similarly, in *Beyond Good and Evil*, he mentions Caesar and Alcibiades as "beautiful expressions" of a nature that does not seek to end the war of opposing drives and value standards in the soul but to exercise a "real mastery and subtlety" in disciplining those drives and value standards (*BGE* 200; see also *TI*, "Expeditions," 49, on Goethe). Likewise, in his notes, Nietzsche compares Caesar and Napoleon to artists who "remain objective, hard, firm, severe in carrying through an idea" (*WP* 975). And the "Roman Caesar with Christ's soul" refers to the creator who possesses the "rulers' virtues that master even one's benevolence and pity" (*WP* 983; see also 905). As is often the case with Nietzsche, political examples function as metaphors for psychological and creative processes.[42]

With respect to the relative happiness of the aristocratic few and the democratic many, Nietzsche makes clear in his later writings, as he did in *Human, All Too Human*, that the former suffer more and bear a heavier burden than the latter: "Life becomes harder and harder as it approaches the *heights*—the coldness increases, the responsibility increases" (*A* 57). Virtually the whole of the second half of the chapter "What Is Noble" in *Beyond Good and Evil* is taken up with all-too-personal reflections on the vulnerability, corruption, isolation, and loneliness of the noble human being. Nietzsche writes there that "the corruption, the ruination of the higher men, of the souls of the stranger type, is the rule: it is terrible to have such a rule before one's eyes" (*BGE* 269); and "it almost determines the order of rank *how* profoundly human beings can suffer. . . . Profound suffering makes noble; it separates" (*BGE* 270). Nietzsche's notes tell much the same story: the great individual suffers more, bears more, and fails more than other human beings (*WP* 887, 965, 971, 987). At the other end of the spectrum, Nietzsche does not begrudge the mediocre their happiness: "For the mediocre it is happiness to be mediocre. . . . It would be quite unworthy of a more profound mind to see an objection in mediocrity as such. It is even the *prime* requirement for the existence of exceptions; a high culture is conditional upon it." For this reason, he considers it a duty for the exceptional human being to treat the mediocre with gentleness (*A* 57; see also *WP* 893).

Running throughout Nietzsche's reflections on the few and the many is the question of the order of rank. It is to the establishment of an order of rank that his aristocratic great politics is ultimately directed. This is what differentiates Nietzsche's moral-political position from the individualism with which it is often confused. He states the difference succinctly: "My philosophy aims at an ordering of rank: not an individualistic morality. The ideas of the herd should rule in the herd—but not reach out beyond it" (*WP* 287). The highest human beings have an entirely different system of values. The idea that what is right for one person is fair for another Nietzsche associates with liberals like John Stuart Mill. The idea of reciprocity advocated by the latter he considers a "piece of gross vulgarity: precisely that something I do may not and could not be done by another, that no balance is possible . . . that in a deeper sense one never gives back, because one is something unique and does only unique things—this fundamental conviction contains the cause of aristocratic segregation from the masses" (*WP* 926). In attacking the idea of reciprocity that is central to liberalism, Nietzsche is attacking not only Mill but also—perhaps even especially—Rousseau.

Connected with his rejection of individualistic morality, Nietzsche also displays an equivocal attitude toward freedom. As with individualistic morality, his doubts about freedom stem largely from the primacy of the order of rank in his political philosophy. As he puts it in a note: "My ideas do not revolve around the degree of freedom that is granted to the one or to the other or to all, but around the degree of *power* that the one or the other should exercise over others or over all, and to what extent a sacrifice of freedom, even enslavement, provides the basis for the emergence of a *higher type*" (*WP* 859). Nietzsche's most revealing remarks on freedom appear in *Twilight of the Idols*, where he spells out the sort of freedom he repudiates and the sort of freedom he embraces. To the former belongs the "claim to independence, to free development, to *laisser aller*" (*TI*, "Expeditions," 41). This is freedom as liberalism conceives of it, and it stands in opposition to the antiliberal "will to tradition, to authority, to centuries-long responsibility" (*TI*, "Expeditions," 39). Independence is only for the great-souled; small souls must obey (*WP* 984). As for the notion of freedom Nietzsche embraces, he defines it largely in terms of self-overcoming and will to power. It involves indifference to "hardship, toil, privation, even to life" and the ability to master one's instincts, especially the instinct for happiness. Such freedom is measured by the "resistance which has to be overcome, by the effort it costs to stay *aloft*. One would have to seek the highest type of free man where the greatest resistance is constantly being overcome: five steps from tyranny, near the threshold of the danger of servitude" (*TI*, "Expeditions," 38).

Nietzsche's equivocal attitude toward freedom brings us back once more to the comparison with Rousseau, for whom freedom is the central value of political life. Though Rousseau's conception of freedom is far from the simple *laisser-aller* or freedom to do what one pleases that Nietzsche attributes to liberalism, it nevertheless valorizes the independence of the individual and not being subject to the will of another. Such a conception of freedom is still too negative and individualistic for Nietzsche. He conceives of political community less in terms of individual liberty protected by the rule of law than in terms of the teleocratic pursuit of a goal that requires self-overcoming and social hierarchy to achieve. In a certain sense, his political philosophy is more communitarian than Rousseau's—uniting individuals, either consciously or unconsciously, in a common project to enhance the human type. It is also far more ambiguous and experimental, which is saying a great deal, given how elusive Rousseau's own political philosophy is. It is a temptation to think beyond the indeterminateness and aimlessness of liberalism and restore to politics an ennobling task.

6

Conclusion

From its inception, Enlightenment modernity has suffered from a certain narrowness and flatness in its conception of the human being. No matter how realistic, the rationally self-interested individual of Hobbes and Locke, driven by the desire for self-preservation and security of property, has always seemed an impoverished and uninspiring image of what it is to be a human being. It is to the critique of this image and the creation of a new one that speaks more profoundly to the depths and heights of the human soul that the moral and political thought of Jean-Jacques Rousseau and Friedrich Nietzsche is primarily addressed.

Rousseau was the first to diagnose the problem of the modern human being in terms of what he called the "bourgeois," a figure driven by the desire to be first in the race, obsessed with how he is perceived by others, and consequently dependent on others' opinions and alienated from himself. He also provided a penetrating genealogy of how *amour propre* in this deformed sense came to dominate human beings, putting the greatest emphasis on the institution of private property and the inequality to which it gave rise. From this genealogy came the indication of a solution—actually, several solutions—to the problem of human dependence, alienation, unhappiness, and unfreedom.

In the first instance, Rousseau argued that personal dependence could be overcome through the establishment of a legitimate political community based on democratic freedom and equality guaranteed by the rule of law. He did not underestimate the difficulties of establishing such a republic in the Europe of his day, and therefore he devised a private education that would allow the individual to achieve freedom from harmful personal dependence even in the absence of a legitimate republic. Central to this educational solution to the problem of the bourgeois was the family and especially the healthy interdependence of husband and wife. Finally, forsaken by fatherland and friends, Rousseau came up with the most radical solution to the problem of human self-alienation: that of the solitary walker who experiences the sweet sentiment of existence in communion with nature. This last solution has sometimes been taken as Rousseau's definitive solution to the problem of human self-alienation,[1] but in fact it is only one solution addressed to the most unpromising of circumstances. It is because human beings confront different circumstances more or less favorable to freedom and happiness that Rousseau came up with three different solutions instead of just one.

More than one hundred years later, Nietzsche picked up where Rousseau left off and leveled an equally devastating critique of the modern bourgeois. For him, though, this uninspiring figure was defined less by his alienating dependence on others than by his lack of direction, aim, or goal and the consequent meaninglessness or nihilism of his life. Nietzsche, too, provided a genealogy of the modern human being's corruption; but unlike Rousseau, he placed the blame not on inequality but on morality—especially Christian morality—which had reduced human beings to gentle and featureless herd animals. He encapsulated his difference with his great predecessor by claiming that whereas for Rousseau "this pitiable civilization is to blame for our *bad* morality," for him, Nietzsche, "our *good* morality is to blame for this pitiableness of our civilization" (*D* 163).

This difference in their respective critiques and genealogies of modernity's discontents led Nietzsche to a very different set of prescriptions to cure them. From the outset, he found the solution to our nihilistic predicament in exceptional human beings whose existence and creativity would restore a sense of purpose, greatness, and meaning to humanity. Unlike Rousseau, he sought a solution in culture rather than politics; but as I have insisted throughout this book, "culture" is not to be construed narrowly in terms of great art or literature but in terms of rich, creative human beings who enhance the species by opening up new possibilities for living. And what more than anything else is required to make such human beings possible, according to Nietzsche, is an overturning of Judeo-Christian morality and a radical revaluation of values based on the will to power. All of this is part of his deeply original doctrine of self-creation. And though such a doctrine is ultimately cultural in nature, he constructed a highly unorthodox, not to say ambiguous, politics grounded in the order of rank to support it.

Rousseau and Nietzsche, then, present us with two of the most important and influential critiques of Enlightenment modernity as well as two of the most original projects to reform it. I have detailed their respective critiques and moral-political reforms in the foregoing chapters, bringing out where they converge and where they diverge. It remains now to offer some sort of assessment. I begin with Rousseau.

In the twenty-first century, Rousseau continues to speak powerfully to our predicament in many different ways. His critique of the inauthentic bourgeois caught in the rat race, driven to compete with his fellows, and forced to conform to a societal image that bears no relation to who he really is, still resonates and captures a good deal of our modern alienation, anxiety, and unhappiness. Equally compelling is his tracing of these problems back to the root problem of social inequality; Marx and Rawls, in different ways, are both the heirs of Rousseau in this regard. Rousseau's solutions to the problems he identifies also retain a certain power. His republican vision of politics represents a serious attempt to overcome the personal dependence created by social inequality, balancing the claims of individual liberty and communal solidarity. His education of Emile results in a morally autonomous human being capable of resisting the alienating pressures of the modern world. And his depiction of the romantic relationship between Sophie and Emile presents an appealing image of human interdependence that counters the selfish individualism of modern bourgeois life.

This is not to say that Rousseau's solutions are without their difficulties. Some of these are practical, having to do with the implementation of his solutions. Ever since Benjamin Constant's 1819 lecture, "The Liberty of the Ancients Compared with That of the Moderns," it has been a commonplace that Rousseau's republican vision of politics works only for small, homogeneous states and is totally inapplicable to large, diverse modern states. Likewise, critics point out that it would be impractical to provide the sort of individual, cradle-to-marriage-bed education Emile receives to every child in society. I do not think these objections go very deep. They fail to grasp the imaginative character of Rousseau's philosophy and to appreciate his awareness of the very practical difficulties they highlight. More serious are the feminist criticisms of Rousseau's sexual politics. Though motivated by a legitimate desire to overcome the problem of individualism in modern society, the complementary role Rousseau assigns to women no longer strikes either men or women as satisfying the claims of equality or justice he seeks to uphold. Perhaps most serious, however, is that neither Rousseau's critique nor his solutions address the deepest problems of modernity. This becomes evident when they are compared with Nietzsche's.

Nietzsche's critique of modernity speaks directly to the most fundamental problem that afflicts us today: the absence of a civilizational purpose, goal, or meaning in a world in which God is dead and all metaphysical supports have

collapsed. In such a situation, everything that looks like a solution in Rousseau's view—liberal democracy, freedom from personal dependence, social
equality, romantic love, and even the solitary enjoyment of the sweet sentiment of existence—only exacerbates the fundamental problem of modern
aimlessness and nihilism, according to Nietzsche. What we need is a new goal
that enables human beings to overcome themselves and their petty desires
for comfortable self-preservation, a goal that will lead to a "*new greatness* of
man, a new untrodden way to his enhancement" (*BGE* 212). Nietzsche finds
such a goal in the production of a superior human being—an *Übermensch*, if
you will—who constantly overcomes himself, who experiments with himself,
who creates himself; a human being who experiences more, suffers more, and
ultimately enjoys more as a result of his creative existence and who understands that the experiencing, suffering, and enjoying are all interconnected
and therefore would not sacrifice any of them. This is not the morally autonomous human being of Rousseau, much less Kant. It is a human being
who embodies a rich conception of individuality that makes Mill's conception look psychologically crude and ethically conventional by comparison.

Nietzsche's doctrine of self-creation yields an understanding of the relation between the sexes and a vision of politics that are both suggestive and
problematic. With respect to the first, Nietzsche follows Rousseau in stressing the differences between the sexes and their complementarity. But unlike
Rousseau, he does not see this complementarity as being in the service of the
moralization or socialization of humanity; rather, he sees it as giving rise to a
creative antagonism that promotes the enhancement of the species. Though
some feminist scholars have argued that there is a disconnect between Nietzsche's nonegalitarian views on men and women and the nonessentialist
thrust of his philosophy as a whole, we have seen that those views are actually quite consistent with his general intention to deepen the differences and
distances between types of human being. More specifically, these differences
correspond to the dialectical relationship between science and art, truth and
appearance, depth and surface, seriousness and play that runs through his
philosophy. The compatibility of Nietzsche's understanding of the relation
between the sexes with his philosophy as a whole does not, however, render
it any more acceptable to contemporary notions. Though it raises thought-
provoking questions about the standard liberal-egalitarian understanding of
the relation between the sexes, Nietzsche's image of woman remains one of
the most perplexing aspects of his reimagination of the human.

Nietzsche's aristocratic politics are not so easily dismissed. By restoring
a common purpose to politics, they attempt to overcome the individualism
and aimlessness of liberalism in general and Rousseau's republicanism in

particular. Insofar as they reflect a set of values rather than a body of political institutions, Nietzsche's aristocratic politics are also perfectly compatible with democracy; the latter serves as a broad and sturdy base comprising the mediocre many to enable the aristocratic few to engage in the experiments of self-creation that serve not only their own needs but enhance the species as a whole and ultimately redeem democracy itself. Nevertheless, as suggestive as Nietzsche's aristocratic politics are, it is never entirely clear how they would actually work. The idea of a set of aristocratic values that is completely divorced from the surrounding democratic political institutions seems highly problematic from a sociological point of view. And the tremendous gulf between the mediocre many and the aristocratic few would seem not only to render the existence and influence of the latter quite precarious but also to destroy the possibility of any sort of common life. Finally, Nietzsche's preoccupation with culture and the cultivation of the individual, which he shares with the whole *Bildung* tradition of German thought going back to Humboldt and Goethe, leads him to neglect politics in the mundane, institutional, and utterly necessary sense.[2] We who live in the shadow of the atrocities of the twentieth century and the looming crises of the twenty-first do not have that luxury.

By pointing out these difficulties in their projects, I in no way mean to diminish the significance of Rousseau and Nietzsche for our moral and political self-understanding. The guiding premise of this book has been that they are necessary authors for precisely such self-understanding; they are the most important creators and explorers of the late-modern moral and political imagination. We do not go to Rousseau and Nietzsche primarily for answers, but because they ask the right questions and put their fingers on real problems and weaknesses in the dispensation of Enlightenment modernity. Their reformist projects are not so much blueprints to be executed as invitations to imagine alternatives to what we currently assume to be fixed and unalterable reality. They use their unmatched literary gifts to shake us out of our dogmatic slumber and inspire us to think differently, more imaginatively, and more boldly. Like the greatest writers, they enrich our understanding of what it is to be a human being. They keep before us the image of the human, when everything around us conspires to erase it.

Notes

Chapter 1

1. Henry Maine, *Ancient Law* (New York: Henry Holt, 1906), 84.

2. Leo Strauss, "The Living Issues of German Postwar Philosophy," in Heinrich Meier, *Leo Strauss and the Theological Political Problem* (Cambridge: Cambridge University Press, 2006), 137. See also Allan Bloom, *Love and Friendship* (New York: Simon & Schuster, 1993), 157.

3. Karl Löwith, *From Hegel to Nietzsche: The Revolution in Nineteenth-Century Thought*, trans. David E. Green (New York: Holt, Rinehart and Winston, 1964), 235. For other discussions of the problem of the bourgeois in Rousseau's thought, see Allan Bloom, introduction to *Emile, or On Education*, trans. Bloom (New York: Basic Books, 1979), 4–6; Allan Bloom, "Rousseau's Critique of Liberal Constitutionalism," in *The Legacy of Rousseau*, ed. Nathan Tarcov and Clifford Orwin (Chicago: University of Chicago Press, 1997), 146–47; Arthur Melzer, *The Natural Goodness of Man: On the System of Rousseau's Thought* (Chicago: University of Chicago Press, 1990), 63–65; Werner Dannhauser, "The Problem of the Bourgeois," in *The Legacy of Rousseau*, ed. Clifford Orwin and Nathan Tarcov (Chicago: University of Chicago Press, 1997), 3–8; and Stephen Smith, *Modernity and Its Discontents: Making and Unmaking the Bourgeois from Machiavelli to Bellow* (New Haven: Yale University Press, 2016), 16–17.

4. Pierre Manent, *Modern Liberty and Its Discontents*, ed. and trans. Daniel J. Mahoney and Paul Seaton (Lanham, MD: Rowman & Littlefield, 162–63). In emphasizing this reformist aspect of Rousseau's philosophy, my interpretation could not be further from the pessimistic interpretation of Judith Shklar, who calls Rousseau "one of the greatest of the nay-sayers," whose only interest was "to judge and condemn without giving any thought to programs of action" (*Men and Citizens: A Study of Rousseau's Social Theory* [1969; Cambridge: Cambridge University Press, 1985], 1).

5. Charles Taylor, *The Ethics of Authenticity* (Cambridge, MA: Harvard University Press, 1992), 26; Taylor, *Sources of the Self: The Making of the Modern Identity* (Cambridge, MA: Harvard University Press, 1989), 363.

6. Taylor, *Sources of the Self*, 447–55.

7. On Nietzsche's relationship to Voltaire and Rousseau, see Peter Heller, "Nietzsche in His Relation to Voltaire and Rousseau," in *Studies in Nietzsche and the Classical Tradition*, ed. James C. O'Flaherty, Timothy F. Sellner, and Robert M. Helm (Chapel Hill: University of North Carolina Press, 1979): 109–33.

8. See, for example, Keith Ansell-Pearson, *Nietzsche Contra Rousseau: A Study of Nietzsche's Moral and Political Thought* (Cambridge: Cambridge University Press, 1991), 21, 25–31, 49–51.

9. W. D. Williams, *Nietzsche and the French: A Study of the Influence on Nietzsche's French Reading on His Thought and Writing* (Oxford: Blackwell, 1952), xxi; see also 127–29. In a similar vein, Jacques Derrida asks, "Is it not remarkable that Nietzsche . . . should have hated Rousseau?" Derrida, *Of Grammatology*, corrected ed., trans. Gayatri Chakravorty Spivak (Baltimore: Johns Hopkins University Press, 1997), 342n18.

10. W. D. Williams, *Nietzsche and the French*, 169–70.

11. Leo Strauss, *Rousseau*, transcript for "Seminar on Rousseau (1962): Rousseau, Autumn 1962," ed. Jonathan Marks, 353, https://leostrausscenter.uchicago.edu/rousseau-autumn-1962/. Other scholars who emphasize the affinities between Rousseau and Nietzsche include Melzer, *Natural Goodness of Man*, 287–88; Laurence Cooper, *Eros in Plato, Rousseau, and Nietzsche: The Politics of Infinity* (University Park, PA: Penn State University Press, 2008); and Heinrich Meier, *On the Happiness of the Philosophic Life: Reflections on Rousseau's Rêveries in Two Books*, trans. Robert Berman (Chicago: University of Chicago Press, 2016), taken together with his *Nietzsches Vermächtnis: "Ecce Homo" und "Der Antichrist": Zwei Bücher über Natur und Politik* (München: C. H. Beck, 2019).

12. See Löwith: "As a critic of the existing world, Nietzsche was to the nineteenth century what Rousseau had been to the eighteenth. He is a Rousseau in reverse: a Rousseau, because of his equally penetrating criticism of European civilization, and in reverse, because his critical standards are the exact opposite of Rousseau's ideal man" (*From Hegel to Nietzsche*, 260). Other scholars who bring out important differences as well as the similarities between Rousseau and Nietzsche include Ansell-Pearson, *Nietzsche Contra Rousseau*; Katrin Froese, *Rousseau and Nietzsche: Toward an Aesthetic Morality* (Lanham, MD: Lexington Press, 2001); and Richard Velkley, "The Tension in the Beautiful: On Culture and Civilization in Rousseau and German Philosophy," in *The Legacy of Rousseau*, ed. Nathan Tarcov and Clifford Orwin (Chicago: University of Chicago Press, 1997), 65–86.

13. Taylor's judgment on the relative merits of Rousseau and Nietzsche is never fully or explicitly spelled out. In *Sources of the Self* and *The Ethics of Authenticity*, he associates Rousseau with several of the constituent goods of modern moral identity—for example, the affirmation of ordinary life in the form of sentiment and family life, and inwardness in the form of conscience. And though he credits Nietzsche with contributing to the development of the "subtler languages" of the creative imagination in the nineteenth century, he also worries about Nietzsche's encouragement of the slide to subjectivism and nihilism that culminates in Derrida's and Foucault's postmodern philosophies. Above all, he cannot follow Nietzsche in his rejection of the modern ethic of benevolence that seeks to reduce human suffering. Similarly, in Taylor, "The Immanent Counter-Enlightenment," in *Canadian Political Philosophy*, ed. Ronald Beiner and Wayne Norman (Oxford: Oxford University Press, 2001), 386–99, while he agrees with much of Nietzsche's critique of the primacy of life in the exclusive humanism of the seventeenth and eighteenth centuries, he does not accept the valorization of suffering, death, and even violence that Nietzsche's antihumanism seems to encourage.

14. See Ansell-Pearson, *Nietzsche Contra Rousseau*, 34, 38–43, 98, 200–24, 229. See also Keith Ansell-Pearson, *An Introduction to Nietzsche as Political Thinker* (Cambridge: Cambridge University Press, 1994), 39–44, 95–97, 148–55, 161–62.

15. See Steven Pinker, *Enlightenment Now: The Case for Reason, Science, Humanism, and Progress* (New York: Viking, 2018).

16. Melzer, *Natural Goodness of Man*, xii; see also 287–88. For Melzer, as for Strauss (see *Natural Right and History* [Chicago: University of Chicago Press, 1953], 252–53), this is not necessarily a good thing. See also Froese, who claims that "Rousseau and Nietzsche are virulent critics of modernity and at the same time remain two of its most passionate defenders" (*Rousseau and Nietzsche*, 177)

17. I have made something like this argument in Paul Franco, *Nietzsche's Enlightenment: The Free-Spirit Trilogy of the Middle Period* (Chicago: University of Chicago Press, 2011).

18. Arthur Melzer, "Rousseau and the Modern Cult of Sincerity," in *The Legacy of Rousseau*, ed. Nathan Tarcov and Clifford Orwin (Chicago: University of Chicago Press, 1997), 292.

19. Daniel Bell, *The Cultural Contradictions of Capitalism*, 20th anniversary ed. (New York: Basic Books, 1996), 19, 120–45; Allan Bloom, *The Closing of the American Mind: How Higher Education Has Failed Democracy and Impoverished the Souls of Today's Students* (New York: Simon and Schuster, 1987), 141–216.

20. Taylor, *Ethics of Authenticity*, 23.

21. Ansell-Pearson puts this point well: "To be heirs of the writings of Rousseau and Nietzsche is to be the inheritors of two of the most powerful and disturbing critiques of civilization that the modern period has produced. Indeed, I would go so far as to contend that part of what it means to be a modern man or woman . . . is to take up the task of engaging in some kind of confrontation (*Auseinandersetzung*) with the paradoxical and ambiguous teachings of Rousseau and Nietzsche" (*Nietzsche Contra Rousseau*, 1).

Chapter 2

1. In his fine book *Rousseau's Critique of Inequality: Reconstructing the "Second Discourse"* (Cambridge: Cambridge University Press, 2014), Frederick Neuhouser seems to accept uncritically that growing social inequality is the fundamental problem of our age.

2. Leo Strauss and the scholars who follow him closely put heavy emphasis on this historical aspect of Rousseau's conception of human nature; see Leo Strauss, *Natural Right and History*, 271–74; Strauss, "Three Waves of Modernity," in *An Introduction to Political Philosophy: Ten Essays*, ed. Hilail Gildin (Detroit: Wayne State University Press, 1989), 89–90; Marc Plattner, *Rousseau's State of Nature: An Interpretation of the "Discourse on Inequality"* (Dekalb: Northern Illinois University Press, 1979), 51; and Melzer, *The Natural Goodness of Man*, 49–50. Among non-Straussian interpreters who emphasize this historical aspect, see Asher Horowitz, *Rousseau, Nature, and History* (Toronto: University of Toronto Press, 1987), 46–49.

3. Several scholars have raised doubts regarding Rousseau's claims about the purely conjectural character of his account of the state of nature; see Strauss, *Natural Right and History*, 267n32; Plattner, *Rousseau's State of Nature*, 17–25; Heinrich Meier, "*The Discourse on the Origin and Foundations of Inequality among Men*: On the Intention of Rousseau's Most Philosophical Work," *Interpretation* 16 (1988–89): 218–19; and Eve Grace, "Built on Sand: Moral Law in Rousseau's *Second Discourse*," in *The Challenge of Rousseau*, ed. Grace and Christopher Kelly (Cambridge University Press, 2013), 171–73. Victor Gourevitch has convincingly countered these arguments in "Rousseau's Pure State of Nature," *Interpretation* 16 (1988–89): 23–59, concluding that Rousseau's "quest for the putative state of nature is a thought-experiment, a systematic 'bracketing' of all artifice and of all moral needs and relations. . . . It is an exercise in 'analysis,'" the aim of which is not to establish a historical fact but "to extrapolate to the limits or conditions of humanity" (37). See also Alessandro Ferrara, *Modernity and Authenticity: A Study of the Social and Ethical Thought of Jean-Jacques Rousseau* (Albany, NY: SUNY Press, 1993), 30–31.

4. In an effort to sustain their strictly scientific, materialist, and antidualist reading of Rousseau, Strauss and his followers turn Rousseau's hesitations here into full-fledged doubts; see Strauss, *Natural Right and History*, 264–66; Plattner, *Rousseau's State of Nature*, 41–46; and Grace, "Built on Sand," 182–89.

5. Allan Bloom describes Rousseau's teaching on pity in *Emile* as "hardheaded softness" (introduction to *Emile*, 18).

6. Strauss uses this phrase to encapsulate the meaning of the Rousseauian doctrine of man's natural goodness (see *Natural Right and History*, 271).See also Victor Gourevitch's criticism of this aspect of Strauss's interpretation of Rousseau in "On Strauss and Rousseau," in *The Challenge of Rousseau*, ed. Eve Grace and Christopher Kelly (Cambridge: Cambridge University Press, 2013), 147–67.

7. On how the pure state of nature serves as a positive model or standard for Rousseau's moral and political theory, see Gourevitch, "Rousseau's Pure State of Nature," 56–59; John Scott, "The Theodicy of the *Second Discourse*: The 'Pure State of Nature' and Rousseau's Political Thought," *American Political Science Review* 86 (1992), 697, 708–9; and Neuhouser, *Rousseau's Critique of Inequality*, ch. 3. Strauss, too, argues that the state of nature serves as a positive standard for Rousseau's moral and political theory (*Natural Right and History*, 282–84); but as Gourevitch points out, he tends to reduce the normative principles articulated by the state of nature to the lowest common denominator of self-preservation rather than freedom ("On Strauss and Rousseau," 159–61). In "Built on Sand," Grace denies that Rousseau's pure state of nature has any normative value or relation to moral law.

8. On the contradiction of society as the source of human vice, see Melzer, *Natural Goodness of Man*, 53–54, 57–58, 69–85.

9. See Melzer, *Natural Goodness of Man*, 70n. Many commentators note that Rousseau does not regard *amour propre* as simply bad but ascribes to it a crucial positive role in love, patriotism, and other higher activities; see esp. N. J. H. Dent, *Rousseau: An Introduction to His Psychological, Social and Political Theory* (Oxford: Basil Blackwell, 1988); Laurence Cooper, *Rousseau, Nature, and the Problem of the Good Life* (University Park, PA: Penn State University Press, 1999), ch. 4; and Frederick Neuhouser, *Rousseau's Theodicy of Self-Love: Evil, Rationality, and the Drive for Recognition* (Oxford: Oxford University Press, 2008). Both Dent and Neuhouser cite a note in Bloom's edition of *Emile* (483–84) as a prominent example of the mistaken, wholly negative view of *amour propre* (see Dent, *Rousseau*, 53–54; Neuhouser, *Rousseau's Theodicy of Self-Love*, 15). It is hard to believe, though, that the translator of *Emile* would be unaware of the positive potential of *amour propre*, and indeed he was not; see Bloom, *Love and Friendship*, 51–52; and Bloom, "Rousseau's Critique of Liberal Constitutionalism," 148.

10. The concept of the "feeling of power" (*Machtgefühl* or *Gefühl der Macht*) suddenly comes to the fore in Nietzsche's notes from the summer of 1880, when he was writing *Daybreak* (see *KSA* 9:4 [170–254]; see also [284, 299, 301, 314, 322]).

11. On the founding of states by men of power, see also *HH* 99. Here Nietzsche sides with Machiavelli and Hegel against the social contract theorists; see G. W. F. Hegel, "The German Constitution," in *Hegel's Political Writings*, trans. T. M. Knox (Oxford: Clarendon Press, 1964), 217–23. See also Daniel Conway, "How We Became What We Are: Tracking the 'Beasts of Prey,'" in *On the Genealogy of Morals: Critical Essays*, ed. Christa Davis Acampora (Lanham, MD: Rowman and Littlefield, 2006).

12. Here I disagree with Paul Cantor, who claims that "Nietzsche's account of the slave revolt in morality fails to explain exactly how the slaves manage to pull off this trick" (*Shakespeare's Roman Trilogy: The Twilight of the Ancient World* [Chicago: University of Chicago Press, 2017],

105). See also Catherine Zuckert, who asks, "How could the slaves ever have convinced their lion-like masters to adopt a pacific, self-effacing morality?" ("Nietzsche on the Origin and Development of the Distinctively Human," *Polity* 16 [1983]: 55).

13. Neuhouser, *Rousseau's Critique of Inequality*, 208–9.

14. Obviously, this is a question on which people will differ. In *Rousseau's Critique of Inequality*, Neuhouser makes a strong case for the contemporary relevance of Rousseau's critique and genealogy of modern society (see esp. ch. 5). Neuhouser also seems to point to Rawls as the solution to the problems Rousseau identifies.

Chapter 3

1. In his classic treatment of the subject, *Sincerity and Authenticity* (Cambridge, MA: Harvard University Press, 1972), Lionel Trilling makes a distinction between the two ideals: while the former ultimately serves a moral and social purpose—the individual should be true to himself in order to avoid being (in Polonius's famous words) "false to any man"—the latter assumes a more subversive and adversarial relationship to one's surrounding society. Trilling associates Rousseau with the ideal of sincerity and Nietzsche with the ideal of authenticity.

2. Bell, *The Cultural Contradictions of Capitalism*, 19, 120–45; Bloom, *The Closing of the American Mind*, 141–216. Arthur Melzer seems to take a similarly critical position with respect to the modern "obsession with sincerity"—which he does not distinguish from authenticity ("Rousseau and the Modern Cult of Sincerity," in *The Legacy of Rousseau*, ed. Nathan Tarcov and Clifford Orwin [Chicago: University of Chicago Press, 1997]). On Rousseau's "new ethic of sincerity and spontaneity," see Melzer, *Natural Goodness of Man*, 21–22. Trilling, too, is quite critical of the ideal of authenticity—as distinguished from sincerity—especially in the form defended by psychoanalytic writers like Norman O. Brown, R. D. Laing, and Michel Foucault, who equate insanity with authenticity (*Sincerity and Authenticity*, 167–72).

3. Taylor, *Ethics of Authenticity*, 23. Ferrara also defends the ideal of authenticity against "neoconservative" critiques by David Riesman, Philip Rieff, Daniel Bell, Christopher Lasch, and Richard Sennett (*Modernity and Authenticity: A Study of the Social and Ethical Thought of Jean-Jacques Rousseau* (Albany, NY: SUNY Press, 1989), x, 7–24).

4. Here I differ with Melzer, who states that for Rousseau, "the true self is not the moral self" ("Rousseau and the Modern Cult of Sincerity," 289); as well as Ferrara, who differentiates authenticity from moral autonomy, associating the former with the Freudian id and the latter with the repressive ego (*Modernity and Authenticity*, 83–90, 93–109).

5. Again, see Löwith on Rousseau's epoch-making statement of the "problem of the bourgeois" (*From Hegel to Nietzsche*, 235).

6. Cooper argues that the sentiment of existence, not happiness, is the sovereign good for Rousseau (*Rousseau, Nature, and the Problem of the Good Life*, 19–29). In this chapter, I treat the two ideas as practically inseparable, the sentiment of existence—the feeling and awareness of being alive—encapsulating what Rousseau means by happiness.

7. Contrary to Ernst Cassirer's classic interpretation of Rousseau as a proto-Kantian thinker in *The Question of Jean-Jacques Rousseau*, trans. Peter Gay (New York: Columbia University Press, 1954).

8. *On the Basis of Morality*, trans. E. F. J. Payne (Indianapolis: Hackett, 1999), 183.

9. On the unity of Rousseau's conception of happiness in the various desirable lives he presents, from the virtuous citizen to the bourgeois householder and solitary dreamer, see Stephen

Salkever, "Rousseau and the Concept of Happiness," *Polity* 11 (1978): 27–45. For insightful discussions of the sentiment of existence, see Melzer, *Natural Goodness of Man*, 33–45; Cooper, *Rousseau, Nature, and the Problem of the Good Life*, 29–40; Cooper, *Eros in Plato, Rousseau, and Nietzsche*, ch. 5; Eve Grace, "The Restlessness of 'Being': Rousseau's Protean Sentiment of Existence," *History of European Ideas* 27 (2001): 133–51; and Meier, *On the Happiness of the Philosophic Life*, ch. 4.

10. Strauss does not think Rousseau regarded it as a defect; he argues that for Rousseau, the highest life is that of the solitary dreamer (*Natural Right and History*, 263, 290–94). See also Meier, *On the Happiness of the Philosophic Life*.

11. See, for example, Cassirer, *The Question of Jean-Jacques Rousseau*; and Andrew Levine, *The Politics of Autonomy: A Kantian Reading of Rousseau's "Social Contract"* (Amherst, MA: University of Massachusetts Press, 1976).

12. For illuminating discussions of Rousseau's account of compassion or pity, see Clifford Orwin, "Rousseau and the Discovery of Political Compassion," in *The Legacy of Rousseau*, ed. Nathan Tarcov and Clifford Orwin (Chicago: University of Chicago Press, 1997), 296–320; Richard Boyd, "Pity's Pathologies: Rousseau and the Limits of Democratic Compassion," *Political Theory* 32 (2004): 519–46; and Jonathan Marks, "Rousseau's Discriminating Defense of Compassion," *American Political Science Review* 101 (2007): 727–39.

13. See Jonathan Marks, "The Divine Instinct? Rousseau and Conscience," *Review of Politics* 68 (2006), 566–67, 581–84 (quotation on 566); Melzer, *Natural Goodness of Man*, 30n1; Arthur Melzer, "The Origin of the Counter-Enlightenment: Rousseau and the New Religion of Sincerity," *American Political Science Review* 90 (1996) 352–58; Clifford Orwin, "Rousseau on the Sources of Ethics," in *Instilling Ethics*, ed. Norma Thompson (Lanham, MD: Rowman and Littlefield, 2000), 69–72; and Meier, *On the Happiness of the Philosophic Life*, 266–73.

14. Many scholars doubt that the faith professed by the Savoyard vicar in *Emile* simply coincides with Rousseau's own; see Leo Strauss, "On the Intention of Rousseau," in *Hobbes and Rousseau: A Collection of Essays*, ed. M. Cranston and R. S. Peters (Garden City, NY: Anchor, 1972), 285–87; Shklar, *Men and Citizens*, 108–23; Bloom, introduction to *Emile*, 20; Bloom, *Love and Friendship*, 71–86; Peter Emberley, "Rousseau Versus the Savoyard Vicar," *Interpretation* 14 (1986): 299–329; Melzer, *Natural Goodness of Man*, 30n1; Melzer, "Origin of the Counter-Enlightenment," 355; Jeffrey Macy, "God Helps Those Who Help Themselves," *Polity* 24 (1992): 615–32; Marks, "The Divine Instinct?," 566; and Meier, *On the Happiness of the Philosophic Life*, ch. 2 and Second Book.

15. There are several factors that make it difficult to answer this question definitively. In the first place, it is hard to ferret out Rousseau's own religious beliefs apart from what he has written. Second, even the vicar does not make dogmatic claims about the objective truth of his faith but, rather, bases it on psychological need and subjective sentiment: "Doubt about the things it is important for us to know is too violent a state for the human mind, which does not hold out in this state for long. It decides in spite of itself one way or the other and prefers to be deceived rather than to believe nothing" (*E* 268; see also LV 242–43). In the end, the vicar (and Rousseau) offers a theology that grows out of and supports the demands of morality. In this way, his profession of faith anticipates the moral theology of Kant. And like Kant, Rousseau does not seem to doubt the truth of the morality grounded in conscience that the theology is meant to support.

16. Cooper, *Rousseau, Nature, and the Problem of the Good Life*, 84–85, makes a similar point.

17. On the interdependence of reason and conscience, see Ferrara, *Modernity and Authenticity*, 77; Joseph Reisert, *Jean-Jacques Rousseau: A Friend of Virtue* (Ithaca, NY: Cornell University

Press, 2003), 20–21, 118–20; and Denise Schaeffer, *Rousseau on Education, Freedom, and Judgment* (University Park, PA: Penn State University Press, 2014), 108–24. This emphasis on the role of reason in Rousseau's ethics contrasts with Melzer's view of Rousseau's "extreme denigration of reason" and "cult of feeling" (*Natural Goodness of Man*, 44–45). This latter view of Rousseau's romantic antirationalism goes all the way back to Irving Babbitt (*Rousseau and Romanticism* [Boston: Houghton Mifflin, 1919], 77–79, 114–79, 217–19, 353–55).

18. But compare Kant on moral self-esteem, self-approbation, and respect in the *Critique of Practical Reason*, ed. Mary Gregor (Cambridge: Cambridge University Press, 1997), 62–75, 96.

19. In his letter to D'Offreville, Rousseau is careful to say that virtue does not always or automatically lead to happiness: "Above all, Sir, consider that one should never strain things beyond the truth, nor confuse, as the Stoics did, happiness with virtue. . . . It is false that the good are all happy in this world" (LO 264). Nevertheless, one cannot be happy without virtue (see *J* 300).

20. See Melzer, "Rousseau and the Modern Cult of Sincerity," 286–89. See also Jean Starobinski, *Jean-Jacques Rousseau: Transparency and Obstruction*, trans. Arthur Goldhammer (Chicago: University of Chicago Press, 1988), 19, 63–64, 198–200.

21. Again, contrary to Ferrara's sharp distinction between authenticity and moral autonomy (*Modernity and Authenticity*, 83–90, 93–109).

22. In *Rousseau and Nietzsche*, Froese sees self-creation as the "cornerstone" of both Rousseau's and Nietzsche's conceptions of selfhood (1–2). But as I try to show in this and the following section, self-creation in the radical Nietzschean sense doesn't really apply to the moral conception of the self found in Rousseau. Much has been written on Nietzsche's doctrine of self-creation, from Alexander Nehamas's pathbreaking discussion in *Nietzsche: Life as Literature* (Cambridge, MA: Harvard University Press, 1985) to Brian Leiter's denial that the doctrine can be taken literally in the light of Nietzsche's fatalism, in "The Paradox of Fatalism and Self-Creation in Nietzsche," in *Willing and Nothingness: Schopenhauer as Nietzsche's Educator*, ed. Christopher Janaway (Oxford: Clarendon Press, 1998), 217–57. I take up the scholarship on this question in Paul Franco, "Becoming Who You Are: Nietzsche on Self-Creation," *Journal of Nietzsche Studies* 49 (2018): 52–77, on which much of this section and the following two are based.

23. Shklar articulates the difference between Rousseau and the nineteenth-century tradition of romantic individuality with characteristic bluntness: "With Everyman as his deepest concern, Rousseau remained closer to Locke's individualism than to that later liberalism which shared the romantic passion for individuality. Rousseau was not in the least interested in the unique personality crushed by mediocrity, nor in the creative imagination stifled by common sense, nor again in the artist-hero persecuted by the philistines. The quite undistinguished universal man, who only wants felicity and who only experiences suffering claimed all his sympathy" (*Men and Citizens*, 54).

24. James Conant, "Nietzsche's Perfectionism: A Reading of *Schopenhauer as Educator*," in *Nietzsche's Postmoralism: Essays on Nietzsche's Prelude to Philosophy's Future*, ed. Richard Schacht (Cambridge: Cambridge University Press, 2001), nicely brings out this "exemplary" function of Nietzsche's great human beings.

25. Nehamas, *Nietzsche: Life as Literature*, 182.

26. Ruth Abbey raises this question in *Nietzsche's Middle Period* (Oxford: Oxford University Press, 2000), 32–33.

27. It is important to bear in mind here that the word *science* (*Wissenschaft*) in German is not limited to the natural sciences but includes the human sciences (*Geisteswissenschaften*) such as history, philology, and philosophy. Nietzsche likewise uses *physics* in an extended or inclusive

sense, similar to Walter Bagehot in *Physics and Politics* (1872), a book with which Nietzsche was very familiar. In a later note from the winter of 1883/84, Nietzsche clarifies his understanding of the relationship between science and self-creation. On the one hand, he reiterates the negative, purifying role science plays: "Science—this has been up to now the elimination of the complete confusion of things by means of hypotheses which 'explain' everything. . . . Morality was just this sort of *simplification*: it taught that humans were *recognizable, familiar.*—Now we have destroyed morality—we have become *completely obscure* to ourselves! I know that I know nothing of *myself. Physics* reveals itself as an *act of charity* for the emotions." On the other hand, he also assigns a more positive role to science in the process of self-creation: "Science . . . gains a new allure after morality has been eliminated—we have to *orient* our lives around it in order to *preserve* consistency for ourselves. This results in a kind of *practical contemplation* about **the conditions** *of our existence* as those who know" (*KSA* 10:24 [18]; see also *GS* 7). Nevertheless, Nietzsche denies that science can ever provide goals for action: "Can science provide goals? No . . . our drives form according to our ideal and with the help of science. [It is] as artists [that we] create our ideal" (*KSA* 9:8 [2]; see also [98]).

28. Leo Strauss nicely brings out the relationship between the unknowability or elusiveness of the self and creativity in his lectures *On Nietzsche's "Thus Spoke Zarathustra"*, ed. Richard Velkley (Chicago: University of Chicago Press, 2017): "The self [is] the elusive depth of man. There could not be creativity if there were not such an elusive depth. Creativity implies elusiveness" (96–97).

29. In his letter to Heinrich Köselitz of August 20, 1882, Nietzsche writes that he has changed several things in the final corrections to *The Gay Science*, including "the conclusions to the 2nd and 3rd books" (*SB* 6:238).

30. In the 1886 preface to the first volume of *Human, All Too Human*, Nietzsche speaks of a "tremendous . . . health that may not dispense even with sickness as a means and fish-hook of knowledge." He calls this *"great* health, that superfluity which grants to the free spirit the dangerous privilege of living *experimentally* and of being allowed to offer itself to adventure" (*HH* 1, preface, 4; see also *GS* 382).

31. Robert Pippin makes this point about the crucial role of self-overcoming versus aesthetic self-creation in Nietzsche's conception of the free self ("How to Overcome Oneself: Nietzsche on Freedom," in *Nietzsche on Freedom and Autonomy*, ed. Ken Gemes and Simon May [Oxford: Oxford University Press, 2009], 69–88).

32. Keith Ansell-Pearson has recently argued that "an ethos of Epicurean enlightenment pervades Nietzsche's middle writings," an ethos that deploys the tools of reason to deliver human beings from irrational fears and anxieties and ultimately achieve the serene contentment of ataraxia; see *Nietzsche's Search for Philosophy: On the Middle Writings* (London: Bloomsbury Press, 2018), esp. 3–4. This seems to me to underestimate the role of suffering in Nietzsche's conception of happiness. In the aphorism "Epicurus" in *The Gay Science*, Nietzsche states that the happiness Epicurus experiences while gazing at the sea "could only be invented by a man who was suffering continually" (*GS* 45). This suffering is not something to be conquered or escaped; rather, it is continually experienced by the philosopher as part of the quest for knowledge, allowing—and perhaps even demanding—from time to time momentary respites in which he delights at the surface of things (cf. *GS* 107 and preface, 4).

33. For all of this, see Bernard Reginster's insightful analysis of the will to power in *The Affirmation of Life: Nietzsche on Overcoming Nihilism* (Cambridge, MA: Harvard University Press, 2006), ch. 3.

34. Alexander Nehamas, too, sees the eternal recurrence as very much bound up with Nietz-sche's theory of self-creation, though again he interprets the latter in terms of aesthetic coher-ence rather than self-overcoming (*Nietzsche: Life as Literature*, ch. 5).

35. Here again, Reginster's analysis in *The Affirmation of Life*, chs. 5–6, is illuminating.

Chapter 4

1. See Mary Wollstonecraft, *A Vindication of the Rights of Woman*, in *"A Vindication of the Rights of Men" and "A Vindication of the Rights of Woman"*, ed. Sylvana Tomaselli (Cambridge: Cambridge University Press, 1995).

2. See the section on the family in G. W. F. Hegel, *Elements of the Philosophy of Right*, ed. Allen Wood (Cambridge: Cambridge University Press, 1991); and the chapters on women in Tocqueville's *Democracy in America*, ed. and trans. Harvey C. Mansfield and Delba Winthrop (1835/1840; Chicago: University of Chicago Press, 2000).

3. Quoted in Richard Lansdown, introduction to *The Bostonians*, by Henry James (London: Penguin Books, 2000), xiv.

4. The locus classicus of the misogynistic interpretation of Rousseau's views on women is Susan Moller Okin, *Women in Western Political Thought* (1979; Princeton: Princeton University Press, 1992), chs. 5–8. See also Nannerl Keohane, "'But for Her Sex . . .': The Domestication of Sophie," *University of Ottawa Quarterly* 49: 390–400; Carol Pateman, *The Sexual Contract* (Palo Alto: Stanford University Press, 1988), chs. 4–5; and Sarah Kofman, "Rousseau's Phallocratic Ends," *Hypatia* 3 (1988): 123–36. Interpretations of Nietzsche's views on women as misogynistic include Ofelia Schutte, *Beyond Nihilism: Nietzsche without Masks* (Chicago: University of Chi-cago Press, 1984), ch. 7; Ellen Kennedy, "Women as *Untermensch*," in *Women in Western Political Philosophy: Kant to Nietzsche*, ed. Kennedy and Susan Mendus (New York: St. Martin's Press, 1987), 179–201; Carol Diethe, "Nietzsche and the Woman Question," *History of European Ideas* 11 (1989): 865–75; Diethe, *Nietzsche's Women: Beyond the Whip* (Berlin: Walter de Gruyter, 1996), 63–71; Bruce Detwiler, *Nietzsche and the Politics of Aristocratic Radicalism* (Chicago: University of Chicago Press, 1990), 15; Keith Ansell-Pearson, "Nietzsche, Woman and Political Theory," in *Nietzsche, Feminism, and Political Theory*, ed. Paul Patton (London: Routledge, 1993), 28–37; Penelope Deutscher, "'Is it not remarkable that Nietzsche . . . should have hated Rousseau?': Woman, Femininity: Distancing Nietzsche from Rousseau," in *Nietzsche, Feminism, and Political Theory*, ed. Paul Patton (London: Routledge, 1993), 162–88; and C. Heike Schotten, *Nietzsche's Revolution: Décadence, Politics, and Sexuality* (New York: Palgrave Macmillan, 2009), chs. 4–5.

5. Sympathetic accounts of Rousseau's views on women include Joel Schwartz, *The Sexual Politics of Jean-Jacques Rousseau* (Chicago: University of Chicago Press, 1984); Susan Meld Shell, "*Emile*: Nature and the Education of Sophie," in *The Cambridge Companion to Rousseau*, ed. Pat-rick Riley (Cambridge: Cambridge University Press, 2001): 272–301; Helena Rosenblatt, "On the 'Misogyny' of Jean-Jacques Rousseau: The *Letter to D'Alembert* in Historical Context," *French Historical Studies* 25 (2002): 91–114; and Schaeffer, *Rousseau on Education, Freedom, and Judg-ment*, chs. 6–7. Amazingly, sympathetic accounts of Nietzsche's views on women far outnumber sympathetic accounts of Rousseau's. These sympathetic accounts tend to focus not on Nietz-sche's overtly antifeminist pronouncements about women, but on his more feminist-friendly deconstruction of the phallocentric, logocentric, and dualistic biases of Western philosophy. Jacques Derrida led the way in this regard with *Spurs/Éperons*, trans. Barbara Harlow (Chicago: University of Chicago Press, 1979). See also Sarah Kofman, "Baubô: Theological Perversion and

Fetishism," in *Nietzsche's New Seas*, ed. Michael Gillespie and Tracy Strong (Chicago: University of Chicago Press, 1988), 175–202; Schutte, *Beyond Nihilism*; Daniel Conway, *"Das Weib An Sich*: The Slave Revolt in Epistemology," in *Nietzsche, Feminism, and Political Theory*, ed. Paul Patton (London: Routledge, 1993), 110–29; Deutscher, " 'Is it not remarkable' "; Lynne Tirrell, "Sexual Dualism and Women's Self-Creation: On the Advantages and Disadvantages of Reading Nietzsche for Feminists," in *Nietzsche and the Feminine*, ed. Peter Burgard (Charlottesville, VA: University of Virginia Press, 1994), 158–82; Kathleen Higgins, "Gender in *The Gay Science*," in *Feminist Interpretations of Friedrich Nietzsche*, ed. Kelly Oliver and Marilyn Pearsall (University Park, PA: Penn State University Press, 1998), 130–51; Maudemarie Clark, "Nietzsche's Misogyny," in *Feminist Interpretations of Friedrich Nietzsche*, 187–98; and Debra Bergoffen, "Nietzsche Was No Feminist . . . ," in *Feminist Interpretations of Friedrich Nietzsche*, 225–35.

6. The Goncourt brothers agreed with Nietzsche on this point: "Woman in the eighteenth century is the principle that governs, the reason that directs, the voice that commands; she is the universal and fatal cause, the origin of events, the source of things"; quoted in French in Lieselotte Steinbrügge, *The Moral Sex: Woman's Nature in the French Enlightenment*, trans. Pamela E. Selwyn (New York and Oxford: Oxford University Press, 1995), 109n2 (my translation).

7. Okin claims that Rousseau's introduction of the division of labor between the sexes at this point in the *Second Discourse* is sudden and "without justification" (*Women in Western Political Thought*, 112–13). Shell shows more convincingly why this development was not only natural but desirable from the point of view of women (*"Emile*: Nature and the Education of Sophie," 279–84).

8. Wollstonecraft does not draw the same conclusion. She acknowledges that the inferiority of women to men with respect to physical strength renders them "in some degree, dependent on men in the various relations of life; but why should it be increased by prejudices that give a sex to virtue"? (*Vindication of the Rights of Woman*, 78).

9. See Wollstonecraft, *Vindication of the Rights of Woman*, chs. 2–3. Wollstonecraft tends to exaggerate the superficiality of Rousseau's conceptions of adornment and coquetry, referring, for example, to his fondness for "the pretty foot and enticing airs of his little favorite" and his reduction of woman to a "coquettish slave" (94).

10. Wollstonecraft merely repeats Rousseau's point rather than critiquing it, when she asks, if women are treated no better than animals or children, "can they be expected to govern a family with judgment?" (*Vindication of the Rights of Woman*, 77; see also 169). Froese fails to appreciate this aspect of Rousseau's education of woman when she argues that he "deprives Sophie of developing a moral backbone of her own" (*Rousseau and Nietzsche*, 77). Schaeffer, *Rousseau on Education, Freedom, and Judgment*, ch. 6, emphasizes the role of reason and judgment in the education of woman.

11. Virginia Woolf captures this art of the hostess in her depiction of Mrs. Ramsey presiding over a dinner party in *To the Lighthouse* (1927; New York: Harcourt, 1981), ch. 16.

12. Schwartz emphasizes this positive aspect of sexual differentiation and interdependence in *The Sexual Politics of Jean-Jacques Rousseau*.

13. See Okin, *Women in Western Political Thought*, 163; and Penny Weiss, *Gendered Community: Rousseau, Sex, and Politics* (New York: NYU Press, 1993), chs. 1, 3–4.

14. Steinbrügge makes a parallel point: "Woman's move into the male world of work has created an actual vacuum, one which manifests itself . . . in the loss . . . of particular norms and behaviors. 'Kindness, gentleness, modesty, the readiness to make sacrifices': Women today, socially equal to men, identify as little with this canon of virtues . . . as most men ever did. The necessity for these virtues has nonetheless by no means disappeared" (*The Moral Sex*, 107).

15. See Okin, *Women in Western Political Thought*, ch. 8; Ferrara, *Modernity and Authenticity*, ch. 5; and Froese, *Rousseau and Nietzsche*, 77–81.

16. Wollstonecraft, *Vindication of the Rights of Woman*, 114

17. For Wollstonecraft's view that friendship rather than love or passion is the ultimate basis of marriage, see *Vindication of the Rights of Woman*, 98–101, 150–51. She even quotes the passage from the end of *Emile*, calling it "a just description of a comfortable couple" (170). On the eighteenth century's new understanding of marriage as based on "affection, true companionship between husband and wife, and devoted concern for the children," see Taylor, *Sources of the Self*, 289–91; see also Rousseau's *New Heloise* as an example of this new understanding.

18. Schwartz, *The Sexual Politics of Jean-Jacques Rousseau*, 114. For a good discussion of *Julie*, see Schwartz, ch. 5 in general

19. See, for example, Bloom, *Love and Friendship*, 156.

20. Abbey emphasizes the ways in which Nietzsche's views in his middle works are not misogynistic or antifeminist, in contrast with his views in his later works (*Nietzsche's Middle Period*, 107–8, 120–21).

21. Abbey argues that Nietzsche does not subscribe in his middle works to an essentialist understanding of the nature of women but grasps how that nature has been conditioned by social circumstances (*Nietzsche's Middle Period*, 110–19).

22. See Wollstonecraft, *Vindication of the Rights of Woman*, 75, 87.

23. Diethe explores these friendships in *Nietzsche's Women*. In addition to Lou Salomé, she discusses Nietzsche's relationships with Malwida von Meysenbug, Meta von Salis, and Resa von Schirnhofer.

24. See Derrida, *Spurs*, 41–55; Tirrell, "Sexual Dualism and Women's Self-Creation"; and Higgins, "Gender in *The Gay Science*."

25. Here I disagree with Tirrell's attempt to see Nietzsche as a nascent feminist in the mold of Simone de Beauvoir, who enjoins women "to stop being male-defined and to actively engage in creating their own identities" ("Sexual Dualism and Women's Self-Creation," 167–68, 176–78). See also Higgins, "Gender in *The Gay Science*," 144.

26. See R. Hinton Thomas, "Nietzsche, Women and the Whip," *German Life and Letters* 34 (1980): 117–25; Kathleen Higgins, "The Whip Recalled," *Journal of Nietzsche Studies* 12 (1996): 1–18; and Laurence Lampert, *Nietzsche's Teaching: An Interpretation of "Thus Spoke Zarathustra"* (New Haven: Yale University Press, 1986), 66–69.

27. In his original plans for *Beyond Good and Evil*, Nietzsche envisaged an entire chapter on "*Das Weib an sich*" (Woman as such), corresponding to the chapter on "Woman and Child" in *Human, All Too Human*; see *KSA* 12:2 [43, 44, 53]. See also Laurence Lampert, *Nietzsche's Task: An Interpretation of "Beyond Good and Evil"* (New Haven: Yale University Press, 2001), 232n32.

28. Clark makes this point in "Nietzsche's Misogyny," but she goes on to mistakenly claim that Nietzsche does not take his observations about women in *BGE* to be true in any sense but merely honest expressions of his feelings of anger and resentment.

29. See Schutte, *Beyond Nihilism*, ch. 7; see also Tirrell, "Sexual Dualism and Women's Self-Creation; and Schotten, *Nietzsche's Revolution*.

Chapter 5

1. Victor Gourevitch, introduction to *Rousseau: "The Social Contract" and Other Later Political Writings*, ed. Gourevitch (Cambridge: Cambridge University Press, 1997), ix.

2. In the case of Rousseau, see Isaiah Berlin, *Freedom and Its Betrayal: Six Enemies of Human Liberty* (London: Chatto & Windus, 2002), 28–52; Robert Nisbet, "Rousseau and Totalitarianism," *Journal of Politics* 5 (1943): 93–114; Bertrand Russell, *A History of Western Philosophy* (New York: Simon and Schuster, 1945), ch. 19; J. L. Talmon, *The Origins of Totalitarian Democracy* (London: Secker & Warburg, 1952), 38–49; Lester Crocker, *Rousseau's "Social Contract": An Interpretive Essay* (Cleveland: Case Western Reserve Press, 1968); and Melzer, *Natural Goodness of Man*, ch. 12. In the case of Nietzsche, see Russell, *A History of Western Philosophy*, ch. 25; Werner Dannhauser, *Nietzsche's View of Socrates* (Ithaca: Cornell University Press, 1974), 29–31, 38–39; Dannhauser, "Friedrich Nietzsche," in *History of Political Philosophy*, 3rd ed., ed. Leo Strauss and Joseph Cropsey (Chicago: University of Chicago Press, 1987), 848–49; Detwiler, *Nietzsche and the Politics of Aristocratic Radicalism*; Ansell-Pearson, *Nietzsche Contra Rousseau*, 34, 210–11, 215, 223–24, 229; Ansell-Pearson, *Nietzsche as Political Thinker*, 39–44, 95–97, 148–55, 161–62; Ruth Abbey and Fredrick Appel, "Nietzsche and the Will to Politics," *Review of Politics* 60 (1998): 83–114; Fredrick Appel, *Nietzsche Contra Democracy* (Ithaca: Cornell University Press, 1999); Don Dombowsky, *Nietzsche's Machiavellian Politics* (London: Palgrave Macmillan, 2004); and Michael Gillespie, *Nietzsche's Final Teaching* (Chicago: University of Chicago Press, 2017), ix, xiii–xiv, 20–21, 38, 48, 59, 172–73, 176–77, 198–99.

3. On the Tocqueville–Nietzsche relationship, see Paul Franco, "Tocqueville and Nietzsche on the Problem of Human Greatness in Democracy," *Review of Politics* 76 (2014): 439–67.

4. The place of natural law in Rousseau's political philosophy has been the subject of fierce debate among scholars in the twentieth century. See C. E. Vaughan, introduction to *The Political Writings of Jean-Jacques Rousseau*, ed. Vaughan (Cambridge: Cambridge University Press, 1915); Robert Derathé, *Jean-Jacques Rousseau et la science politique de son temps* (Paris: Presses universitaires de France, 1950); Alfred Cobban, "New Light on the Political Thought of Rousseau," *Political Science Quarterly* 66 (1951): 272–84; Strauss, *Natural Right and History*, 266–82; Roger Masters, *The Political Philosophy of Rousseau* (Princeton: Princeton University Press, 1968), 76–89, 158–65, 316–18; Maurizio Viroli, *Jean-Jacques Rousseau and the Well-Ordered Society*, trans. Derek Hanson (Cambridge: Cambridge University Press, 1988), 132–48; Melzer, *Natural Goodness of Man*, ch. 8; Robert Wokler, "Rousseau's Pufendorf: Natural Law and the Foundations of Commercial Society," in *Rousseau, the Age of Enlightenment, and Their Legacies*, ed. Bryan Garsten (Princeton: Princeton University Press, 2012), ch. 6; Gourevitch, introduction to *"The Social Contract" and Other Later Political Writings*, x–xvii; and Helena Rosenblatt, *Rousseau and Geneva: From the "First Discourse" to the "Social Contract," 1749–1762* (Cambridge: Cambridge University Press, 1997), chs. 3–4.

5. Hegel, *Elements of the Philosophy of Right*, 258R; G. W. F. Hegel, *Lectures on the History of Philosophy*, trans. E. S. Haldane and F. H. Simson (Lincoln: University of Nebraska Press, 1995), 3:401–2.

6. On Rousseau's conception of freedom as the absence of dependence on the wills of others, see Viroli, *Rousseau and the Well-Ordered Society*, 11, 150–51; and Frederick Neuhouser, "Freedom, Dependence, and the General Will," *Philosophical Review* 102 (1993): 373–91.

7. On equality as a means to secure political freedom, see Gourevitch, introduction to *"The Social Contract" and Other Later Political Writings*, xix.

8. For illuminating discussions of this passage, see Neuhouser, "Freedom, Dependence, and the General Will," 366–73; and David Lay Williams, *Rousseau's "Social Contract": An Introduction* (Cambridge: Cambridge University Press, 2014), 54–58.

9. Interestingly, moral freedom is not mentioned in the parallel discussion of freedom in the *Geneva Manuscript* (see GenMS 1:3).

10. See Berlin, *Freedom and Its Betrayal*, 31–49; and Isaiah Berlin, "Two Concepts of Liberty," in *Four Essays on Liberty* (Oxford: Oxford University Press, 1969), 131–54.

11. On Rousseau's attempt to ground justice in individual self-interest, see Horowitz, *Rousseau, Nature, and History*, 183–206; Viroli, *Rousseau and the Well-Ordered Society*, 118–32; and Reisert, *Rousseau: A Friend of Virtue*, 124–37.

12. On the intimate connection between law and freedom from personal dependence in Rousseau's political philosophy, see Viroli, *Rousseau and the Well-Ordered Society*, 11, 148–52; Neuhouser, "Freedom, Dependence, and the General Will," 373–91; and Gourevitch, introduction to *"The Social Contract" and Other Later Political Writings*, xx–xxi.

13. On the relationship between Rousseau's theoretical justification of the legitimate state and the practical means of bringing it into existence and preserving it, see Viroli, *Rousseau and the Well-Ordered Society*, 187–226. On Rousseau's practical concern with motivating people to do what is right or just, see Reisert, *Rousseau: A Friend of Virtue*, 22–26.

14. D. L. Williams, in *Rousseau's "Social Contract"*, 68, 110–12, criticizes Crocker and Talmon for this misunderstanding.

15. On the incompatibility of extreme economic inequality with freedom and the rule of law, see Viroli, *Rousseau and the Well-Ordered Society*, 4–6; Neuhouser, *Rousseau's Critique of Inequality*, 198–208; and D. L. Williams, *Rousseau's "Social Contract"*, 60–63, 79, 102.

16. See Walter Kaufmann, *Nietzsche: Philosopher, Psychologist, Antichrist*, 4th ed. (Princeton: Princeton University Press, 1974). See also Nehamas, *Nietzsche: Life as Literature*; Peter Bergmann, *Nietzsche, "the Last Antipolitical German"* (Bloomington: Indiana University Press, 1987); Leslie Thiele, *Friedrich Nietzsche and the Politics of the Soul: A Study of Heroic Individualism* (Princeton: Princeton University Press, 1990); and Thomas Brobjer, "Critical Aspects of Nietzsche's Relation to Politics and Democracy," in *Nietzsche, Power, and Politics: Rethinking Nietzsche's Legacy for Political Thought*, ed. Herman Siemens and Vasti Roodt (Berlin: Walter de Gruyter, 2008): 205–30.

17. Brian Leiter, *Nietzsche on Morality*, 2nd ed. (London: Routledge, 2015), 237. Martha Nussbaum offers a particularly crude version of the thesis that Nietzsche has no political philosophy, arguing that he lacks six of the seven elements necessary for "serious political thought" ("Is Nietzsche a Political Thinker?," *International Journal of Philosophical Studies* 5 [1997]: 1–13).

18. Bernard Williams, *Shame and Necessity* (Berkeley: University of California Press, 2008), 10. See also Williams, "'There Are Many Kinds of Eyes,'" in *The Sense of the Past* (Princeton: Princeton University Press, 2006), 326–27.

19. The locus classicus of this "aristocratic radical" interpretation of Nietzsche's politics is Detwiler's *Nietzsche and the Politics of Aristocratic Radicalism*. For similar interpretations, see Dannhauser, *Nietzsche's View of Socrates*, 29–31, 38–39; Dannhauser, "Friedrich Nietzsche," 848–49; Ansell-Pearson, *Nietzsche as Political Thinker*, 39–44, 95–97, 148–55, 161–62; Abbey and Appel, "Nietzsche and the Will to Politics," 83–114; Appel, *Nietzsche Contra Democracy*; Dombowsky, *Nietzsche's Machiavellian Politics*; and Gillespie, *Nietzsche's Final Teaching*, ix, xiii–xiv, 20–21, 38, 48, 59, 172–73, 176–77, 198–99.

20. See Mark Warren, *Nietzsche and Political Thought* (Cambridge, MA: MIT Press, 1991); William Connolly, *Identity/Difference* (Ithaca: Cornell University Press, 1991); Bonnie Honig, *Political Theory and the Displacement of Politics* (Ithaca: Cornell University Press, 1993); David Owen, *Nietzsche, Politics and Modernity* (London: Sage, 1995); and Lawrence Hatab, *A Nietzschean Defense of Democracy: An Experiment in Postmodern Politics* (Chicago: Open Court, 1995).

21. While my interpretation shares much with Hugo Drochon's in *Nietzsche's Great Politics* (Princeton: Princeton University Press, 2016), he sometimes exaggerates the systematic

character of Nietzsche's theory of the state (see, e.g., 51). In this regard, my position is closer to that of Herman Siemens, "Yes, No, Maybe So . . . Nietzsche's Equivocations on the Relation between Democracy and '*Grosse Politik*,'" in *Nietzsche, Power, and Politics*, ed. Siemens and Vasti Roodt (Berlin: Walter de Gruyter, 2008), 231–33, 263–64.

22. Ansell-Pearson, *Nietzsche as Political Thinker*, 155.

23. I take these terms from John Rawls, *A Theory of Justice*, rev. ed. (Cambridge, MA: Belknap Press, 1999/1971), 22, 285–92; and Michael Oakeshott, "On the Character of a Modern European State," in *On Human Conduct* (Oxford: Clarendon Press, 1975), 203, 224, 232, 281, 282, 307, 311, respectively. Both refer to a political system organized in terms of a substantive purpose independent of the self-chosen purposes of individuals. Oakeshott contrasts *teleocracy* with *nomocracy*, a political order based on noninstrumental or nonpurposive rules or laws.

24. Compare Hegel, *Elements of the Philosophy of Right*, §324, on the "ethical moment of war."

25. On this shift, see Franco, *Nietzsche's Enlightenment*, ch. 1.

26. See, for example, Ansell-Pearson, *Nietzsche Contra Rousseau*, 215–19; and David Owen, "Nietzsche, Ethical Agency and the Problem of Democracy," in *Nietzsche, Power, and Politics: Rethinking Nietzsche's Legacy for Political Thought*, ed. Herman Siemens and Vasti Roodt (Berlin: Walter de Gruyter, 2008), 159–65.

27. See Detwiler, *Nietzsche and the Politics of Aristocratic Radicalism*, esp. ch. 8; see also Ansell-Pearson, who takes a somewhat ambivalent position on the relationship between the politics of the middle and later writings, arguing on the one hand that there is not a radical break between them, and on the other that "in his 'mature' thinking [Nietzsche] jettisons [his] former insights and places his hopes for a regeneration of humanity on a new legislation and new enslavement" (*Nietzsche as Political Thinker*, 95, 162; see also 96–97).

28. Tocqueville, *Democracy in America*, 3.

29. For a similar view of the place of democracy in *Human, All Too Human*, see Drochon, *Nietzsche's Great Politics*, 78–79.

30. In a later note from August–September 1885, Nietzsche clearly distinguishes between the superficial individualism of democracy and genuine individuality. The former, which conforms to the demands of equal rights, "rejects the *truly great* human beings. . . . Its unfairness consists of a rage without bounds *not* against the tyrants and demagogues . . . but against the *noble* humans who despise the praise of the many. The demand for equal rights (e.g., to be allowed to sit in judgment over everything) is *anti-aristocratic*" (*KSA* 11:40 [26]).

31. In his notebooks from 1880/81, Nietzsche refers several times to the prospect of humanity turning into sand, often in connection with Herbert Spencer's belief that human evolution consists in the progress from egoism to altruism or to the ideal point where the two merge into each other (*KSA* 9:1 [123], 6 [163], 8 [103], 11 [40]).

32. Herbert Siemens calls this the "pivotal text" in the development of Nietzsche's attitude toward democracy ("Nietzsche's Critique of Democracy," *Journal of Nietzsche Studies* 38 [2009]: 25–27).

33. Siemens makes a similar point in "Nietzsche's Critique of Democracy," 21.

34. Here I reject Laurence Lampert's claim that the teaching on the *Übermensch* in *Zarathustra* is a merely provisional teaching that is ultimately rendered obsolete by the teaching on the eternal recurrence (*Nietzsche's Teaching: An Interpretation of "Thus Spoke Zarathustra"* [New Haven: Yale University Press, 1986], 19–21, 80–82, 258). Without the new ideal of the *Übermensch*, the idea of the eternal recurrence would be unendurable, the endless repetition of

wastefulness, pointlessness, and meaningless, in accordance with the teaching of the soothsayer. Only the *Übermensch* can fully affirm and incorporate the idea of the eternal recurrence, like the shepherd who bites off the head of the serpent. Nietzsche articulates the correlativity of his teachings on eternal return and the *Übermensch* in a note from 1883: "We discover that the only way to bear [the idea of the eternal recurrence] is to create a being *that bears it.* . . . We created the weightiest thought—*now let us create the being* for whom the thought is light and blissful!" (*KSA* 10:21 [6]). See also Robert Pippin, "Irony and Affirmation in Nietzsche's *Thus Spoke Zarathustra*," in *Nietzsche's New Seas*, ed. Michael Gillespie and Tracy Strong (Chicago: University of Chicago Press, 1988), 45–71, which treats the idea of the *Übermensch* ironically as a "solution that deconstructs itself" (56).

35. On the relation between the historical sense and future orientation, see *GS* 337, where Nietzsche mentions the idea of a "new nobility" for the first time (see also *KSA* 9:12 [76], 15 [17, 70]).

36. Strauss also emphasizes the nonpolitical character of Nietzsche's conception of the new nobility and criticizes it for its abdication of political responsibility (*On Nietzsche's "Thus Spoke Zarathustra"*, 152–54, 203–4).

37. Daniel Conway, *Nietzsche and the Political* (London: Routledge, 1997), 3. See also Siemens, "Nietzsche's Critique of Democracy," 25–27.

38. Maudemarie Clark makes this point very effectively in "Nietzsche's Antidemocratic Rhetoric," *Southern Journal of Philosophy* 37 (1999), supplement: 119–41. In this article, she also makes some telling criticisms of the meritocratic democratic implications Hatab draws from Nietzsche's political philosophy (131–37).

39. On this development, compare *GS* 356, where Nietzsche describes the breakdown of rigidly fixed social roles in democratic ages and the rise of the belief that the individual "can do just about everything and *can manage almost any role*," as a result of which the individual "experiments with himself, improvises, makes new experiments, enjoys his experiments; and all nature ceases and becomes art." Nietzsche goes on to argue that this democratic actor's faith is detrimental to the projects of the "great architects" of society, which "require thousands of years for their completion." Such projects demand a different faith, "that man has value and meaning only insofar as he is *a stone in a great edifice*; and to that end he must be *solid* first of all, a 'stone'—and above all not an actor!" Therefore, he concludes, "what will not be built any more henceforth, and *cannot* be built any more, is—a society in the old sense of that word; to build that, everything is lacking, above all the material. *All of us are no longer material for a society*; this is a truth for which the time has come." Part of the ambiguity of this aphorism lies in what Nietzsche means by "society in the old sense of that word." William Connolly argues that the aphorism shows that Nietzsche did not think a "hierarchical, ordered culture of nobility could be rebuilt in the modern age" ("Nietzsche, Democracy, Time," in *Nietzsche, Power, and Politics: Rethinking Nietzsche's Legacy for Political Thought*, ed. Herman Siemens and Vasti Roodt [Berlin: Walter de Gruyter, 2008], 119–24; quotation on 119). But the passages referenced in the text above suggest that Nietzsche ultimately saw a way in which just such a culture could be constructed on the basis of this democratic actor's faith. On the relation of this aphorism to Nietzsche's aristocratic great politics, see Drochon, *Nietzsche's Great Politics*, 81–82, 125–26.

40. Ansell-Pearson, *Nietzsche Contra Rousseau*, 34, 209–12, 229; quotation on 210. See also Ansell-Pearson, *Introduction to Nietzsche as Political Thinker*, 41–43, 153–55.

41. On Nietzsche's vision of future society as consisting of two radically separate spheres—a high, cultural one and a lower, democratic one—see Drochon, *Nietzsche's Great Politics*, 4, 20–21, 88–104.

42. Here I disagree with Paul Glenn's claim that Nietzsche's use of the example of Napoleon proves that his higher man is to be understood as a political leader who uses the "state as the medium of his self-overcoming and spiritual growth" ("Nietzsche's Napoleon: The Higher Man as Political Actor," *Review of Politics* 63 [2001]: 140, 150, 155–56; quotation on 156). Dombowsky argues that Nietzsche advocates a "Napoleonic Caesarism," in which "political authority [is] exercised through a state apparatus" (*Nietzsche's Machiavellian Politics*, 110–13, 166–67); see also Dombowsky, "Nietzsche as Bonapartist," in *Nietzsche, Power, and Politics*: 347–70; Abbey and Appel, "Nietzsche and the Will to Politics," 92–94; and Appel, *Nietzsche Contra Democracy*, 119–21.

Chapter 6

1. See Strauss, *Natural Right and History*, 255, 263, 290–94; and Meier, *On the Happiness of the Philosophic Life*.

2. On the German *Bildung* tradition and its susceptibility to political irresponsibility, see W. H. Bruford, *The German Tradition of Self-Cultivation: "Bildung" from Humboldt to Thomas Mann* (Cambridge: Cambridge University Press, 1975); and Wolf Lepenies, *The Seduction of Culture in German History* (Princeton: Princeton University Press, 2006).

Works Cited

Abbey, Ruth. *Nietzsche's Middle Period*. Oxford: Oxford University Press, 2000.

Abbey, Ruth, and Fredrick Appel. "Nietzsche and the Will to Politics." *Review of Politics* 60 (1998): 83–114.

Ansell-Pearson, Keith. *An Introduction to Nietzsche as Political Thinker*. Cambridge: Cambridge University Press, 1994.

———. *Nietzsche Contra Rousseau: A Study of Nietzsche's Moral and Political Thought*. Cambridge: Cambridge University Press, 1991.

———. *Nietzsche's Search for Philosophy: On the Middle Writings*. London: Bloomsbury Press, 2018.

———. "Nietzsche, Woman and Political Theory." In *Nietzsche, Feminism, and Political Theory*, edited by Paul Patton. London: Routledge, 1993.

Appel, Fredrick. *Nietzsche Contra Democracy*. Ithaca: Cornell University Press, 1999.

Babbitt, Irving. *Rousseau and Romanticism*. Boston: Houghton Mifflin, 1919.

Bell, Daniel. *The Cultural Contradictions of Capitalism* 20th anniversary ed. New York: Basic Books, 1996.

Bergmann, Peter. *Nietzsche, "the Last Antipolitical German"*. Bloomington: Indiana University Press, 1987.

Bergoffen, Debra. "Nietzsche Was No Feminist . . ." In *Feminist Interpretations of Friedrich Nietzsche*, edited by Kelly Oliver and Marilyn Pearsall. University Park, PA: Penn State University Press, 1998.

Berlin, Isaiah. *Freedom and Its Betrayal: Six Enemies of Human Liberty*. London: Chatto & Windus, 2002.

———. "Two Concepts of Liberty." In *Four Essays on Liberty*. Oxford: Oxford University Press, 1969.

Bloom, Allan. *The Closing of the American Mind: How Higher Education Has Failed Democracy and Impoverished the Souls of Today's Students*. New York: Simon and Schuster, 1987.

———. Introduction to *Emile, or On Education*, translated by Bloom. New York: Basic Books, 1979.

———. *Love and Friendship*. New York: Simon & Schuster, 1993.

———. "Rousseau's Critique of Liberal Constitutionalism." In *The Legacy of Rousseau*, edited by Nathan Tarcov and Clifford Orwin. Chicago: University of Chicago Press, 1997.

Boyd, Richard. "Pity's Pathologies: Rousseau and the Limits of Democratic Compassion." *Political Theory* 32 (2004): 519–46.

Brobjer, Thomas. "Critical Aspects of Nietzsche's Relation to Politics and Democracy." In *Nietzsche, Power, and Politics: Rethinking Nietzsche's Legacy for Political Thought*, edited by Herman Siemens and Vasti Roodt. Berlin: Walter de Gruyter, 2008.

Bruford, W. H. *The German Tradition of Self-Cultivation: "Bildung" from Humboldt to Thomas Mann*. Cambridge: Cambridge University Press, 1975.

Cantor, Paul. *Shakespeare's Roman Trilogy: The Twilight of the Ancient World*. Chicago: University of Chicago Press, 2017.

Cassirer, Ernst. *The Question of Jean-Jacques Rousseau*. Translated by Peter Gay. New York: Columbia University Press, 1954.

Clark, Maudemarie. "Nietzsche's Antidemocratic Rhetoric." *Southern Journal of Philosophy* 37 (1999), supplement: 119–41.

———. "Nietzsche's Misogyny." In *Feminist Interpretations of Friedrich Nietzsche*, edited by Kelly Oliver and Marilyn Pearsall. University Park, PA: Penn State University Press, 1998.

Cobban, Alfred. "New Light on the Political Thought of Rousseau." *Political Science Quarterly* 66 (1951): 272–84.

Conant, James. "Nietzsche's Perfectionism: A Reading of *Schopenhauer as Educator*." In *Nietzsche's Postmoralism: Essays on Nietzsche's Prelude to Philosophy's Future*, edited by Richard Schacht. Cambridge: Cambridge University Press, 2001.

Connolly, William. *Identity/Difference* (Ithaca: Cornell University Press, 1991.

———. "Nietzsche, Democracy, Time." In *Nietzsche, Power, and Politics: Rethinking Nietzsche's Legacy for Political Thought*, edited by Herman Siemens and Vasti Roodt. Berlin: Walter de Gruyter, 2008.

Conway, Daniel. "*Das Weib An Sich*: The Slave Revolt in Epistemology." In *Nietzsche, Feminism, and Political Theory*, edited by Paul Patton. London: Routledge, 1993.

———. "How We Became What We Are: Tracking the 'Beasts of Prey.'" In *On the Genealogy of Morals: Critical Essays*, edited by Christa Davis Acampora. Lanham, MD: Rowman and Littlefield, 2006.

———. *Nietzsche and the Political*. London: Routledge, 1997.

Cooper, Laurence. *Eros in Plato, Rousseau, and Nietzsche: The Politics of Infinity*. University Park, PA: Penn State University Press, 2008.

———. *Rousseau, Nature, and the Problem of the Good Life*. University Park, PA: Penn State University Press, 1999.

Crocker, Lester. *Rousseau's "Social Contract": An Interpretive Essay*. Cleveland: Case Western Reserve Press, 1968.

Dannhauser, Werner. "Friedrich Nietzsche." In *History of Political Philosophy*, 3rd ed., edited by Leo Strauss and Joseph Cropsey. Chicago: University of Chicago Press, 1987.

———. *Nietzsche's View of Socrates*. Ithaca: Cornell University Press, 1974.

———. "The Problem of the Bourgeois." In *The Legacy of Rousseau*, edited by Clifford Orwin and Nathan Tarcov. Chicago: University of Chicago Press, 1997.

Dent, N. J. H. *Rousseau: An Introduction to His Psychological, Social and Political Theory*. Oxford: Basil Blackwell, 1988.

Derathé, Robert. *Jean-Jacques Rousseau et la science politique de son temps*. Paris: Presses universitaires de France, 1950.

Derrida, Jacques. *Of Grammatology*. Corrected ed. Translated by Gayatri Chakravorty Spivak. Baltimore: Johns Hopkins University Press, 1997.

———. *Spurs/Éperons*. Translated by Barbara Harlow. Chicago: University of Chicago Press, 1979.

Detwiler, Bruce. *Nietzsche and the Politics of Aristocratic Radicalism*. Chicago: University of Chicago Press, 1990.

Deutscher, Penelope. "'Is it not remarkable that Nietzsche . . . should have hated Rousseau?': Woman, Femininity: Distancing Nietzsche from Rousseau." In *Nietzsche, Feminism, and Political Theory*, edited by Paul Patton. London: Routledge, 1993.

Diethe, Carol. "Nietzsche and the Woman Question." *History of European Ideas* 11 (1989): 865–75.

———. *Nietzsche's Women: Beyond the Whip*. Berlin: Walter de Gruyter, 1996.

Dombowsky, Don. "Nietzsche as Bonapartist." In *Nietzsche, Power, and Politics: Rethinking Nietzsche's Legacy for Political Thought*, edited by Herman Siemens and Vasti Roodt. Berlin: Walter de Gruyter, 2008.

———. *Nietzsche's Machiavellian Politics*. London: Palgrave Macmillan, 2004.

Drochon, Hugo. *Nietzsche's Great Politics*. Princeton: Princeton University Press, 2016.

Emberley, Peter. "Rousseau Versus the Savoyard Vicar." *Interpretation* 14 (1986): 299–329.

Ferrara, Alessandro. *Modernity and Authenticity: A Study of the Social and Ethical Thought of Jean-Jacques Rousseau*. Albany, NY: SUNY Press, 1993.

Franco, Paul. "Becoming Who You Are: Nietzsche on Self-Creation." *Journal of Nietzsche Studies* 49 (2018): 52–77.

———. *Nietzsche's Enlightenment: The Free-Spirit Trilogy of the Middle Period*. Chicago: University of Chicago Press, 2011.

———. "Tocqueville and Nietzsche on the Problem of Human Greatness in Democracy." *Review of Politics* 76 (2014): 439–67.

Froese, Katrin. *Rousseau and Nietzsche: Toward an Aesthetic Morality*. Lanham, MD: Lexington Press, 2001.

Gillespie, Michael. *Nietzsche's Final Teaching*. Chicago: University of Chicago Press, 2017.

Glenn, Paul. "Nietzsche's Napoleon: The Higher Man as Political Actor." *Review of Politics* 63 (2001): 129–58.

Gourevitch, Victor. "Rousseau's Pure State of Nature." *Interpretation* 16 (1988–89): 23–59.

———. Introduction to *Rousseau: "The Social Contract" and Other Later Political Writings*, edited by Gourevitch. Cambridge: Cambridge University Press, 1997.

———. "On Strauss and Rousseau." In *The Challenge of Rousseau*, edited by Eve Grace and Christopher Kelly. Cambridge: Cambridge University Press, 2013.

Grace, Eve. "Built on Sand: Moral Law in Rousseau's *Second Discourse*." In *The Challenge of Rousseau*, edited by Grace and Christopher Kelly. Cambridge University Press, 2013.

———. "The Restlessness of 'Being': Rousseau's Protean Sentiment of Existence." *History of European Ideas* 27 (2001): 133–51.

Hatab, Lawrence. *A Nietzschean Defense of Democracy: An Experiment in Postmodern Politics*. Chicago: Open Court, 1995.

Hegel, G. W. F. "The German Constitution." In *Hegel's Political Writings*, translated by T. M. Knox. Oxford: Clarendon Press, 1964.

———. *Elements of the Philosophy of Right*. Edited by Allen Wood. Cambridge: Cambridge University Press, 1991.

————. *Lectures on the History of Philosophy*. Translated by E. S. Haldane and F. H. Simson. Lincoln: University of Nebraska Press, 1995.

Heller, Peter. "Nietzsche in His Relation to Voltaire and Rousseau." In *Studies in Nietzsche and the Classical Tradition*, edited by James C. O'Flaherty, Timothy F. Sellner, and Robert M. Helm. Chapel Hill: University of North Carolina Press, 1979.

Higgins, Kathleen. "Gender in *The Gay Science*." In *Feminist Interpretations of Friedrich Nietzsche*, edited by Kelly Oliver and Marilyn Pearsall. University Park, PA: Penn State University Press, 1998.

————. "The Whip Recalled." *Journal of Nietzsche Studies* 12 (1996): 1–18.

Honig, Bonnie. *Political Theory and the Displacement of Politics*. Ithaca: Cornell University Press, 1993.

Horowitz, Asher. *Rousseau, Nature, and History*. Toronto: University of Toronto Press, 1987.

Kant, Immanuel. *Critique of Practical Reason*. Edited by Mary Gregor. Cambridge: Cambridge University Press, 1997.

Kaufmann, Walter. *Nietzsche: Philosopher, Psychologist, Antichrist*. 4th ed. Princeton: Princeton University Press, 1974.

Kennedy, Ellen. "Women as *Untermensch*." In *Women in Western Political Philosophy: Kant to Nietzsche*, edited by Kennedy and Susan Mendus. New York: St. Martin's Press, 1987.

Keohane, Nannerl. "'But for Her Sex . . .': The Domestication of Sophie." *University of Ottawa Quarterly* 49: 390–400.

Kofman, Sarah. "Baubô: Theological Perversion and Fetishism." In *Nietzsche's New Seas*, edited by Michael Gillespie and Tracy Strong. Chicago: University of Chicago Press, 1988.

————. "Rousseau's Phallocratic Ends." *Hypatia* 3 (1988): 123–36.

Lampert, Laurence. *Nietzsche's Teaching: An Interpretation of "Thus Spoke Zarathustra"*. New Haven: Yale University Press, 1986.

————. *Nietzsche's Task: An Interpretation of "Beyond Good and Evil"*. New Haven: Yale University Press, 2001.

Lansdown, Richard. Introduction to *The Bostonians*, by Henry James. London: Penguin Books, 2000.

Leiter, Brian. *Nietzsche on Morality*. 2nd ed. London: Routledge, 2015.

————. "The Paradox of Fatalism and Self-Creation in Nietzsche." In *Willing and Nothingness: Schopenhauer as Nietzsche's Educator*, edited by Christopher Janaway. Oxford: Clarendon Press, 1998.

Lepenies, Wolf. *The Seduction of Culture in German History*. Princeton: Princeton University Press, 2006.

Levine, Andrew. *The Politics of Autonomy: A Kantian Reading of Rousseau's "Social Contract"*. Amherst, MA: University of Massachusetts Press, 1976.

Löwith, Karl. *From Hegel to Nietzsche: The Revolution in Nineteenth-Century Thought*. Translated by David E. Green. New York: Holt, Rinehart and Winston, 1964.

Macy, Jeffrey. "God Helps Those Who Help Themselves." *Polity* 24 (1992): 615–32.

Maine, Henry. *Ancient Law*. New York: Henry Holt, 1906.

Manent, Pierre. *Modern Liberty and Its Discontents*. Edited and translated by Daniel J. Mahoney and Paul Seaton. Lanham, MD: Rowman & Littlefield.

Marks, Jonathan. "The Divine Instinct? Rousseau and Conscience." *Review of Politics* 68 (2006): 564–85.

————. "Rousseau's Discriminating Defense of Compassion." *American Political Science Review* 101 (2007): 727–39.

Masters, Roger. *The Political Philosophy of Rousseau*. Princeton: Princeton University Press, 1968.

Meier, Heinrich. *"The Discourse on the Origin and Foundations of Inequality among Men*: On the Intention of Rousseau's Most Philosophical Work." *Interpretation* 16 (1988–89): 211–28.

———. *Nietzsches Vermächtnis: "Ecce Homo" und "Der Antichrist": Zwei Bücher über Natur und Politik*. München: C. H. Beck, 2019.

———. *On the Happiness of the Philosophic Life: Reflections on Rousseau's "Rêveries" in Two Books*. Translated by Robert Berman. Chicago: University of Chicago Press, 2016.

Melzer, Arthur. *The Natural Goodness of Man: On the System of Rousseau's Thought*. Chicago: University of Chicago Press, 1990).

———. "Rousseau and the Modern Cult of Sincerity." In *The Legacy of Rousseau*, edited by Nathan Tarcov and Clifford Orwin. Chicago: University of Chicago Press, 1997.

———. "The Origin of the Counter-Enlightenment: Rousseau and the New Religion of Sincerity." *American Political Science Review* 90 (1996) 352–58.

Nehamas, Alexander. *Nietzsche: Life as Literature*. Cambridge, MA: Harvard University Press, 1985.

Neuhouser, Frederick. "Freedom, Dependence, and the General Will." *Philosophical Review* 102 (1993): 373–91.

———. *Rousseau's Critique of Inequality: Reconstructing the "Second Discourse"*. Cambridge: Cambridge University Press, 2014.

———. *Rousseau's Theodicy of Self-Love: Evil, Rationality, and the Drive for Recognition*. Oxford: Oxford University Press, 2008.

Nisbet, Robert. "Rousseau and Totalitarianism." *Journal of Politics* 5 (1943): 93–114.

Nussbaum, Martha. "Is Nietzsche a Political Thinker?" *International Journal of Philosophical Studies* 5 (1997): 1–13.

Oakeshott, Michael. "On the Character of a Modern European State." In *On Human Conduct*. Oxford: Clarendon Press, 1975.

Okin, Susan Moller. *Women in Western Political Thought*. Princeton: Princeton University Press, 1992. First published 1979.

Orwin, Clifford. "Rousseau and the Discovery of Political Compassion." In *The Legacy of Rousseau*, edited by Nathan Tarcov and Clifford Orwin. Chicago: University of Chicago Press, 1997.

———. "Rousseau on the Sources of Ethics." In *Instilling Ethics*, edited by Norma Thompson. Lanham, MD: Rowman and Littlefield, 2000.

Owen, David. "Nietzsche, Ethical Agency and the Problem of Democracy," in *Nietzsche, Power, and Politics: Rethinking Nietzsche's Legacy for Political Thought*, edited by Herman Siemens and Vasti Roodt. Berlin: Walter de Gruyter, 2008.

———. *Nietzsche, Politics and Modernity*. London: Sage, 1995.

Pateman, Carol. *The Sexual Contract*. Palo Alto: Stanford University Press, 1988.

Pippin, Robert. "How to Overcome Oneself: Nietzsche on Freedom." In *Nietzsche on Freedom and Autonomy*, edited by Ken Gemes and Simon May. Oxford: Oxford University Press, 2009.

———. "Irony and Affirmation in Nietzsche's *Thus Spoke Zarathustra*." In *Nietzsche's New Seas*, edited by Michael Gillespie and Tracy Strong. Chicago: University of Chicago Press, 1988.

Pinker, Steven. *Enlightenment Now: The Case for Reason, Science, Humanism, and Progress*. New York: Viking, 2018.

Plattner, Marc. *Rousseau's State of Nature: An Interpretation of the "Discourse on Inequality"*. Dekalb: Northern Illinois University Press, 1979.

Rawls, John. *A Theory of Justice*. Rev. ed. Cambridge, MA: Belknap Press, 1999/1971.

Reginster, Bernard. *The Affirmation of Life: Nietzsche on Overcoming Nihilism*. Cambridge, MA: Harvard University Press, 2006.

Reisert, Joseph. *Jean-Jacques Rousseau: A Friend of Virtue*. Ithaca, NY: Cornell University Press, 2003.

Rosenblatt, Helena. "On the 'Misogyny' of Jean-Jacques Rousseau: The *Letter to D'Alembert* in Historical Context." *French Historical Studies* 25 (2002): 91–114.

———. *Rousseau and Geneva: From the "First Discourse" to the "Social Contract," 1749–1762*. Cambridge: Cambridge University Press, 1997.

Russell, Bertrand. *A History of Western Philosophy*. New York: Simon and Schuster, 1945.

Salkever, Stephen. "Rousseau and the Concept of Happiness." *Polity* 11 (1978): 27–45.

Schaeffer, Denise. *Rousseau on Education, Freedom, and Judgment*. University Park, PA: Penn State University Press, 2014.

Schopenhauer, Arthur. *On the Basis of Morality*. Translated by E. F. J. Payne. Indianapolis: Hackett, 1999.

Schotten, C. Heike. *Nietzsche's Revolution: Décadence, Politics, and Sexuality*. New York: Palgrave Macmillan, 2009.

Schutte, Ofelia. *Beyond Nihilism: Nietzsche without Masks*. Chicago: University of Chicago Press, 1984.

Schwartz, Joel. *The Sexual Politics of Jean-Jacques Rousseau*. Chicago: University of Chicago Press, 1984.

Scott, John. "The Theodicy of the *Second Discourse*: The 'Pure State of Nature' and Rousseau's Political Thought." *American Political Science Review* 86 (1992): 696–711.

Shell, Susan Meld. "*Emile*: Nature and the Education of Sophie." In *The Cambridge Companion to Rousseau*, edited by Patrick Riley. Cambridge: Cambridge University Press, 2001.

Shklar, Judith. *Men and Citizens: A Study of Rousseau's Social Theory*. Cambridge: Cambridge University Press, 1985/1969.

Siemens, Herman. "Nietzsche's Critique of Democracy." *Journal of Nietzsche Studies* 38 (2009): 20–37.

———. "Yes, No, Maybe So . . . Nietzsche's Equivocations on the Relation between Democracy and '*Grosse Politik*.'" In *Nietzsche, Power, and Politics: Rethinking Nietzsche's Legacy for Political Thought*, edited by Herman Siemens and Vasti Roodt. Berlin: Walter de Gruyter, 2008.

Smith, Stephen B. *Modernity and Its Discontents: Making and Unmaking the Bourgeois from Machiavelli to Bellow*. New Haven: Yale University Press, 2016.

Starobinski, Jean. *Jean-Jacques Rousseau: Transparency and Obstruction*. Translated by Arthur Goldhammer. Chicago: University of Chicago Press, 1988.

Steinbrügge, Lieselotte. *The Moral Sex: Woman's Nature in the French Enlightenment*. Translated by Pamela E. Selwyn. New York and Oxford: Oxford University Press, 1995.

Strauss, Leo. "The Living Issues of German Postwar Philosophy." In Heinrich Meier, *Leo Strauss and the Theological Political Problem*. Cambridge: Cambridge University Press, 2006.

———. *Natural Right and History*. Chicago: University of Chicago Press, 1953.

———. "On the Intention of Rousseau." In *Hobbes and Rousseau: A Collection of Essays*, edited by M. Cranston and R. S. Peters. Garden City, NY: Anchor, 1972.

———. *On Nietzsche's "Thus Spoke Zarathustra"*. Edited by Richard Velkley. Chicago: University of Chicago Press, 2017.

———. "Three Waves of Modernity." In *An Introduction to Political Philosophy: Ten Essays*, edited by Hilail Gildin. Detroit: Wayne State University Press, 1989.

———. *Rousseau*. Transcript for "Seminar on Rousseau (1962): Rousseau, Autumn 1962. Edited by Jonathan Marks. https://leostrausscenter.uchicago.edu/rousseau-autumn-1962/.

Talmon, J. L. *The Origins of Totalitarian Democracy*. London: Secker & Warburg, 1952.

Taylor, Charles. *The Ethics of Authenticity*. Cambridge, MA: Harvard University Press, 1992.

———. "The Immanent Counter-Enlightenment." In *Canadian Political Philosophy*, edited by Ronald Beiner and Wayne Norman. Oxford: Oxford University Press, 2001.

———. *Sources of the Self: The Making of the Modern Identity*. Cambridge, MA: Harvard University Press, 1989.

Thiele, Leslie. *Friedrich Nietzsche and the Politics of the Soul: A Study of Heroic Individualism*. Princeton: Princeton University Press, 1990.

Thomas, R. Hinton. "Nietzsche, Women and the Whip." *German Life and Letters* 34 (1980): 117–25.

Tirrell, Lynne. "Sexual Dualism and Women's Self-Creation: On the Advantages and Disadvantages of Reading Nietzsche for Feminists." In *Nietzsche and the Feminine*, edited by Peter Burgard. Charlottesville, VA: University of Virginia Press, 1994: 158–82.

Tocqueville, Alexis. *Democracy in America*. Edited and translated by Harvey C. Mansfield and Delba Winthrop. Chicago: University of Chicago Press, 2000. First published 1835/1840.

Trilling, Lionel. *Sincerity and Authenticity*. Cambridge, MA: Harvard University Press, 1972.

Vaughan, C. E. Introduction to *The Political Writings of Jean-Jacques Rousseau*, edited by Vaughan. Cambridge: Cambridge University Press, 1915.

Velkley, Richard. "The Tension in the Beautiful: On Culture and Civilization in Rousseau and German Philosophy." in *The Legacy of Rousseau*, edited by Nathan Tarcov and Clifford Orwin. Chicago: University of Chicago Press, 1997.

Viroli, Maurizio. *Jean-Jacques Rousseau and the Well-Ordered Society*. Translated by Derek Hanson. Cambridge: Cambridge University Press, 1988.

Warren, Mark. *Nietzsche and Political Thought*. Cambridge, MA: MIT Press, 1991.

Weiss, Penny. *Gendered Community: Rousseau, Sex, and Politics*. New York: NYU Press, 1993.

Williams, Bernard. *Shame and Necessity*. Berkeley: University of California Press, 2008.

———. "'There Are Many Kinds of Eyes.'" In *The Sense of the Past*. Princeton: Princeton University Press, 2006.

Williams, David Lay. *Rousseau's "Social Contract": An Introduction*. Cambridge: Cambridge University Press, 2014.

Williams, W. D. *Nietzsche and the French: A Study of the Influence on Nietzsche's French Reading on His Thought and Writing*. Oxford: Blackwell, 1952.

Wokler, Robert. "Rousseau's Pufendorf: Natural Law and the Foundations of Commercial Society." In *Rousseau, the Age of Enlightenment, and Their Legacies*, edited by Bryan Garsten. Princeton: Princeton University Press, 2012.

Wollstonecraft, Mary. *A Vindication of the Rights of Woman*. In *"A Vindication of the Rights of Men" and "A Vindication of the Rights of Woman"*, edited by Sylvana Tomaselli. Cambridge: Cambridge University Press, 1995.

Woolf, Virginia. *To the Lighthouse*. New York: Harcourt, 1981. First published 1927.

Zuckert, Catherine. "Nietzsche on the Origin and Development of the Distinctively Human." *Polity* 16 (1983): 48–71.

Index